DEMOCRACY AND AUTHORITARIANISM IN PERU

Also by Maxwell A. Cameron

■ ■ ■ ■ ■

THE POLITICAL ECONOMY OF NORTH AMERICAN FREE TRADE
(editor with Ricardo Grinspun)

DEMOCRACY AND AUTHORITARIANISM IN PERU

POLITICAL COALITIONS AND SOCIAL CHANGE

Maxwell A. Cameron

ST. MARTIN'S PRESS
NEW YORK

Chapter 2, "Evolving Social Bases of Party Competition," reprints, with modifications, *Bulletin of Latin American Research*, Vol. 10, No. 3, Maxwell A. Cameron, "Political Parties and the Worker-Employer Cleavage: The Impact of the Informal Sector on Voting in Lima, Peru," pp. 293–313, copyright 1991, with kind permission of Elsevier Science Ltd, The Boulevard, Langford Lane, Kidlington OX5 1GB, UK.

Chapter 3, "The Center, Populism, and the Informal Sector," draws upon, and reprints portions of, *Canadian Journal of Latin American and Caribbean Studies*, Vol. 16, No. 31, Maxwell A. Cameron, "The Politics of the Urban Informal Sector in Peru: Populism, Class and 'Redistributive Combines,'" with kind permission of the *Canadian Journal of Latin American and Caribbean Studies*.

Chapter 4, "Alliance Bargaining in the Democratic Front," reprints, with modifications, *Comparative Political Studies*, Vol. 25, No. 2, July 1992, Maxwell A. Cameron, "Rational Resignations: Coalition Building in Peru and the Phillippines," pp. 229–250, copyright 1992, with kind permission of Sage Publications, Inc.

First published in the United States of America 1994

Printed in the United States of America

ISBN 0-312-12153-9

Library of Congress Cataloging-in-Publication Data

Cameron, Maxwell A.
    Democracy and authoritarianism in Peru : political coalitions and
social change / Maxwell A. Cameron.
    p. cm.
    Includes bibliographical references and index.
    ISBN 0-312-12153-9
    1. Democracy—Peru. 2. Peru—Politics and government—1980-
3. Authoritarianism—Peru. I. Title.
JL3481.C36 1994
320.985—dc20   94-9119
                                                          CIP

Interior design by Digital Type & Design

For my Mom

CONTENTS

I. Introduction

II. Social Bases of Shifting Coalitions

III. Crisis in the Left and the Right

IV. Instability of Democracy

V. Conclusion

ACRONYMS AND ABBREVIATIONS

ANP	Asamblea Nacional Popular
APS	Acción Política Socialista
AP	Acción Popular
APRA	Alianza Popular Revolucionaria Americana
ASI	Acuerdo Socialista de Izquierda
CADE	Conferencia Anual de Ejecutivos
CCD	Congreso Constituyente Democrático
CETALM	Central de Trabajadores Ambulantes de Lima Metropolitana
CISEPA	Centro de Investigaciones Sociológicas, Económicas, Políticas, y Antropológicas
CITE	Confederación Intersectorial de Trabajadores Estatales
CODE	Convergencia Democrática
CONFIEP	Confederación Nacional de Instituciones Empresariales del Perú
CUAVES	Comunidad Urbana Autogestionaria de Villa El Salvador
CGTP	Confederación General de Trabajadores Peruanos
DESCO	Centro de Estudios y Promoción del Desarrollo
DIRCOTE	Dirección Contra Terrorismo
FEDEVAL	Federación Departamental de Vendedores Ambulantes de Lima
FIM	Frente Independiente Moralizador
FNTC	Frente Nacional de Trabajadores y Campesinos
FOCEP	Frente Obrero, Campesino, Estudiantil y Popular
FONCRESI	Fondo de Crédito del Sector Informal
FRE	Frente Agrícola del Perú
FREDEMO	Frente Democrático
FRENATRACA	Frente Nacional de Trabajadores y Campesinos
GDP	Gross Domestic Product
IBOPE	Instituto Brasileiro de Pesquisa
IDESI	Instituto para Desarrollo del Sector Informal
ILD	Instituto Libertad y Democracia
ILO	International Labour Office
IMF	International Monetary Fund
IS	Izquierda Socialista
IU	Izquierda Unida
JNE	Jurado Nacional de Elecciones

MAS	Movimiento de Afirmación Socialista
MDI	Movimiento Democrático de Izquierda
MIA	Movimiento Independiente Agrícola
MIR	Movimiento Izquierda Revolucionaria
MRTA	Movimiento Revolucionario Tupac Amaru
MSNP	Movimiento Socialista No-Partidarizado
OAS	Organization of American States
PAIT	Programa de Apoyo de Ingreso Temporal
PAP	Partido Aprista Peruano—see APRA
PCP	Partido Comunista del Perú
PCP-SL	Partido Comunista del Perú—Sendero Luminoso
PCR	Partido Comunista Revolucionario
PDC	Partido Demócrata Cristiano
PFL	Partido da Frente Liberal—Brazil
PMDB	Partido do Movimento Democrático Brasileiro
PPC	Partido Popular Cristiano
PPR	Partido Progressista Reformador—Brazil
PREALC	Programa Regional del Empleo para América Latina y el Caribe
PROEM	Programa Metropolitano de Empleo
PRT	Partido Revolucionario de los Trabajadores
PSDB	Partido Social Democrático Brasileiro
PSR	Partido Socialista Revolucionario
PT	Partido dos Trabalhadores—Brazil
PUM	Partido Unificado Mariáteguista
SINAMOS	Sistema Nacional de Apoyo a la Movilización Social
SODE	Solidaridad y Democracia
SSHRCC	Social Sciences and Humanities Research Council of Canada
UASP	Unidad de Acción Sindical y Popular—Guatemala
UNIR	Unión de Izquierda Revolucionaria
UNO	Unión Nacional Odriísta
URNG	Unidad Revolucionaria Nacional Guatemalteca
VR	Vanguardia Revolucionaria

LIST OF TABLES AND FIGURES

ACKNOWLEDGMENTS

Financial support for this research came from a Social Sciences and Humanities Research Council of Canada (SSHRCC) Doctoral Fellowship. That fellowship supported three years of graduate studies and made it possible for me to spend a year in Peru while writing my doctoral dissertation. A subsequent research grant from the SSHRCC financed a return trip to Peru to complete the research for the manuscript. An Inter-American Foundation Master's Fellowship helped me to begin research on Peru in an earlier field trip. A grant from Carleton University assisted the completion of the project and supported travel, and a leave of absence enabled me to complete the writing. Funding from these sources enabled me to spend nearly two years in Peru between 1986 and 1993. Carleton University also provided funding for methodological training at the Hoover Summer Program in International Politics. A number of the chapters were written or revised during a Visiting Research Fellowship at the Center for U.S.-Mexican Studies at the University of California at San Diego in 1991. Although these institutions made the research and writing possible, they are not responsible for the findings or interpretations presented in this book.

David Collier and Vinnie Aggarwal—the political scientists on my doctoral dissertation committee at the University of California at Berkeley—were extremely encouraging and stimulating mentors. Kim Voss—the sociologist on the committee—gave detailed and helpful feedback on sociological aspects of the analysis. Graduate students at Berkeley were a constant source of stimulation and intellectual challenge. Conversations with Francisco Durand, Timothy Scully, Peter Kingstone, Andy Gould, Ronald Archer, Deborah Norden, David Parker, Cynthia Sanborn, María Cook, Mina Silberberg, Deborah Yashar, Yemile Mizrahi, and other students at Berkeley and Stanford, were very helpful during the formulative stages of the project. I had the opportunity to present parts of this manuscript in seminars at Carleton University, Duke University, Queen's University, the University of California at San Diego, and the Instituto de Estudios Peruanos. The comments of Lorraine Eden, David Long, Ozay Mehmet, Peter Lange, Herbert Kitschelt, Julio Cotler, Catherine Legrand, Fernando Rospigliosi, Francisco Verdera, and Romeo Grompone were especially useful.

Jean Daudelin read and commented on the introduction. Jack Citrin, Scott Mainwaring, David Parker, Rafael Roncagliolo, Timothy Scully, Susan Stokes, Lewis Taylor, and Alicia Unger read and commented on earlier drafts of chapter 2 of this manuscript. David Scott Palmer made helpful suggestions on an earlier version of chapter 3. Gretchen Casper and Maureen A. Molot commented on a draft of chapter 4. George Tsebelis made very keen observations on chapters 4 and 5. Shane Hunt commented on a draft of chapter 6, and Cynthia McClintock commented on a draft of chapter 8. Paul Drake, Fen O. Hampson, Philip Mauceri, Liisa North, Robert Koep, Matthew Shugart, and Andrew Zimbalist read and commented on an earlier draft of the entire manuscript. Their insights substantially improved the final product.

I am grateful to Jorge Bernedo, Abel Centurión Marchena, William Sánchez, Delma Del Valle, Daniel Chiri, and María Polo in the Employment Office (Dirección General de Empleo) of the Ministry of Labor in Peru for the elaboration of data on the informal sector. Without their help the collection of data for this book would not have been possible. I was affiliated with the Pontificia Universidad Católica del Perú during 1985–1986 and 1987–1988. It provided an extremely congenial environment for research. I am grateful to the staff of the Centro de Investigaciones Sociológicas, Económicas, Políticas, y Antropológicas (CISEPA). Gordon Adams, David Heath, Silvia Matos, Chong Min Park, William Postma, Jeff Walker, and Stephen Nairne provided indispensable research assistance. Alfredo Torres Guzman was extremely generous with the information gathered by his public opinion firm, APOYO S.A. The Peruvian embassy in Ottawa kept me informed with a steady stream of official documents after the events of April 5, 1992, some of which found their way into this book.

The research for this book was partly based on many interviews, conducted between 1986 and 1993, with numerous politicians, government officials, business executives, trade unionists, and academics. I owe the greatest debt of gratitude to Alberto Adrianzén, Francisco Aguilar, Carmen Rosa Balbi, Eduardo Ballón, Alfonso Barrantes, Hector Béjar, Fernando Belaúnde Terry, Alberto Bustamante, Eduardo Cáceres, Eliana Chávez O'Brien, Pablo Checa, Javier Diez Canseco, Enrique Espinoza, Carlos Franco, Vitaliano Gallardo, Manuel Glave, Francisco Guerra, Narda Henriquez, Claudio Herzka, Christine Hünefeldt, Juan Larco, Ricardo Letts, Sinesio López, Carlos Monge, Jorge Nieto, Guillermo Nolasco, Aldo Panfichi, Peri Paredes, Jorge Parodi, Henry Pease García, Susana Pinilla, Gonzalo Portocarrero, Nestor Ríos, Rafael Roncagliolo, Denis Sulmont, Alejandro Toledo, Teresa Tovar, Richard Webb, Carlos Wendorf, and Odett Zamolloa. I am especially grateful to Fernando Tuesta for providing data on elections from the second edition of his *Perú Político en Cifras* prior to its publication. None of the above individuals, however, are responsible for errors or deficiencies in the analysis that follows.

Parts of chapter 2 are reprinted with modifications from "Political Parties and the Worker-Employer Cleavage: the Impact of the Informal Sector on

Voting in Lima, Peru," *Bulletin of Latin American Research,* Vol 10, No. 3, 1991, and chapter 3 draws on "The Politics of the Urban Informal Sector in Peru: Populism, Class and 'Redistributive Combines,'" *Canadian Journal of Latin American and Caribbean Studies,* Vol 16, No. 31, 1991. In both chapters, new election data are used that were not available when the articles were first published, and in places the analysis has been updated. Chapter 4 is reprinted, with modifications, from "Rational Resignations: Coalition Building in Peru and the Philippines," *Comparative Political Studies,* Vol 25, No. 2, 1992. All articles are reprinted with kind permission.

I wish to express my gratitude to Fabiola Bazo for her insights, which have enriched this book, and her patience and support during the writing. Likewise, Jorge Bazo Peña, Lucrecia Escudero de Bazo, Jorge Bazo Escudero, and Ricardo Bazo Escudero always provided the most generous hospitality during my visits to Peru. Ricardo Bazo captured the leitmotif of the book with the picture he drew for the cover. Finally, this book is dedicated to my Mom, Ann Cameron, for encouraging my interest in Latin America, for friendship and moral support, and for being a wonderful example.

PART I

INTRODUCTION

. 1 .

BETWEEN DEMOCRACY AND AUTHORITARIANISM IN PERU

Under what conditions is democracy stable? What forces undermine or reinforce democratic institutions? How stable is democracy in Latin America? This book suggests answers to these questions in the context of Peru, one of Latin America's least stable democracies (Dietz 1992; Mauceri 1994; McClintock 1989, 1993, 1994; Cotler 1993; Tuesta 1994b). It seeks to identify the micro- and macrocauses that explain the gradual breakdown of democracy in the period between the 1980 transition from authoritarian rule and the 1992 suspension of the constitution and closure of Congress by President Alberto Fujimori.[1]

The stability of democracy has been the focus of considerable theoretical and empirical attention in Latin American studies and in comparative politics generally, especially since the transition from authoritarian rule in Latin America during the 1980s (Hagopian 1993; Higley and Gunther 1992; Levine 1988; Mainwaring et al. 1992; O'Donnell et al. 1986; O'Donnell 1992; Smith 1991; Remmer 1990; Diamond et al. 1989; Cueva 1988; Malloy and Seligson 1987; Petras and Herman 1986; Foxley 1986; Huntington 1984). Peru is an important case of democratization in Latin America. It was the first country to initiate a transition from authoritarian rule in the 1970s, and the first Latin American country to abandon the democratic institutions created in that transition process. On April 5, 1992, Alberto Fujimori suspended the 1979 constitution, closed Congress, and seized near-dictatorial powers (Abugattás et al. 1992; Acurio et al. 1992; Balbi 1993a; Ferrero Costa 1993; Gorriti 1993; Mauceri 1994). In 1993 a new legislature, called the Democratic Constituent

Congress (CCD), was elected that significantly modified the constitution to strengthen executive power (López 1993: 37–8). One of the most astonishing aspects of Peru's departure from the rule of law was the breadth of popular support received by Fujimori (Tovar 1992).

A pair of distinctive, yet complementary, theoretical perspectives have emerged from the debate on Latin America's prospects for democratic consolidation. Together they help explain the puzzle of democratic instability in Peru. The first perspective is sociological, in the tradition of Barrington Moore, Jr. (1966), and has a strongly structuralist orientation; it suggests democracy is stable when social conditions increase the political power of the working class and other subordinate groups (Rueschemeyer, Stephens, and Stephens 1992). The second perspective is rooted in microeconomic analysis, and starts from the perspective of the individual actor; it argues that democracy is stable when it is in the interest of all relevant political actors (Przeworski 1985, 1986, 1991; Conaghan 1992: 229–34). These two perspectives are rarely explored within a single framework or study.

This book seeks to combine macrosocial and microeconomic perspectives to provide a distinctively *political* explanation of problems in the consolidation and breakdown of democracy. It argues that the breakdown of democracy in Peru is partly due to changes in the class structure that have created social conditions unfavorable to democratic consolidation. It also traces the mechanisms through which democracy has been undermined by exploring the choices and strategies of political actors in response to changing structural conditions. In short, it attempts to provide an account of the crisis of Peruvian democracy that integrates structural constraints and political choices. The following sections compare and contrast macrosocial and microeconomic perspectives on democratic consolidation, present an overview of the argument, and outline the organization of the book.

MACROSOCIAL EXPLANATIONS OF DEMOCRATIC CONSOLIDATION

Dietrich Rueschemeyer, Evelyne Huber Stephens, and John D. Stephens's (1992) account of the relation between capitalist development and democracy synthesizes cross-national quantitative and comparative historical research. Social class is a central category in their analysis because class inequality stands in tension with political democracy (1992: 41–51). The prospects for democracy depend on the balance of power among contending classes: those who gain from democracy will promote and defend it, while those with the most to lose will resist it (1992: 57). Thus, capitalist development is associated with the rise of democracy because of two structural effects: "it strengthens the working class as well as other subordinate classes, and it weakens large landowners" (1992: 58).

Rueschemeyer, Stephens, and Stephens provide a plausible and impressive synthesis of existing comparative historical and cross-national research (see Kitschelt 1992: 1030–1 for a review). Unlike some of the earlier work in the cross-national quantitative tradition (for example, Seligson 1987), Rueschemeyer, Stephens, and Stephens are careful to specify causal paths and mechanisms that link economic development and the consolidation of democracy. Their chapter on Latin America demonstrates how different types of export economies led to different patterns of initial democratization after the consolidation of state power in the nineteenth century and during the onset of industrialization (1992: 159). Once political institutions were formed, however, "they assumed a life of their own and became important determinants of regime outcomes" in subsequent sequences of breakdown and reconstitution that followed the initial establishment of democracy (1992: 159). A key variable for Rueschemeyer, Stephens, and Stephens is the "level of threat perception" by the economic elites faced with rising pressure from subordinate classes. Parties play a key role in the consolidation of democracy because they are able to mediate pressures in ways that reduce the level of threat perceived by the elites (1992: 168): "Democracy could be consolidated only where there were two or more strong competing political parties at least one of which effectively protected dominant class interests" (1992: 9).[2]

Rueschemeyer, Stephens, and Stephens anticipate objections to their emphasis on the power of the subordinate classes in developing countries where organized labor is weak:

> If indeed the size and role of the urban working class is typically smaller, how is this continuing effect of development on democratization to be explained? While we do not think that this objection invalidates the balance of class power approach, there is little question that democratization in the early developing countries of Europe was quite different in its specifics than similar developments in the Third World today. . . . Yet while the working class is typically smaller in today's Third World countries, the urban population with its better chances to communicate and organize very often is not; in fact, the urban subordinate classes in peripheral countries today may be larger than their counterparts in the countries that developed earlier. (1992: 77)

Rueschemeyer, Stephens, and Stephens recognize that the size of the informal sector has typically been larger in Latin America than in developed countries at an earlier period (1992: 180), a fact with "important implications both for the strength of civil society and for the political articulation of the middle and working classes" (1992: 180). Indeed, "dependent industrialization led to the emergence of a comparatively small industrial working class. At the same time there was a very large urban informal sector of self-employed and of people employed in very small enterprises. This made labor organization exceedingly difficult" (1992: 220).

The political power and capacity for collective action of workers was further reduced by the economic crisis in the 1980s. In a large number of Latin American countries the growth of the informal sector[3] was one manifestation of an economic crisis that changed the balance of power among classes by undermining the trade union movement, limiting the capacity for collective action of subordinate classes, diminishing the relevance of orthodox leftist ideology, and weakening parties of the left based on organized labor (see Portes 1981; Portes et al. 1989; Touraine 1987). As Manuel Castells and Alejandro Portes observed, one of the effects of the informal economy "is the undermining of the power of organized labor in all spheres: economic bargaining, social organization, and political influence" (1989: 31). Another effect is that "the more the informal economy expands, the more the class structure of each society becomes blurred" (Castells and Portes 1989: 31); as a result, "classes, old and new, may become defined more by their struggles than by their structure, and collective actors will appeal to their social projects and visions rather than to common positions in the work process" (Castells and Portes 1989: 32). The blurring of the class structure and the recomposition of collective actors around new projects and visions resulted in coalition instability, and new political alliances (Annis and Franks 1989); increased the volatility of electoral outcomes (Degregori and Grompone 1991); and provided a potential social base for both populist (Carbonetto et al. 1988; Carbonetto 1986) and neoliberal economic policies (De Soto 1989a, 1989b; Ghersi ed. 1989).

The structural-historical approach of Rueschemeyer, Stephens, and Stephens's work provides a powerful explanation for the relationship between development and democracy in Latin America. What are its implications for the future of democracy in the region? They claim, "Inequality and poverty have increased in the 1980s and thus the room for tolerance and compromise has shrunk" (1992: 155). Moreover, although Peru entered the decade with relatively cohesive political parties, by the end of the 1980s it was clear that "clientelistic parties without strong ties to civil society are subject to rapid decay, particularly if confronted as incumbents with difficult economic problems" (1992: 215).

The stability of democracy in contemporary Latin America crucially depends on how political parties adapt to the disintegration of class-based organizations and the growth of the informal economy. A major purpose of this book is to supplement and extend Rueschemeyer, Stephens, and Stephens' argument by examining a case where a structural effect of capitalist development—the strength of the working class as well as other subordinate classes—has been reversed by a decade of economic crisis and decline.

MICROECONOMIC EXPLANATIONS OF DEMOCRATIC CONSOLIDATION

The goal of Adam Przeworski's 1991 *Democracy and the Market* is to provide a theory of democratic stability with solid microfoundational credentials. For Przeworski, democracy is a system "in which parties lose elections" (1991: 10). The central question of any theory of democracy is, why do the losers comply with outcomes they do not like? How are such outcomes enforced in a system in which no single player can dictate the results of electoral competition? The answer, according to Przeworski, lies neither in fear of repression nor in an idealistic adherence to democratic norms, but in the self-interested action of the players. Democracy is consolidated "when compliance—acting within the institutional framework—constitutes the equilibrium of the decentralized strategies of all the relevant political forces" (1991: 26).

Under what conditions would the relevant forces find it in their interests to agree to submit to the uncertain interplay of democratic institutions? Przeworski argues that democratic institutions may "offer to the relevant political forces a prospect of eventually advancing their interests that is sufficient to incite them to comply with immediately unfavorable outcomes. Political forces comply with present defeats because they believe that the institutional framework that organizes the democratic competition will permit them to advance their interests in the future" (1991: 19). Thus, democracy gives an inter-temporal dimension to conflict, providing current losers the hope that in the future they may aspire to power.

Noncompliance involves seeking to alter the outcomes of the democratic process *ex post facto,* or engaging in actions that reduce the confidence of others in democratic institutions. This perspective implies that for democracy to be stable it must "deliver the goods." That is, "if some important political forces have no chance to win distributional conflicts and if democracy does not improve the material conditions of losers, those who expect to suffer continued deprivation under democratic institutions will turn against them" (1991: 32).

Choice-theoretic approaches, such as that of Przeworski, have the advantage of theoretical clarity and parsimony (Tsebelis 1990: 40). Often, clarity and parsimony give way to oversimplification. However, more formal exposition of theory makes mistakes more easily detected and corrected. Above all, choice-theoretic models focus attention on the often-neglected strategic dimension of politics, and encourage social scientists to probe the preferences, strategies, choices, and motivations of individual actors. In short, game theory provides microfoundations for social inquiry.

Critics of rational choice argue that the focus on actors and events leads to a neglect of structures and history. Preferences, power resources, and identities are all taken as given. The problem-solving, static quality of choice-theoretic approaches leads many to reject them as inherently conservative, even though rational-choice theorists span a broad ideological spectrum (Geddes 1993: 3). However, insufficient attention has been devoted to exploring ways of combining choice-theoretic and structural-historical analysis.

A *prima facie* case can be made that Przeworski's view of democracy is generally consistent with the work of Rueschemeyer, Stephens, and Stephens. Both macrosocial and microeconomic perspectives provide alternative ways of understanding the importance of democratic institutions from a social-democratic perspective. Both explicitly reject the Leninist critique of democracy (Rueschemeyer, Stephens, and Stephens 1992: 43; Przeworski 1991: 41); and both see democracy as inherently conservative because of the need to protect the interests of economic elites in order to secure compliance with the democratic rules of the game. This insight provides the point of departure for an effort at synthesis.

TOWARD A SYNTHESIS

Social class must be a central category in the analysis of democracy in capitalist societies (Marshall 1953). The concepts of class formation and class alliances have been building-blocks in many of the major theories of regime change in Latin America (O'Donnell 1973, 1988a, 1988b; Collier 1979; Collier and Collier 1991; Bergquist 1986; Rueschemeyer, Stephens, and Stephens 1992). If the central argument made by Rueschemeyer, Stephens, and Stephens (1992) is that democracy is stable when social conditions empower the working class and other subordinate groups, then democracy will be unstable when social conditions undermine the power of workers and subordinate groups.

The economic crisis in Peru in the 1980s should have resulted in a less stable democracy. The breakdown of democracy in Peru in 1992 provides evidence in support of this thesis. Yet the shifting balance of class forces did not lead mechanically to the breakdown of the party system. An account of the crisis of democracy in Peru must explain the *process* whereby structural conditions that undermine collective action by workers and subordinate groups undermine the stability of democracy. Parties play a particularly important role in pressing for inclusion, organizing collective action, and mediating conflict (Adrianzén 1992; Cotler 1988; Pásara 1993). The focus of this analysis is on why traditional political parties and coalitions of the Left and the Right[4] were unable to adjust to changes in the electorate that were caused by the informalization of the economy.[5]

Peru is an ideal case for examining the political impact of the growth of the informal sector.[6] The growth of the informal economy surpassed anything witnessed elsewhere in Latin America (Carbonetto et al. 1988: Annex 1, table 2; De Soto 1989a; Chávez 1990b). Political parties, which had been organized around the class cleavage, were unable to adapt to the new circumstances created by the economic crisis—the decline of class-based organizations and ideology, and the growth of the informal sector. To understand this, it is necessary to recall the character of the party system that emerged in 1980, at the end of 12 years of military rule.

The military government lowered the voting age to 18 years in 1978, and the 1979 constitution extended the franchise to illiterate voters. More than a decade of urbanization and industrial expansion resulted in a more urban, working-class electorate. The new balance of class forces led to the formation of a powerful left-wing coalition (Stephens 1983). The mobilization and radicalization of working-class protest under military rule was channelled by the Left into pressures to expand democratic participation. A tripolar electorate—with parties located at the left, center, and right—emerged in the 1980s. The inclusion of organized labor and the popular sectors under the umbrella of the Left awakened hopes for a more democratic and participatory political system.

The expectation that the inclusion of labor under the umbrella of the Left would contribute to democratic consolidation was short-lived. The economic crisis in the 1980s weakened linkages between the parliamentary Left and workers. A decade of economic recession beginning in 1982 resulted in a dramatic decline in the numbers and power of organized labor and, simultaneously, the growth of the informal economy.

The growth of the informal sector and the decline of organized labor did not weaken the salience of class in Peruvian elections, but it undermined the ability of the Left to represent a broad working-class constituency, and it contributed to a shift in the preferences of the electorate from the left toward so-called independent candidates without an explicit ideological program. Moreover, a confrontation between the Partido Comunista del Perú—Sendero Luminoso (PCP-SL, or, the Shining Path) and the armed forces exacerbated the ambivalence of the Left toward democracy.[7]

The severity of the crisis undermined class identities and class-based collective action at the same time that it increased underemployment, income inequality, and absolute levels of poverty (Chossudovsky 1991; Salcedo 1992; Chávez O'Brien 1990b; Vega-Centeno 1990; Amat y León 1985, 1987). A growing number of strategically important voters located themselves ideologically in the center-left of the spectrum, or refused to locate themselves on an ideological spectrum at all. Class remained a powerful predictor of the vote, yet class-based parties were unable to retain the loyalty of their supporters among the working class and informal sector. Working-class and informal-sector voters lost interest in candidates of the Left, were never drawn to the Right, and became increasingly attracted to candidates who defined themselves as "outsiders."

During the 1980s, the center-left became the best location for candidates seeking a broad majority of the vote. Yet centrist parties were discredited by their inability to manage the economy or control political violence. A volatile "floating" electorate at the center, capable of swinging left or right, found itself without political representation. Extremist political parties failed to reflect shifting voter preferences and move toward the center of the party system, and thus could not attract voters in the informal sector. This created an opportunity for political "outsiders" to enter the political system. The result was a fragmentation of the party system; political parties failed to adjust to the shifting preferences of the electorate, leading to a collapse of the Peruvian party system.

The Left failed to represent the new groups emerging in the context of prolonged economic crisis, thus debilitating pressures for democratization. The Right also had difficulty surviving under democracy. It had been politically marginalized by social changes in the 1970s under military rule; after the transition to democracy, it struggled to create a political party capable of protecting dominant-class interests and overcoming the social and ethnic isolation of these groups. However, the Right was unable to build a broader coalition with subordinate groups capable of winning elections. The Right failed to acquire the political strength to win elections, thus weakening the commitment of the economic elite to democracy. The failure of the Right, Center, and Left created a democracy nobody wanted.

The flight from the formal economy and the breakdown of the traditional party system were two sides of the same coin. One cannot understand the fragmentation of the political parties and coalitions of the Left and Right in Peru without understanding the growth of the informal economy. The growth of the informal sector undermined partisan loyalties, broke the tenuous linkages between parties and civil society, interrupted traditional channels of communication between elites and masses, weakened political parties based on the class cleavage, and contributed to the formation of a huge "floating" or "independent" electorate that was not represented by the programs, appeals, and symbols of traditional class-based political parties. The class cleavage remained a powerful predictor of the vote, but increasingly voters in the working class and informal sector shifted their loyalties to independent candidates without a clearly defined ideology.

The result of the economic collapse in Peru was unprecedented coalition instability, culminating in the disintegration of the most powerful political forces on both the Left and Right. Paralyzed by internal factions, ambivalent about democracy, and unable to agree on how to reach out to the informal sector, both the Left and Right failed to deter anti-system entrants into the political system who were better able to construct broad new coalitions that appealed to the needs of a changing, increasingly centrist, and less class-struggle oriented electorate. When the class-based party system crumbled, a drastic shift toward a more authoritarian style of government occurred. Alberto Fujimori was able to exploit the weakness of political parties to reject the democratic rules of the game. Business and popular support for Fujimori's self-coup on April 5, 1992 unequivocally demonstrated that democracy was not, to use Przeworski's terminology, "an equilibrium of the decentralized strategies of all the relevant political forces" (Przeworksi 1991: 26).

ORGANIZATION OF THE BOOK

Chapter 2 begins with an examination of the social bases of the Peruvian party system in the 1980s, and presents evidence for the salience of the class cleavage in party competition. The chapter goes on to analyze internal tensions within the Left between revolutionaries and reformists, and within the Right between conservatives and liberals, drawing on the work of Adam Przeworski and John Sprague (1986) on the dilemmas of social democratic parties in Europe. Chapter 2 also illustrates how factional tensions were related to the structure of opportunities for electoral competition created by the expansion of the informal sector, just as the growth of the middle sectors created factional tension among social democrats in Europe. The consequences for democratic stability, however, were radically different.

Chapter 3 describes the political parties that successfully used their location at the center of the political spectrum to construct winning electoral coalitions between 1980 and 1990. It traces their electoral success to their ability to occupy the center or center-left of the political spectrum. However, it also draws attention to the failure of these parties to provide stable and effective government. Major policy oscillations—due to the failure of alternative economic models to create sustained, equitable growth—intensified social conflict and discredited centrist parties. Moreover, the informalization of the economy made it difficult for any political party to establish a reliable social base with an increasingly disorganized, heterogeneous, and unpredictable urban electorate.

Chapters 4 and 5 analyze the internal factional strife within the Left and the Right in greater detail. Why was there resistance within each coalition to taking the steps necessary to occupy the center of the spectrum? Analysis of the bargaining among the factions highlights how the divisions within these coalitions were related to the tension between the leaders of strong party machines and candidates with wider electoral appeal seeking to transcend the limits of traditional class politics. Different answers are given as to why these coalitions were unable to break out of their "ghettos" at the periphery of the party system. Simple game-theoretic models are used to illustrate strategic choices facing factional leaders.

Chapter 6 applies a simple model of spatial competition that brings together the elements of the previous chapters into a systematic analysis of the 1990 presidential election. On the one hand, chapters 4 and 5 demonstrated the inability of the Left and Right to move away from the ideological hinterland at the extremes of the political spectrum—despite evidence of the strategic importance of voters in the center. On the other hand, chapter 3 illustrates the failure of centrist parties to govern effectively and manage the economy competently. In chapter 6 we see the consequences of this situation in the 1990 elections. As predicted by the model, a new entrant into the political system, Alberto Fujimori, successfully occupied the center of the electoral spectrum and went on to win in an election that upset the existing party system.

Chapter 7 asks how an anti-system candidate like Fujimori could emerge with such wide support. Fujimori consistently rejected alliances with established political parties that would have enabled him to govern by coalition or to implement legislation by negotiation with the legislative wing of government. Instead, he preferred to rule by decree, in an authoritarian style, to rely on the armed forces, and to strengthen his image by attacking unpopular institutions.

Chapter 8 addresses the implication of the rise of Fujimori for Peruvian democracy. The chapter then traces the causes of the Fujimori self-coup to his inability to pass legislation in the Congress, the growth of opposition to orthodox economic policies, and the continuing expansion of the Shining Path. It argues that the palace coup was a direct result of the coalition instability analyzed in previous chapters. Fujimori was able to successfully attack Peru's "traditional political parties," with substantial support from the business elite as well as workers and other subordinate groups. As a result, democracy was seriously eroded. Yet Fujimori retained support from the electorate because he continued to occupy the center of the political spectrum. The chapter explores similarities and differences between the Peruvian *autogolpe* (self-coup), the crackdown on Parliament in Russia in October 1993, the Guatemala coup attempt in May 1992, and the decision by President Franco in Brazil to decline an "invitation" to implement a Peruvian-style coup in October 1993.

Chapter 9 summarizes the argument of the book and evaluates its main findings. No other country in Latin America—with the possible exception of Nicaragua—experienced the level of economic decline, growth of the informal economy, or political violence that occurred in Peru in the 1980s. The results do not encourage a sanguine view of the prospects for the stability of democracy in Latin America, but they do provide lessons for democratic leaders facing uncertain choices in circumstances inhospitable to democratic consolidation.

PART II

SOCIAL BASES OF SHIFTING COALITIONS

The two chapters in this section examine the social bases of the political coalitions that emerged in Peru's fledgling democracy after military rule ended in 1980. Chapter 2 shows the importance of the class cleavage as a predictor of voting results in the 1980s, but also indicates that the growth of the informal economy contributed to the erosion of the class cleavage and thus threatened the viability of class-based parties.

Chapter 3 argues that, notwithstanding the importance of class in Peruvian elections, the political center—especially the center-left—remained the center of political gravity in Peru. Those parties that were successful in winning presidential elections in the 1980s were centrist parties. However, their failure in office created a dangerous vacuum at the center of the political spectrum.

.2.

Evolving Social Bases of Party Competition

A major victim of the growth of the informal sector during the 1980s in Peru was the party system that had been organized around the class cleavage since the late 1970s. The growth of the informal sector exacerbated tensions within the Left between revolutionaries and reformists, and within the Right between conservatives and liberals. The tension between revolutionaries and reformists concerned whether the Left should turn to what some regarded as "petty bourgeois" sectors for electoral support, or continue to build an organized base with the urban and rural proletariat. The tension between conservatives and liberals concerned whether the Right should seek a pro-free market alliance between the formal and informal sectors, or build upon the ties of conservative parties to their bases of support among employers and the middle class in the formal sector. The factions that resisted change in both the Left and the Right were those with control over powerful party machines tied to specific interests in society—organized workers, employers, or the middle sectors. The leaders who promoted change sought potentially wider support from formally "unorganized" sectors of society which, because of their numbers, were decisive in determining electoral outcomes.

In their analysis of European social democracy, Przeworski and Sprague (1986) note that socialist parties either stick with their working-class base and are condemned to minority status in Parliament, or they also appeal to middle class groups and risk alienating their core working class supporters. The saliency of class in shaping electoral outcomes is "a cumulative consequence of strategies pursued by political parties of the left" (Przeworski 1985: 14). If political parties do not mobilize workers as a class, but as "the people" or "the masses," then "workers are less likely to identify themselves as class members" (Przeworski 1985: 27). Typically, socialist parties alternate between radical and reformist postures, remaining "sentenced to perpetual electoral defeats" or diluting their class orientation (Przeworski and Sprague 1986: 3).

Is Przeworski and Sprague's analysis relevant, as suggested by Gibson (1990: 213–215), to parties of the Right in Latin America? Conservative parties that represent the specific interests of business and the middle sectors often must seek to build coalitions with the urban and rural poor in order to win electoral majorities. This is especially true where the majority of the electorate is poor. Does the Right risk alienating core supporters among the economic and political elites by moderating its position and seeking working-class allies? More broadly, can Przeworski and Sprague's argument be applied to a country like Peru, with a different social structure and a political system that is undergoing a violent crisis?

To answer these questions, this chapter is divided into five parts. The first part describes the major currents within the Left and the Right. The second shows how the Left and Right competed for opposed poles of the class vote in the 1980s. The third discusses the dilemmas created by the informal sector for ideological parties, while the fourth analyses the evolution of the Right and the Left, illustrating the importance both forces placed on winning support from the informal sector in the 1980s. The final section deals with the 1990 elections.

THE LEFT AND RIGHT IN PERU

In the 1960s the working class and the middle sectors were represented in Parliament by three multiclass parties: The Alianza Popular Revolucionaria Americana (APRA), the Unión Nacional Odriísta (UNO), and Acción Popular (AP). APRA had the support of organized labor; much of the unorganized working class supported UNO through clientelistic neighborhood associations; and AP had the support of white-collar employees and other middle sector groups. In the 1980s two new political actors competed like centrifugal forces to occupy the opposed poles of the class vote in Peru—the Marxist Izquierda Unida (IU) coalition, and the right-wing Partido Popular Cristiano (PPC).

The Left

The IU, formed in September 1980, was an electoral front formally composed of six registered political parties. There were three major factions in the IU. The first, often referred to as the "revolutionary bloc," was composed of the Partido Unificado Mariateguista (PUM), the Unión de Izquierda Revolucionaria (UNIR) and the Frente Obrero, Campesinos, Estudiantil y Popular (FOCEP). The second group, the "reformist bloc," was led by Alfonso Barrantes Lingan.

His Acuerdo Socialista coalition included the Partido Socialista Revolucionaria (PSR) and the Partido Comunista Revolucionaria (PCR). The third faction of IU was composed of the Partido Comunista del Perú (PCP) and legally non-registered independent groups (Movimiento de Afirmación Socialista, or MAS, and Acción Política Socialista, APS).[1]

The Right

The PPC was closely associated with business, white-collar, and professional groups in Lima. It was founded in December 1966 by the twice-elected mayor of Lima, Luis Bedoya Reyes. As a breakaway group from within the Partido Demócrata Cristiano (PDC), the PPC rapidly surpassed the PDC in membership and electoral performance. It formed important alliances with other parties—including a coalition with President Fernando Belaúnde Terry's AP between 1980 and 1984—and in November 1984 it united with a group of disgruntled Apristas to become the Convergencia Democrática (CODE), which subsequently disbanded.[2]

The PPC, which produced some of Peru's most distinguished legislators, promoted free enterprise and respect for private property. Yet it was unable to expand its appeal beyond an elite and middle sector constituency to less privileged voters. In 1985 the PPC won 10 percent of the popular vote, most of which came from a few wealthy districts of Lima. Thus, the PPC expressed the interests and ideology of Peru's urban upper-middle class (Bernales 1980: 68, 70; Amat y León 1985: 5–6; Tuesta 1994b).

In 1987 the Movimiento Libertad (henceforth Libertad), was formed by Mario Vargas Llosa in response to the attempted nationalization of the banks by the APRA government. The formation of Libertad intensified the competition within this small political space. Thus, in 1988, AP and the PPC joined a coalition with Libertad called the Frente Democrático (FREDEMO) to compete in the April 1990 presidential election (Durand 1990: 2). FREDEMO also brought together business and professional associations, research centers, conservative Catholic groups, and part of the intelligentsia, in an effort to build a broad movement for market-oriented solutions to Peru's problems (Durand 1990). In June 1989 Vargas Llosa was proclaimed presidential candidate for FREDEMO.

PARTY COMPETITION IN THE 1980s: THE CLASS CLEAVAGE

Party competition in the 1980s contrasted with that of the 1960s.[3] Voting results from Lima—where over one-third of Peru's electorate lived—indicate that class was a salient determinant of voting in the 1980s after military rule. The tables presented below demonstrate remarkably strong, stable, and statistically significant ecological correlations between the size of major social groups in Lima and the shares of the vote for ideological parties. This section is devoted to describing these findings.

According to table 2.1, the correlation between the percent of workers in electoral districts and support for the Left in the 1980s was extraordinarily high—markedly higher than that seen when APRA ran in the 1960s. The PPC was a mirror reflection of IU; votes for the Right (PPC and FREDEMO) were negatively correlated with the percent of workers in districts. Moreover, as table 2.2 illustrates, the right-wing vote was strongly and positively correlated with the percent of employers in districts of Lima.

TABLE 2.1
Ecological Correlations between Percent Manual Workers and Shares of the Vote for the Left and Right in Districts of Metropolitan Lima, 1978-1989

		Left	Right
1989	Municipal	0.904	-0.899
1986	Municipal	0.899	-0.954
1985	Presidential	0.934	-0.928
1983	Municipal	0.927	-0.925
1980	Municipal	0.920	-0.937
1980	Presidential	0.918	-0.921
1978	Constituent Assembly	0.864	-0.834

Pearson's r correlation coefficients: all correlations significant at the 0.005 level.
N = 25 districts.
Sources: See appendix to chapter 2.

TABLE 2.2
Ecological Correlations between Percent Employers and Shares of the Vote for the Left and Right in Districts of Metropolitan Lima, 1978-1989

		Left	Right
1989	Municipal	-0.679	0.904
1986	Municipal	-0.762	0.865
1985	Presidential	-0.749	0.909
1983	Municipal	-0.678	0.850
1980	Municipal	-0.682	0.814
1980	Presidential	-0.670	0.854
1978	Constituent Assembly	-0.747	0.726

Pearson's r correlation coefficients: all correlations significant at the 0.005 level.
N = 25 districts.
Sources: See appendix to chapter 2.

White-collar employees, according to table 2.3, were highly conservative in their electoral allegiances. Voting for the Right was closely associated with the percent of white-collar employees in districts of Lima. This is an interesting finding given the high level of radicalism of white-collar unions. It suggests that support for radical unions by white-collar employees may have been instrumental, and did not necessarily imply agreement with the ideology of the union leadership. David Parker notes that white-collar union leaders often

> espouse ideologies largely not shared by the rank-and-file, yet . . . receive wholehearted support. An employee who identifies himself as middle class and who personally feels little solidarity with manual workers, may . . . submit gladly to the authority of a radical politicized union preaching proletarian struggle. The union protects him and fights for better wages, while he also tries to rise through his employer's good graces. As long as the union uses tactics other than the prolonged strike, this sort of instrumentalism may not only be possible, but may be the only way to survive a crisis. (1987:37–38)

TABLE 2.3
Ecological Correlations between Percent White-Collar Employees and Shares of the Vote for the Left and Right in Districts of Metropolitan Lima, 1978-1989

		Left	Right
1989	Municipal	-0.872	0.794
1986	Municipal	-0.857	0.880
1985	Presidential	-0.909	0.822
1983	Municipal	-0.918	0.850
1980	Municipal	-0.882	0.883
1980	Presidential	-0.910	0.846
1978	Constituent Assembly	-0.846	0.767

Pearson's r correlation coefficients: all correlations significant at the 0.005 level.
N = 25 districts.
Sources: See appendix to chapter 2.

The conservatism of white-collar employees as individual voters helps account for a peculiarity of white-collar union leadership: the combination of radical rhetoric with bread-and-butter demands. The Left acquired control over a number of major white-collar unions in the 1970s, including public employees, bank employees, and teachers. The common interest that held the ideologically heterogeneous rank-and-file together was wage demands. The combination of militance and status consciousness among white-collar workers was often reflected in an acute sense of social differences with respect to the migrant indigenous population and manual labor, combined with a strong sense of solidarity with other white-collar employees in opposition to employers.

Available survey data reinforce the finding that workers and the lower-middle class inclined more to the Left, whereas upper income groups tend to support the Right. Thus, a 1983 survey of 595 subjects found that 30 percent of the "lower-middle class" reported voting for the Left, as opposed to 23 percent of the "upper class" and "upper-middle class"; 39 percent and 52 percent of the "upper-" and "lower-" working class respectively voted for the Left. Support for the Right declined from 33 percent of the "upper" and "upper-middle class" to 24 percent of the "lower-middle class," and then dropped off to 16 percent of the "upper-lower" class and 8 percent of the very lowest stratum (DATUM 1983). Survey data are consistent with voting analyses that have found voter preferences are fairly consistently arrayed along the left-right spectrum, and covary with income.[4] On important and emotionally charged political issues there is striking variation in the opinions of Peruvians across upper-, lower- and middle-income strata.[5]

In short, the data on how manual workers, employers, and white-collar employees vote indicate that the Left and the Right captured the extreme poles of the class cleavage in Peruvian elections over the eleven-year period 1978–1989.[6] Despite political instability in Peru, the worker-employer cleavage remained stable. There was a clear distinction in the social base of the Peruvian Left and Right that corresponded roughly to the division in Peruvian society between social classes. The distinction between manual workers on the one hand, and employers and white-collar employees on the other, was a crucial line of cleavage in Peruvian elections. This critical distinction reflected social, cultural, and ethnic differences in Peruvian society.

THE INFORMAL SECTOR AND THE CLASS CLEAVAGE

The strategic choices of politicians have an independent effect on the saliency of class among voters. In order for individual workers to vote together, political parties and other organizations must actively encourage class identification. The problem is that the line that separates workers from the rest of "the people" is very hard to draw, especially where the informal sector is significant.

Przeworski and Sprague define workers narrowly as "manual wage-earners," saying that "the specific definition also involves a bet on our part: a hypothesis that the line of sharpest divisions, of interest and values, lies between narrowly defined manual workers and other wage-earners." The tradeoff between manual workers and white-collar workers in Peru was extremely sharp, confirming Przeworski and Sprague's hypothesis. However, white-collar employees were a smaller segment of the population in Peru than in Western Europe. Indeed, their relative size declined in recent years due to the severe economic crisis. Until the recession in 1982 and 1983, no presidential election had been won without substantial white-collar support; since then white-collar employees have strongly supported a number of losing presidential candidates.

Whereas white-collar workers were of relatively little importance to the Peruvian Left, the informal sector was a critical source of electoral support. Between 1981 and 1986 the size of the wage-earning and salaried population in Lima grew only slightly in absolute terms while the informal sector nearly doubled. In the 25 districts of Lima from which the data are drawn—which encompass 90 percent of the electorate in Lima—the number of manual workers in the formal sector increased during this period from 330,000 to 350,000 and the number of white-collar employees increased from 510,000 to 540,000. The number of people in the informal sector expanded from 440,000 to 730,000 (Alvarado et al. 1987:41).

The startling growth of the informal sector had important political ramifications. It helped Barrantes win the 1983 municipal elections in Lima, and it was a factor in the reorientation of APRA in 1985. The shantytown districts where over a quarter of the economically active population were wage earners provided 523,627 votes to APRA in 1985, half of APRA's total electoral support in Lima (1,038,578 votes). The IU won 294,288 votes in the shantytown districts, or 60 percent of its total (487,748 votes). The combined right-wing (AP plus CODE) share of the vote in the shantytowns, on the other hand, amounted to only 156,492 votes, one-third of its 478,157 vote total.

There is little evidence of any difference between the voting patterns of manual workers and the informal sector. The districts in which each group was concentrated were areas to which the IU tended to appeal. As of 1985 they were also swept by APRA. Table 2.4 demonstrates a high correlation between the size of the stratum engaged in informal economic activities in districts of Lima and shares of the vote for the IU, a correlation which is stable over time and strongest at the municipal level.

Despite the assertion that "informality has turned a large number of people into entrepreneurs" (De Soto 1989a: 243), the informal sector showed no propensity to vote for the PPC. After its presidential victory in 1980, AP tended to draw less support from the informal sector in municipal races. And FREDEMO drew significantly less support from informal sector districts than from middle- and upper-middle class districts in 1989.

TABLE 2.4

Ecological Correlations between Percent Informal Sector and Shares
of the Vote for the Left and Right in Districts of Metropolitan Lima, 1978-1989

		Left	Right
1989	Municipal	0.773	-0.865
1986	Municipal	0.882	-0.865
1985	Presidential	0.872	-0.854
1983	Municipal	0.884	-0.877
1980	Municipal	0.855	-0.874
1980	Presidential	0.823	-0.847
1978	Constituent Assembly	0.783	-0.792

Pearson's r correlation coefficients: all correlations significant at the 0.005 level.
N = 25 districts.
Sources: See appendix to chapter 2.

The results of table 2.4 put to rest the idea that there was any tradeoff—much less a severe one—between appeals to manual wage-earners and the informal sector. There is little evidence of a distinction between how manual workers and the informal sector voted. Left-of-center parties sought to attract both factory workers and the informal sector. Together these segments of the work force accounted for a major fraction of the adult working population (roughly 1,080,000 people in Lima in 1986), and easily represented a plurality of the vote in Lima.[7]

Since there is little evidence of a tradeoff between appeals to the informal sector and to manual workers, why was there resistance within the Left to building an electoral coalition including the informal sector? There was no consensus within the Left on the need to build a broad coalition in order to win elections because of a more fundamental ambivalence within the Left concerning elections and formally democratic state institutions. The best-organized parties within the IU sought to build a powerful mass organization that would achieve a basic, revolutionary transformation of Peruvian society. This faction of the Left was openly sceptical of the value of bourgeois institutions like the Parliament and the electoral process, and tended to regard the need to attract informal-sector votes as secondary to the imperative of building organized trade union and peasant support.

A faction of the Right recognized the need to build a wider coalition than the social groups that typically supported the traditional political parties. However, Mario Vargas Llosa believed he had to form an alliance with AP and the PPC so as not to divide the forces of the Right in the general elections. This decision increased the odds against winning the support of the informal sector. In the next section we examine the evolution of the Left and Right in response to the challenges and opportunities created by the growth of the urban informal sector.

THE EVOLUTION OF THE RIGHT AND LEFT

Reformists and Revolutionaries in the United Left

The political strength of the Left in the 1980s contrasted with its weakness in the 1960s (Stephens 1983: 62–63). As Lewis Taylor notes, the IU "emerged as the largest legal force of the Marxist left in Latin America" (1990: 108). Years of grassroots organizing under military rule were responsible for the "spillover" of confrontational practices from unions into the broader organizations of the shantytowns (Stokes 1991: 91–92).

In the general strikes between 1977 and 1979, shantytown dwellers joined organized labor to protest austerity measures. They coordinated roadblocks, and fought street battles in the northern and southern cones of Lima. The armed forces set a timetable for elections for a Constituent Assembly in 1978, hoping to let off pressure. The convocation of elections forced the Left to choose between participating in the democratic process in order to promote revolutionary change, or abstaining and denouncing the elections as a trap created by the armed forces (Lynch 1992: 133–134). Orthodox Maoist groups,[8] for example, refused to participate; in Ayacucho the Shining Path flatly rejected any participation in elections. For its leader, Abimael Guzmán Reynoso (known to his followers as Presidente Gonzalo), the transition to democracy was a propitious moment to initiate the armed struggle since the armed forces, exhausted and divided after twelve years in government, would be reluctant to be drawn out of the barracks and back into politics.[9]

The legal Left won one-third of the vote in elections for a Constituent Assembly. Stephens observed that the "existence of a large, previously unmobilized electorate also aided the left's success in generating electoral support" (1983: 79). Changes in electoral rules under the 1979 constitution written by the Constituent Assembly further expanded participation in the 1980 presidential elections. The 1979 constitution allowed illiterates to vote for the first time, and the government had lowered the voting age from 21 to 18 years in 1978. Population growth and rural-urban migration in the 1970s dramatically increased the size of the shantytown districts. A new generation of leaders emerged from shantytowns where labor-led mobilizations were especially intense.

The Left, having chosen to participate in elections, found its relationship with the urban working class began to change. As it did, factionalism emerged between what was often referred to in Peru as the "class-struggle oriented

Left,"[10] which retained control over the most powerful party machines and sought to continue to build organized resistance, and the groups in the Left that were more committed to working with Parliamentary institutions. I call these factions "revolutionaries" and "reformists," respectively. There were many differences between these factions; among them was their view of the informal sector.

Reformists. The reformist Left placed a stronger emphasis on winning elections, changing the political system from within, implementing heterodox economic policies, and winning the confidence of business and the armed forces, in order to present a viable electoral alternative. The cautiousness of this perspective was reflected in the joke that "in event of a triumph, it would be necessary to flee the country."[11]

Reformists in the Left also stressed the importance of the informal sector. As the mayor of Lima between 1983 and 1986, Alfonso Barrantes was one of the first politicians to give small sums of credit to the informal sector. Barrantes sought to mobilize the informal sector as part of a broader effort to democratize decision-making and strengthen grassroots organizations. In this view, the informal sector provided an obvious electoral base for a popular democratic coalition against the orthodox recipes of structural adjustment and austerity.

Barrantes spoke with special admiration for the street hawkers. He saw them as more politically sophisticated than industrial workers because they interacted with a larger world of political threats and opportunities, which were embodied in the police, municipalities, legislators, consumers, suppliers, contractors, middlemen, and other "informals." Barrantes sought to represent the aspirations of the informal sector to have political influence and protection. One of Barrantes main allies in the municipality argued that street hawkers "want to be heard by the authorities. They want the doors of local government to be opened. They are very willing to dialogue."[12] Yet, the volatility of voters in the shantytowns around Lima was a major problem for the Left. In part, this was because the Left often tended to take the shantytowns for granted. It was also due to the fact that many shantytown dwellers found the rhetoric of the revolutionary Left excessively radical.

Revolutionaries. The revolutionary Left positioned itself in opposition to both the repression of the armed forces and the terrorist violence of the Shining Path. It argued that the leadership of the class struggle fell to the organized proletariat and the peasantry; the informal sector would have to play a secondary role. Moreover, the emphasis of the reformists on winning the electoral support of the informal sector was seen as part of a "revisionist" preoccupation with forming a government rather than creating a revolutionary situation. For Javier Diez Canseco, the reformists were wrong to focus "attention on occupying the spaces within the old state, penetrating it, occupying the seats of deputies, senators, mayors, regional governments . . ." (1992: 82).

Part of the problem the informal sector posed for the revolutionary Left was that it was extremely difficult to organize. Such a group operated in a world of social relations that were fluid and unstable, often based on kinship ties. The informal sector had few powerful lobbies, and its organizations tend to be ephemeral. Political entrepreneurs complained that the informal sector was hard to organize. Every meeting of the street vendor's federation, for example, was attended by a different group of people. The main concerns of the street hawkers included acquiring patches of sidewalk on which to sell their products without being relocated by the police and gaining credit to expand their operations.

The struggles of the informal sector were not easily assimilated into the framework of conventional class struggle. According to PREALC, "the division between owners of labor and capital characteristic of the formal sector does not predominate in the informal sector" (PREALC 1981: 28).[13] In many instances the unit of production was the family. This reality was often observed by members of the revolutionary bloc of the IU. As one leader of the Confederación General de Trabajadores Peruanos (General Confederation of Peruvian Workers, or CGTP) put it, "how can you organize workers in family units?" He added ominously that the informal sector was a potential "political base for the counterrevolution."[14]

Evolving Relations between Reformists and Revolutionaries

During the 1980s, the most dynamic focus of social protest and mobilization passed from organized labor to a wider range of neighborhood-based social movements in the shantytowns. Grassroots organizations were linked to new policy-making channels to address the needs of the nonunionized masses: "the Left was no longer only denouncing opponents' ideas—it was now presenting well-thought-out and feasible proposals of its own on a wide range of social questions, from the problem of infant nutrition to the lack of municipal finance . . ." (Taylor 1990: 110).

In 1983, under the leadership of Barrantes, the IU won 19 electoral districts in Lima, including the many districts that composed a "red belt" of shantytowns surrounding the city. Barrantes symbolized the transformation of the Peruvian Left. He gave the confrontational style of the Left a respectable face. As Alan García reputedly put it: "Barrantes, with his irony, captures the bad temper of the popular sectors and gives it a more positive sense."[15] By promising to give every needy child in Lima a glass of milk, the new mayor created an extensive set of new organizations in the shantytowns.

One of the council members in Barrantes's administration in the municipality of Lima was Guillermo Nolasco, the first street vendor to win public office in Lima. As a founder of the 10,000-member Federación Departamental de Vendedores Ambulantes de Lima (FEDEVAL), Nolasco personally coordinated a network of informal-sector associations with the policies of the municipality in an effort to meet the demands of the street vendors for markets and credit. The IU established a lending agency—the Programa Metropolitano de Empleo (PROEM)—to provide credit to street hawkers and small businesses. Similar programs were coordinated with the Ministry of Labor, the International Labour Office, the Industrial Bank, and the Bank of Credit (Castillo and Joseph 1987: 40).

Courting the informal sector brought Barrantes into conflict with the revolutionary bloc, to whom credit to small business seemed almost counterrevolutionary. Revolutionary-bloc leaders of the neighborhood committee (Comunidad Urbana Autogestionaria de Villa El Salvador, or CUAVES) in the municipality of Villa El Salvador criticised an ambitious effort to support the informal sector through the formation of an industrial park because it would create a "new petty bourgeoisie."[16] The revolutionary-bloc leaders argued that IU should place less emphasis on electoral competition and more on building a mass front for revolutionary struggle. According to Taylor, the reformist and independent blocs "held that IU should expand its influence and project itself as a future government by demonstrating its effectiveness in administering Lima" (1990: 111). The revolutionaries believed that the municipality "could not be considered the center of class struggle: in a situation where living standards were falling rapidly, energies also needed to be channelled into developing worker and neighbourhood organizations and into protests against the economic policies of the Belaúnde government" (Taylor 1990: 111; see also debate in PUM reported by Roberts 1992: 353–55).

Barrantes "had little organizational base, and the parties which supported him were little more than prominent personalities with retinues of followers and a relatively weak role in Peru's popular organizations. In contrast, UNIR retained its control over the important teachers' union and wielded influence within the peasant movement, while the PUM dominated the largest peasant federation and the powerful miners' union, and increasingly competed with the weakening Communist Party for influence in the largest labor federation, the CGTP" (Roberts 1992: 361–62). In a 1988 Congress, shortly before the 1989–90 electoral cycle, a sector of the PUM (the *zorros,* or foxes, led by Tapia) rejected "those who underestimate the struggle for the government by privileging confrontation and the fortification of the [party] apparatus." (See Roberts 1992: 365). They broke with PUM and joined Bernales's PSR and Dammert's PCR. This exodus shifted the median voter in PUM to the left, radicalizing the party. There was also an influx of Trotskyists into the PUM in the late 1980s (especially Hugo Blanco's Partido Revolucionario de los Trabajadores, PRT).

PUM's Leninist internal party structure was based on "democratic centralism."[17] Yet, Eduardo Cáceres "admitted that the party had been forced to relax its cellular model and accept more open local committees and assemblies as a result of social and economic instability, since the classic 'factory cell' was hardly functional in a context of an increasingly unemployed, informal, and irregular work force." (Roberts 1992: 342, fn. 47).

Ultimately, the divisions of the Left were caused by a deeper ambivalence toward democracy in the revolutionary bloc. The decision of the Shining Path to reject elections and develop a "prolonged people's war" had a major impact on the strategies of the parties of the parliamentary Left throughout the 1980s. The extreme radicalism in the discourse of Maoist parties[18] in IU reflected their ambivalence about democracy in the face of a movement, the Shining Path, that was obviously pursuing a strategy more consistent with Maoist doctrine.[19] On the other hand, the more reformist groups within the Left became increasingly impatient with the "militarism and vanguardism" of the Maoists and other revolutionary groups within the Left. These tensions between the numerous parties that made up the Left existed even before the United Left was formed as a political coalition, and the continuing growth of the Shining Path during the 1980s ensured that they would never be resolved.

In 1989, after its First National Congress was held in Huampaní, the IU formally divided. Barrantes formed the Acuerdo Socialista to compete in the 1989 municipal elections. Divisions within the IU led to a dramatic decline in overall support for the Left from nearly one-third of the vote at the national level in the municipal election of 1986 to half that number in 1989. Ironically, the division in the Left was partly the result of Barrantes's strategy to capture greater support from independent voters. Nearly one-fifth (19 percent) of the electorate in Lima voted for independent candidates at the district level in 1989 (Roncagliolo 1989–1990: 14). Ricardo Belmont, a television personality who had never before held elected office, won the municipality of Lima. By forming a new political party, Barrantes had hoped to maximize his appeal among undecided independent voters. In the presidential race he even offered to make Hernando de Soto, the director of the Instituto Libertad y Democrácia (ILD), his vice-presidential candidate.[20] De Soto declined, but the gesture reflected the extent to which political alignments were recast around efforts to capture independent voters.

Liberals and Conservatives in FREDEMO

The Right can also be divided into factions with very different understandings of the nature and role of the informal economy in the social and political changes they were seeking to promote. The power of the "old right" was based on its control over land and mines, and it was nearly destroyed as a political force by the agrarian reform during military rule; the new right emerged in the 1980s as a more entrepreneurial class based on banks and massive conglomerates, or *grupos de poder económico* (Durand 1990).

Liberals. The Liberal Right refers basically to the Movimiento Libertad, formed in opposition to the nationalization of the banks by President García. From the outset, the Liberal Right was stigmatized by association with bankers and the business elite.[21]

Liberals espoused free-market reforms for Peru, and criticized the rent-seeking and inefficiency caused by excessive and arbitrary state intervention in the economy. They sought to tap the unexploited economic potential in the unregulated activities that had fled the prohibitive "costs" of formality. Few believed that the informal sector would prefer adjustment policies to expansionary policies. However, the informal sector was widely presumed to be more flexible and capable of adapting to a new, deregulated environment created by market reforms. Thus, the policies advocated by the World Bank and the International Monetary Fund (IMF) were seen to have a potential coalition base in the informal sector (Cameron 1992a: 210).

Liberals took "a public choice view" of the informal sector. They believed it would support whatever political coalition offered it the goods and services it needed. Thus, private-bus drivers were organized by liberals against government regulation of ticket prices, mandatory uniforms, and regimented routes. Bus drivers are owners who hire casual workers to sell tickets. They think of themselves as either workers or employers. Some were previously factory workers and readily adopted lobbying tactics—strikes, vitriolic communiques, demonstrations—that reflected working-class culture and trade-union experience. Yet when asked to sign their communiques as "entrepreneurs," they apparently quite willingly accepted that label.[22]

Conservatives. Conservatives were traditional politicians who received benefits and privileges in Peruvian society and feared the dramatic economic reforms espoused by liberals. A conservative view of the informal sector was common in the traditional parties of the Right. Many conservatives were eager to regulate, and if necessary repress, the informal economy on the grounds that it created bad externalities—noise, filth, and congestion in the streets. Such a view was repeatedly articulated by the conservative newspaper *El Comercio*. It appealed to racist prejudices against the rural migrants, who had left the countryside only to find a hostile reception from the elite in Lima (De Soto 1989a: 10–11).

Evolving Relations between Liberals and Conservatives

Mario Vargas Llosa believed that a liberal program would appeal to small industrialists in the informal sector, small agricultural producers, and workers and peasants who saw their fortunes decline as a result of populist policies (A. Vargas Llosa 1991: 22–23). "We wanted to create something that was broader and more flexible than a political party, a movement that would unite everyone who had opposed nationalization, particularly the *informales,* the members of the 'informal' economy—the millions of peasants who, unable to participate in the state's economy, had created their own black market, popular capitalism" (Vargas Llosa 1991: 29–30).

From the outset the Libertad movement was allied with De Soto's ILD. De Soto joined the nascent movement Libertad as soon as Vargas Llosa began to campaign against García's bank nationalization policy. The author of a widely acclaimed book on the informal sector entitled *The Other Path* (De Soto 1989a), and a personal friend of Vargas Llosa, De Soto provided the intellectual foundation of the Libertad movement.

The initiatives of the ILD were designed to win informal-sector support focused on developing lines of credit, land titles, and organizational expertise. The ILD helped organize the drivers of Lima's seven thousand informally operated buses. Under the leadership of FREDEMO supporter Chang Lafock, the bus drivers held a number of major strikes in 1988. In another project, De Soto proposed a new register of home ownership that was adopted in principle by the García government in April 1988. Most houses in Lima were built illegally. The scheme would entitle residents to take out a loan in return for assigning their property rights to an insurance company.[23]

Mario Vargas Llosa shared De Soto's objections to excessive regulation and rent-seeking in the Peruvian economy: "The problem with Peruvian society is the existence of privileges, monopolies, oligopolies, and all the distortions of the market they produce," he said: "We want to eliminate these, because we believe that a society can't develop under a system based on privileges and monopolies, not only for ethical reasons, but also for economic reasons."[24]

Such a perspective made many local business elites uncomfortable. In particular, De Soto's proclivity to label the Peruvian business elite "mercantilists" irritated some of its members, especially after he publicly attacked the Goodyear Tire Company for making substantial profits at the expense of consumers in an artificially protected market (Bromley 1990: 342). Business elites were also uncomfortable with the ILD-sponsored "union of the formal and informal sectors." This initiative was aimed at formalizing an alliance between small and big businesses against arbitrary state intervention in the economy.

De Soto envisaged Libertad, according to Bromley (1990: 341), "as a long-term movement that should develop its own philosophy, cadres, and think-tanks, perhaps targeting the 1995 elections rather than those scheduled for 1990." An association between his think-tank, the ILD, and the electoral opposition could undermine the relationship between the ILD and the government. Sensing the need for a firmer political vehicle, Vargas Llosa formed the FREDEMO coalition. The alliance with AP and PPC prevented the center-right from entering the 1989 and 1990 elections divided, provided a base of support for Vargas Llosa's candidacy, and supplied the political machinery to run the campaign. Vargas Llosa "preferred the political expediency of an alliance with AP and PPC, even though this associated [Libertad] with traditional politicians, parties, and policies, most notably from the second Belaúnde government of 1980–1985—figures whom De Soto had derided in *The Other Path* as 'right-wing mercantilists'" (Bromley 1990: 341).

De Soto disagreed with Vargas Llosa's decision to form an alliance with the traditional parties of the Right, which he felt would weaken the candidate's ability to capture broad support, especially from the urban poor.[25] Some people in FREDEMO felt that "by giving this reason," he provided "an instrument for attacking Vargas Llosa" (Daeschner 1993: 61). However, De Soto did not create this "instrument," and opponents were sure to seize it regardless of De Soto's views.

One of the consequences of the split between Vargas Llosa and De Soto was that the informal sector was allowed to slip out of the FREDEMO message.[26] As one member of FREDEMO said: "Since Mario fought with De Soto, the people surrounding Mario during the campaign thought that they had to fight De Soto's ideas. . . . To continue dealing with the informals was to continue paying attention to De Soto" (Daeschner 1993: 62).

CONCLUSION

The social bases of the Peruvian Left and Right were clearly differentiated in the 1980s. The Left tended to draw support from workers and the informal sector; the Right appealed to white-collar employees and employers. However, tensions emerged within both coalitions between the leaders of established political parties and politicians who sought to transcend the limits of class politics and build broader coalitions with groups outside the formal economy.

During the course of the research a major tradeoff between votes from the manual working class and the informal sector was expected. This expectation was not borne out by the analysis of voting behavior. Thus, the explanation for the divisions within the Left shifted to its ambivalence about democratic institutions. Diverse reactions within the IU to the growth of the informal sector were merely part of a more fundamental debate on whether the Left should commit itself unequivocally to winning elections by building the broadest possible base of support, or accept that Peru was in a state of virtual civil war and prepare for armed action.

The revolutionary bloc believed that electoral competition was only one arena of struggle. Mass popular organizations had to be created or strengthened in the factories, shantytowns, and provinces. Some thought that in a "conjuncture of an expanding civil war, increased state repression and the possibility of a Pinochet-style coup, it would be foolhardy to be 100 per cent committed to a parliamentary system that could collapse at any time" (Taylor 1990: 112). The reformist and independent blocs, by contrast, held that "the prime task was to safeguard Peru's precarious democratic regime against the combined threat of a rightist military coup and the Shining Path. Reforms should therefore be piecemeal and gradual so as not to provoke the military or the right" (Taylor 1990: 112).

The argument by Przeworski and Sprague provided a more accurate description of the dilemmas of the Right than of those of the Left. A major problem for the Right was the need to broaden its base of support to include workers, shantytown dwellers, the provincial voters, and the informal sector. The Peruvian Right faced a tradeoff in appealing beyond its core constituency among employers and white-collar employees to the broader masses of poor voters in the shantytowns and factories.

The difficulty the liberal Right faced was that much of the electorate blamed the conservative parties in the Right for the social and economic problems of the 1980s. Tensions emerged between conservative politicians (in AP and the PPC) and the liberals who viewed the conservatives with disdain as "paternalists" or "statists." Some liberals—De Soto in particular—argued against an alliance with the conservative parties. Yet such a course would have divided the potential electorate of the Right and deprived Vargas Llosa of the party machinery necessary to sustain a national campaign.

The informal sector did not provide a stable base for either of the coalitions that occupied the opposed poles of the ideological spectrum in Peru. The crisis of the traditional political parties of the Right and Left created an unoccupied space in the arena of electoral competition that was quickly filled by politicians and movements with a powerful message of support for the informal sector. The principal winners in recent elections were independent candidates without an anchor in the established party system. Alan García personified this new style of leadership in 1985. Five years later Alberto Fujimori won the presidential election by highlighting his independence from established parties and his close identification with the urban poor. The strength of candidates like García and Fujimori reflected the disenchantment of the electorate with formal institutional arrangements—whether the formal economy or the established party system.

APPENDIX TO CHAPTER 2

SOURCES OF THE DATA

Data on the occupational characteristics of districts of Metropolitan Lima from the 1981 National Census were compiled and correlated with voting results for the seven elections between and 1978 and 1989. Official election results were taken from Tuesta (1987, 1994a). The data are presented in tables II.1, II.2, and II.3 of this appendix. Note that in table II.1 and all subsequent tables, Villa El Salvador includes Villa María del Triunfo. This is because Villa El Salvador was created as a district after the 1981 National Census was taken.

Data on the informal sector at the district level was obtained through the Ministry of Labor, computed on the basis of the Household Surveys of 1986 and 1987 because the National Census does not provide occupational data disaggregated into wage-earners and non-wage-earners. These two surveys were merged to provide a reasonable number of cases for each district. The methodology used was that proposed by Eliana Chávez O'Brien and Jorge Bernedo in "Los Rasgos Esenciales de la Problemática de los Estratos No Organizados de la Economía," *Apuntes,* no. 8, March 1983, Ministry of Labor. The method consists of separating from the total economically active population all extractive sectors, all professional occupations and all firms with more than four to nine workers depending on the category. What remains is the informal sector.

The method adopted is the standard one employed by the Peruvian Ministry of Labor in collaboration with the ILO. It is consistent with the method used by Alejandro Portes (1985), and provides the basis for the authoritative volume by Carbonetto et al (1988). Given existing data, and my purposes, it was the only available approach. The ILD uses a different method which gives the same results. However, I was interested in district-level data for which the Household Survey was the only available source.

Dietz (1985) demonstrates a high level of intercorrelation among the independent variables drawn from the census data. This makes it harder to distinguish with certainty the relative impact of alternative explanatory variables. Aware of this problem, I make no multivariate claims on the basis of these data.

It is possible that antecedent factors explain the voting outcomes; in fact, some of the most interesting questions emerge by considering the characteristics shared by workers in the formal and informal sectors (and not shared with employers and white-collar employees) that might explain why they vote the way they do—for example, residence in shantytowns, status or income levels. These explanations are not explored here, however.

A certain degree of imprecision is introduced into the analysis by virtue of the use of two data sets: the census, and the district election results. However, the demographic overlap is substantial given that voting is compulsory for the entire adult population and rates of abstention are low. In the absence of adequate survey data, there is no alternative to the method adopted.

Table II.1

Percent of Economically Active Population in Occupational Groups and the Informal Sector in Districts of Metropolitan Lima

Districts	Workers	Employers	White-Collar Employees	Informal Sector
Independencia	40.51	0.38	21.63	50.84
Villa El Salvador*	38.91	0.86	18.90	52.98
Comas	37.34	0.56	24.09	47.00
Lurigancho	35.60	1.18	26.74	33.05
San Juan de Lurigancho	35.56	1.02	24.45	54.74
Ate	32.95	1.70	29.64	39.53
El Agustino	32.85	0.56	19.81	63.38
San Juan de Miraflores	30.29	0.90	32.69	44.30
Chorrillos	30.18	0.94	32.70	35.87
San Martín de Porres	28.25	0.81	37.90	44.20
Rímac	27.53	0.85	40.15	44.06
Lima	23.14	1.39	42.45	43.43
La Victoria	20.45	1.87	38.21	47.70
San Luis	19.27	1.61	38.16	35.37
Breña	17.99	2.02	48.99	41.36
Surquillo	16.94	2.66	46.31	34.55
Baranco	16.52	2.05	50.92	10.72
San Miguel	14.28	1.98	53.90	20.82
Surco	14.25	4.36	47.28	24.77
Lince	9.42	2.88	56.43	20.98
Magdalena	7.32	2.54	57.52	23.82
Pueblo Libre	7.73	2.69	59.29	27.15
Jesus María	6.57	2.56	61.77	23.54
Miraflores	4.99	5.90	53.25	16.10
San Isidro	3.68	8.61	48.15	16.61

Sources: Peruvian National Census (1981); Ministry of Labor, Household Survey (1986, 1987).
*Villa El Salvador includes Villa María del Triunfo

Table II.2

Vote for the Left , 1978-1989

Districts	1978c	1980p	1980m	1983m	1985p	1986m	1989m
Independencia	63.8	24.1	49.4	58.2	36.3	54.7	24.5
Villa El Salvador	51.4	19.7	39.5	53.5	30.6	43.6	21.6
Comas	54.6	20.1	43.1	53.8	34.0	45.9	20.7
Lurigancho	40.2	15.1	29.1	44.1	28.0	35.3	20.5
San Juan de Lurigancho	46.6	18.0	39.4	51.2	33.8	43.3	18.0
Ate	32.9	19.5	38.2	50.4	33.9	42.6	18.7
El Agustino	48.3	19.1	41.4	55.3	36.4	48.3	18.9
San Juan de Miraflores	44.3	16.2	36.7	47.3	28.9	41.3	16.4
Chorrillos	33.2	12.0	26.8	36.9	21.3	27.6	8.4
San Martín de Porres	44.3	17.1	38.4	45.6	27.8	44.5	15.0
Rímac	33.3	12.6	29.5	37.3	22.4	33.6	12.8
Lima	30.4	12.0	28.0	35.1	24.4	36.9	13.2
La Victoria	30.4	12.1	27.6	36.2	22.3	33.1	12.3
San Luis	41.4	14.9	31.5	43.4	25.4	37.0	13.6
Breña	27.1	9.9	24.2	31.5	18.3	29.1	11.0
Surquillo	48.0	12.5	28.3	36.8	21.1	31.6	11.0
Barranco	24.9	8.4	21.6	18.8	15.2	22.9	9.5
San Miguel	24.9	9.3	21.8	27.6	14.9	24.4	8.8
Surco	27.5	10.2	22.5	30.4	14.7	21.1	8.6
Lince	21.5	8.0	19.2	26.1	14.5	23.2	8.8
Magdalena	22.4	7.9	19.9	24.6	13.6	21.9	8.3
Pueblo Libre	20.7	7.8	18.7	24.3	13.8	22.2	9.0
Jesus María	20.1	7.8	18.8	24.8	15.4	24.1	10.0
Miraflores	17.5	7.1	15.3	20.3	10.5	17.5	7.1
San Isidro	15.0	6.4	12.5	16.8	8.3	14.4	5.5

c = Constituent Assembly
m = Municipal
p = Presidential

Sources: Tuesta (1987, 1994a).

Table II.3

Vote for the Right (PPC between 1978-1986, FREDEMO in 1989)

Districts	1978c	1980p	1980m	1983m	1985p	1986m	1989m
Independencia	8.6	3.7	6.2	6.4	4.3	6.7	13.3
Villa El Salvador	17.6	5.3	8.0	9.0	7.7	9.1	12.3
Comas	12.0	5.0	9.0	8.0	5.3	9.2	15.4
Lurigancho	23.8	10.1	13.7	14.3	11.6	16.6	28.2
San Juan de Lurigancho	17.5	6.6	10.1	9.9	7.6	13.2	17.3
Ate	23.6	9.4	14.3	13.8	13.4	18.6	21.4
El Agustino	16.0	6.5	9.8	8.9	6.3	9.6	14.8
San Juan de Miraflores	21.6	9.2	13.3	13.8	11.1	16.3	16.9
Chorrillos	35.2	15.9	21.5	23.1	15.9	25.1	20.3
San Martín de Porres	20.7	9.2	12.7	13.4	10.5	16.4	16.5
Rímac	27.9	13.4	18.4	17.4	14.9	24.0	23.1
Lima	34.9	16.4	22.2	21.3	17.2	26.8	23.5
La Victoria	32.7	14.2	19.4	19.7	17.9	26.5	23.0
San Luis	24.6	9.7	15.1	16.2	17.3	26.6	25.9
Breña	35.1	16.3	21.4	21.4	21.2	31.2	28.3
Surquillo	5.1	14.1	20.1	19.3	19.4	28.7	27.4
Barranco	44.0	20.5	28.5	30.2	27.7	36.7	35.5
San Miguel	40.0	18.6	25.9	26.6	28.9	41.5	36.2
Surco	41.5	20.6	28.0	32.0	36.8	48.2	45.7
Lince	45.0	21.1	30.0	29.1	31.8	42.9	39.2
Magdalena	45.3	21.9	29.8	31.3	33.4	45.3	41.2
Pueblo Libre	47.6	22.8	29.7	31.9	35.6	47.4	43.4
Jesus María	45.5	21.3	28.2	31.3	34.2	46.0	42.3
Miraflores	54.8	28.3	34.5	40.8	47.5	57.7	55.8
San Isidro	59.3	32.9	39.1	44.0	55.2	65.1	63.8

c = Constituent Assembly
m = Municipal
p = Presidential

Sources: Tuesta (1987, 1994a).

.3.

THE CENTER, POPULISM, AND THE INFORMAL SECTOR

This chapter examines the two centrist parties that won presidential elections in 1980 and 1985: the center-right Popular Action party (Acción Popular, or AP), and the center-left American Popular Revolutionary Alliance (Alianza Popular Revolucionaria Americana, or APRA). Both parties were successful in their electoral strategies during the 1980s because they were located near the median voter.[1] However, they were unsuccessful in managing the economy, or in confronting the problem of violence and implementing a coherent counter-subversion strategy. The orthodox economic strategy adopted by AP following the economic crisis in 1982–83 shifted the party sharply to the right in the perception of the electorate and created the opportunity for Alan García Pérez to create a massive center-left coalition in 1985.

Particular attention is devoted in this chapter to the reorientation of the populist APRA toward the informal sector in 1985 under President Alan García. The success of García's strategy, and the devastating defeat of AP, deprived the Right of effective political representation in Parliament—a dangerous situation for a fragile democracy, as Rueschemeyer, Stephens, and Stephens have argued (1992: 9).[2] The also chapter examines the success of independent candidate Ricardo Belmont and his movement, Obras (or Works). Belmont won the municipal election in Lima in 1989 and was reelected in 1993.

In the absence of a clear worker-employer relationship, many informal organizations were susceptible to being captured by multiclass coalitions with politicians and political parties. Although neither a cohesive nor a unified social force, the urban informal sector has given rise to demands for institutional change

(Cameron 1992a). These demands have been articulated, not by parties of the Left and Right, but by populist politicians. The informal sector is not an electoral bloc distinct from other lower-income groups. It provides the basis for populist, multiclass electoral coalitions that nevertheless tend to be highly unstable.

Paul Drake distinguishes between populist movements, policies, and governments. Populist movements are defined by "(1) Paternalistic, personalistic, often charismatic leadership and mobilization from the top down; (2) multiclass incorporation of the masses, especially urban workers but also middle sectors; and (3) integrationist, reformist, nationalist development programs for the state to promote simultaneously import-substituting industrialization and redistributive measures for populist supporters" (1991: 36). Populist policies are designed "to ram through rapid industrialization and redistribution" (1991: 37). "In contrast with populist movements or policies, full-blown populist governments with a magnetic inspirational leader, a multiclass urban clientele, and a hothouse program to raise domestic demand and production have been rarer. The classic models are Argentina under Juan Perón (1946–55, 1973–76), Brazil under the democratic period of Getúlio Vargas and his heirs (1951–64), and Peru under Alan García (1985–90)" (1991: 37).

In the following pages we discuss (1) a neoliberal government; (2) a full-fledged populist government; and (3) an independent municipal government without an organized base or coherent ideology.

AP AND THE POLITICS OF NEOLIBERALISM

The results of the 1980 presidential elections returned Fernando Belaúnde Terry to the presidential palace from which he had been unceremoniously expelled by the military on October 3, 1968. AP refrained from participating in the elections for a new Constituent Assembly in 1978. Yet in 1980, AP was returned to power by a wide margin. Belaúnde won 45 percent of the vote against 27 percent for the APRA candidate, Armando Villanueva. None of the remaining candidates won more than 10 percent; the Left was divided behind five different coalitions (Tuesta 1987: 223).

AP was able to achieve a majority in the House of Deputies and the Senate by forming an alliance with Luis Bedoya Reyes and his PPC. One of Belaúnde's first acts as president was to call municipal elections, which were held in November of 1980. Once again, AP won by a large margin, receiving 36 percent of the municipal votes nation-wide, with the now-united Left winning 24 percent, APRA 23 percent, and the PPC 11 percent. In Lima, AP won with Eduardo Orrego as candidate; AP also won a plurality of the vote in 28 of 39 district municipalities in Lima (Tuesta 1987: 220).

The electoral success of AP was largely due to Belaúnde's ability to rise above the sectarian conflicts that dominated Peruvian politics in the 1970s.[3] As Philip Mauceri has argued, "Belaúnde, with his campaign slogan of 'trabajar y dejar trabajar' (work and let work), appeared as a familiar face on the political scene, yet one untouched by the political conflicts of the 1970s" (1991: 85). Belaúnde appealed to the average voter who felt that the military had mismanaged the economy; APRA was perceived as too sectarian, and the Left was seen as too extremist (Rojas 1986: 119).

The data from table 3.1 demonstrate that the support for AP in 1980 tended not to be associated with any particular social class or sector. AP drew its support broadly from across the society, both in the presidential and municipal elections. Only at the municipal level was the size of the informal sector significantly negatively correlated with votes for AP. In this regard, it is noteworthy that Eduardo Orrego, AP's mayoral candidate in Lima, was notoriously conservative in his treatment of and attitudes toward the informal sector during his term as mayor of Lima between 1980 and 1983.

TABLE 3.1
Ecological Correlations between Percent of Economically Active Population in Occupational Groups and the Informal Sector and Shares of the Vote for AP in Metropolitan Lima, 1980–1985

		Workers	Employers	White-Collar Employees	Informal Sector
1985	Presidential	0.243	0.432*	-0.172	0.118
1983	Municipal	0.885**	0.814**	0.800**	-0.868**
1980	Municipal	-0.472*	0.035	0.385*	-0.602**
1980	Presidential	0.076	0.490*	-0.024	-0.200

Pearson's r correlation coefficients:
**significant at the 0.005 level; *significant at the 0.05 level.
N = 25 districts.   Sources: See appendix to chapter 3.

Belaúnde's ability to remain at the center of the political spectrum was, however, restricted by his management of the economic crisis that began in 1982 and his appointment of an orthodox economic team. The priorities set by Manuel Ulloa, Belaúnde's Prime Minister, included trade liberalization, cutbacks on state subsidies, promotion of foreign investment, deregulation, and privatization of state owned enterprises.[4] The government reversed the changes to property rights established under the Velasco government (1968–75) and accelerated the schedule of repayments on the international debt in order to increase the credit-worthiness of the country in international money markets. With export prices rising in the early 1980s, these policies seemed sensible and feasible. Nobody in the Peruvian government anticipated the impending economic collapse (Aggarwal and Cameron 1994).

In 1982–83 prices for Peru's traditional exports (minerals and petroleum) fell, and climatic conditions affected agricultural produce and the fishing industry. At the same time, international interest rates soared, and service on the debt increased correspondingly. Global recession, high interest rates, indiscriminate trade liberalization, and other factors resulted in a decline of 12.3 percent in Peru's Gross Domestic Product (GDP) in 1983. Belaúnde was forced to reschedule Peru's debt under extremely unfavorable terms. Negotiations with the IMF and the banks led to the implementation of harsh austerity measures that resulted in massive labor protest and unrest in the public sector.

When municipal elections were held in 1983 the erosion of support for AP was clear. By then, AP was seen as a right-wing party (see table 3.1). No longer was it perceived as identified with the average voter. AP support became strongly correlated with social classes and sectors. Working-class districts tended not to vote for AP, whereas employers and white-collar workers tended to be strongly associated with AP.

In 1984 Belaúnde began to prepare for his succession; he recognized that AP needed a fresh face, and sought out Mario Vargas Llosa as a potential candidate. Belaúnde's initial proposal was for Vargas Llosa to lead both the PPC and AP in the 1985 presidential election. However, negotiations on Vargas Llosa's candidacy fell through when the PPC refused to accept Vargas Llosa's leadership and instead proposed its own leader, Luis Bedoya, to lead the coalition. "We didn't have any idea of what Vargas Llosa was like," said one PPC activist (Daeschner 1993: 45).

The process of electoral polarization and division in the Right that occurred after the 1983 municipal elections created an opportunity for any political party or leader who could appeal to the center, particularly the center-left. This opportunity was not lost on Alan García. AP and PPC activists would later blame each other for failing to stop García.

GARCIA'S REORIENTATION OF APRA TOWARD THE INFORMAL SECTOR

The reorientation of APRA toward the urban informal sector under the charismatic leadership of Alan García in 1985 signaled the emergence of an important new type of multiclass coalition in the Latin American region. Unlike earlier populist coalitions founded during the period of import-substitution industrialization, this new variant of populism was not based on an expanding industrial work force. Fifty years after the early phase of labor organization,

APRA built a new kind of broad-based popular coalition in the international context of debt and a severe economic recession. As industry contracted, throwing
tens of thousands of workers out of their jobs, the urban informal sector almost
doubled.[5] By 1986 it encompassed nearly half of the work force in Lima.

In 1985 APRA won an absolute majority (53 percent) of the valid votes cast.
It also captured most of the districts of Lima. Support was strongest in the
densely populated shantytowns of Lima, where over half of the city's electorate was concentrated. Table 3.2 shows no relation between the population
in lower-income groups and support for APRA in the period between the formation of a Constituent Assembly under military rule and the municipal election of 1983. Strong correlations emerged for the first time only in 1985 and
1986 with the rise of Alan García.

TABLE 3.2

**Ecological Correlations between Percent of Economically Active Population
in Occupational Groups and the Informal Sector and Shares of the Vote
for APRA in Metropolitan Lima, 1978-1989**

		Workers	Employers	White-Collar Employees	Informal Sector
1989	Municipal	0.695**	-0.833**	-0.505*	0.663**
1986	Municipal	0.835**	-0.850**	-0.714**	0.667**
1985	Presidential	0.714**	-0.913**	-0.518*	0.647**
1983	Municipal	0.233	-0.658**	0.032	0.258
1980	Municipal	0.279	-0.638**	-0.130	0.421*
1980	Presidential	-0.056	-0.411*	0.284	0.095
1978	Constituent Assembly	-0.041	-0.510*	0.179	0.147

Pearson's r correlation coefficients:
**significant at the 0.005 level; *significant at the 0.05 level.
N = 25 districts.   Sources: See appendix to chapter 3.

The urban poor, especially in Lima's shantytowns, were a major source of
support for APRA in the 1985 presidential race.[6] APRA has always had the
solid backing of a broad spectrum of groups—workers, peasants, and the
middle-income groups in the urban and coastal areas. APRA had especially
strong support in the middle class.[7] But the party was weak in Lima and the
central highlands (McDonald and Ruhl 1989: 215). APRA had a powerful
party machine connected to a large regional clientele, yet never once won a
plurality of the vote in Lima in any election prior to 1985 (Tuesta 1986: 38).

Observers have often been struck by how, in the post-authoritarian period,
APRA retained a core of support, which included a wide spectrum of voters:

workers, peasants, middle sectors and parts of the upper bourgeoisie (Bernales 1980: 61). Clearly, APRA lost much of its working support with the emergence of the United Left. However, APRA recovered working-class support in 1985 and 1986. After military rule, in the four elections prior to 1985, APRA's share of the vote did not reflect, as it had in 1963 and 1966, a definite bias toward any social group, except perhaps against employers.

The 1985 reorientation of APRA reflected the personality and leadership of Alan García. The degree to which the party was reoriented toward workers and the informal sector diminished in 1989 when he was no longer the candidate.

García's efforts to build a political base with the urban poor ran against the grain of electoral polarization that was the legacy of military rule in the 1970s. He captured a plurality of the vote in every district except San Isidro and Miraflores—the most exclusive, wealthy districts of Lima. Alan García did not seek to divide Peru's electorate along class lines. During the campaign he focused on local business, the middle sectors, the peasantry, and workers (Bonilla and Drake 1989: 11). He made no rhetorical calls to class division; nor did he directly attack the Left's control over trade unions. García did, however, suggest that unions represented a "privileged minority," located in the top income quarter of the social pyramid (Ballón 1986a).

García sought to form a multiclass coalition that drew support from all classes and sectors. He appealed broadly to the entire electorate with the message: "My commitment is to all Peruvians." But he paid special attention to the informal sector, which he alternately called "the marginal," "the forgotten ones," "the poor," and "the future of the nation." In his inaugural address, García proclaimed himself the president of "the other 70 percent" of the population—"the agricultural and peasant sectors, the unemployed and street vendors, the provincial inhabitants, and the shantytown residents."[8]

In defining his supporters, García referred to "the rural Andean agriculture with its millions of campesinos and sharecroppers and another human group that some people have called the informal sector, which includes the unemployed and underemployed, most of whom are inhabitants of the shantytowns." According to a senior government official, party strategists recognized the linkage between migration and the urban informal sector. Most of those who migrated to Lima in the 1970s came from the northern provinces of Peru where APRA was historically strong. Table 3.2 shows a strong positive correlation between the percent share of the urban informal sector in districts of Lima and votes for APRA in 1985 and 1986.

García sought to occupy the center-left, undercutting IU and winning away its supporters, particularly among provincial migrants in Lima. "We have to distance ourselves from the Left and capture the broad sectors that support it," said the APRA candidate; "the Shining Path has broken up the Left, and this can be seen in its language which is divided between a reformist discourse, as they call it, a social democratic discourse close to APRA, and radical language which, nevertheless, cannot be radical because it has the obligation to differentiate itself from the Shining Path."[9]

Under the leadership of García, APRA attempted to build a "social democratic" coalition based on *concertación* (peak bargaining) with business groups and social assistance to the informal sector (Durand 1990). Business would provide investment for economic recovery and the informal sector would provide votes to maintain the predominance of APRA. García embarked on a demand-stimulus strategy of economic growth aimed at improving the lives of those who lived in the poorer districts in the periphery of Lima, among others. He asked, "for whom will the industrial sector produce if the majority gets poorer by the day?"

The central idea proposed by García was to "give jobs or a chance to earn a living to the hundreds of thousands of unemployed or underemployed people in the shantytowns" in order to attain the "social reactivation of consumption." "We will be building a new nation," García said, "if our agricultural production can meet the consumption needs of those who now have nothing to eat because they have no jobs. This process must take place at the foundations of society, at the lowest level of the social pyramid. The local market will then buy Lima's industrial production, which is slowly dying because of vanishing demand." Offering redistributive justice and nationalist development, García revived populist rhetoric in a new domestic and international environment.

Recent analyses of the reorientation of APRA have drawn upon the literature on populism (Abugattas 1987; Bonilla and Drake 1989; Graham 1990, 1992; Sanborn 1989). Populist coalitions with broad working-class support are common in the history of the Latin American region—some examples are Peronism in Argentina, Vargas's *Estado Novo* in Brazil, and the reformist government of Lázaro Cárdenas in Mexico. However, the term "populism" tends to evoke images from the aftermath of the Depression in the 1930s. Indeed, a recent volume suggested that perhaps "a wave of studies of populism is upon us because historians like to analyze things that are dead. Although a funeral oration for populism may be premature, such movements clearly faded in the 1970s" (Drake in Conniff, ed., 1982: 217; see chapter by Drake in Bonilla and Drake 1989: 14). If "populist" is the correct label for the García government, clearly it is very different from the populism of the 1930s–1960s.

Populist movements are usually associated with an expansion of the organized working class in the early stages of industrial growth. Juan Perón, Lázaro Cárdenas, and Getúlio Vargas each played an important role in the incorporation of an institutionalized labor movement into their respective political systems. By contrast, the García government did not rest on the support of organized labor (Sanborn 1989: 93). García came to power during an international economic recession that slackened employment in the industrial labor market and led to a demobilization of the trade-union movement (Parodi 1986b).

It was not the heterogeneity of García's social base that was unlike earlier populist parties and movements, nor the fact that his strategy cut against the grain of electoral polarization in a society sharply divided along class and ethnic lines.[10] García's populism occurred in the context of a new international and intraurban division of labor. Constructed outside the modern sector, the APRA coalition was strongly connected with the informal economy, the unemployed, and the migrant shantytown population in Lima. With great prescience Julio Cotler (1985: 48) observed that García's victory presaged a decline in class politics, and the rise of new social subjects: "The political system, 'open' to demands from multiple social subjects that do not define their political identity as social classes, will create the conditions for a rejection of 'class-based' social programs and, instead, will favor options that take into account the demands of various social subjects and classes."

The victory of Alan García in the 1985 presidential election was accomplished with broad working-class support for his party. Yet APRA did not make a specific electoral appeal to what he called the "privileged" unionized work force, which was dominated by the Left; nor did he seek to revive old APRA-union linkages using the moribund APRA-union confederation; instead, he made an energetic effort to build a direct and highly personalistic relationship with the unorganized segments of labor.

The success of Alan García's bid to be the candidate of APRA followed Barrantes's successful campaign in the municipal elections of 1983. The victory of Barrantes in 1983 demonstrated the efficacy of appealing to the informal sector. The APRA old guard saw in García someone who could win broad support from the masses without exacerbating social tensions; someone who could bring together his country as well as his party. To do so, García revived the notion of the "oligarchy," and directed his message to the *pueblo*.[11] He claimed that, despite a major land reform in the 1970s, the oligarchy continued to survive in the form of powerful elites tied to financial institutions and the IMF.

In explicitly rejecting appeals to class, García argued that the organized working class was part of that privileged 25 percent of the country that earned 75 percent of the national income, and he claimed to be the president of the informal sector not organized labor. In the districts classified by the Central Reserve Bank as typical shantytown districts, García dramatically increased APRA's vote. Whereas these districts accounted for only 20 percent of APRA's total vote in 1980, in 1985 they accounted for 40 percent. APRA became the dominant force in all districts of Lima, especially those with large informal sector.

Table III.2 in the appendix shows that APRA under García drew support from across all districts of Lima. The class cleavage was a strong predictor of APRA support, but the variance in support for APRA across districts was small. APRA did well in both rich and poor districts of Lima. Therefore, despite the strength of the correlation coefficients shown on table 3.2, the 1985 and 1986 elections illustrate the strategic importance of centrist voters in Peruvian politics.

Once in government, García sought to consolidate his support with the informal sector, using three main instruments: Programa de Apoyo de Ingreso Temporal (PAIT), a job creation program aimed at supplementing lower class incomes; the Instituto para Desarrollo del Sector Informal (IDESI), which gave credit to the informal sector; and the Programa Metropolitano de Empleo (PROEM), a job contracting program that allowed employers to hire workers without providing job security after the three month period stipulated by law (Paredes 1988a, 1988b; Graham 1992: 169–99). Although the last measure seemed unexpectedly "anti-labor," it was consistent with the overall thrust of García's policies. It allowed APRA to reactivate the economy without strengthening the trade union movement; it also held constant the size of the informal sector. The other two policies allowed APRA to directly coopt the informal sector. PAIT provided temporary employment at the minimum wage for over 150,000 workers in Lima alone (Vigier 1986a). IDESI provided credit to over 75,000 recipients in the informal sector (Pinilla 1986).

IDESI, the most ambitious of these programs, was created by an agreement between the International Labour Office and the National Planning Institute in Peru. This agreement created a fund (Fondo de Credito del Sector Informal—FONCRESI) to be administered through the existing financial system (the Central Credit Cooperative, the Bank of the Nation, the Bank of Credit, the Agrarian Bank, and the Municipal Bank). A major accomplishment of this arrangement, according to top IDESI officials, was that informal sector recipients of credit acquired expertise in dealing with private financial institutions to which they had previously been denied access.

The main aim of aid to the informal sector was to strengthen the political support of APRA (Paredes 1988a: 79). Most PAIT jobs were distributed where APRA sought to consolidate its vote at the expense of the Left. PAIT workers were obliged to attend meetings in support of the government at which Aprista symbols were prominently displayed, and were frequently driven en masse to political rallies. On a number of occasions PAIT workers were used in direct confrontations with striking workers and employees in the formal sector. Twice they formed counterdemonstrations at picket lines to harass striking workers.

Temporary jobs did not guarantee political support. In Villa El Salvador, the left-wing municipality insisted on participating in the administration of the PAIT to neutralize its political effect. Many workers participated in pro-APRA rallies organized by the PAIT without feeling any obligation to vote for APRA. Carol Graham has noted that "APRA's connections with these sectors were very shallow and were made even more so by García's populism. The way in which programs . . . were implemented—always from above and with no respect for existing organizations—limited their potential" (1990: 95; see also 1992).

In the case of IDESI, the receipt of credit was apparently not tied to political conditions. The main slogan of IDESI was: "Your work is your collateral." The only condition of continuing credit was prompt repayment of previous loans. With a default rate lower than in the formal sector (a mere 2 percent, according to Pinilla [1988: 45]), many recipients were allowed to return for ever larger loans. Yet, IDESI did serve as a channel between the president and the informal sector. In 1988 it organized meetings between García and informal-sector groups at a point when García's popularity ratings had begun to decline precipitously, even with the popular sectors. In one meeting the president extolled the virtues of the informal sector, and then officially recognized one of its new organizations, the Central de Trabajadores Ambulantes de Lima Metropolitano (CETALM). But although García left a favorable impression on the assembly, there was no guarantee that this would be translated into votes.

It was possible for APRA to build a domestic coalition around confrontation with the IMF without directly challenging the control of the Left over unionized labor because of the electoral weight of the informal sector. Much-anticipated efforts by APRA to recapture control over unions remained blocked, moreover, by the difficulties of extricating the entrenched oligarchy from APRA–dominated unions. By reactivating the economy without strengthening labor, APRA intended to win the support of business—the other major group detrimentally affected by the economic crisis of 1982–83. The coalition with business would have electoral support from the informal sector.

Support for García fell precipitously when the recovery in 1985-87 was followed by a severe recession; the economy contracted by 8.4 percent in 1988, 11.4 percent in 1989, and 4.9 percent in 1990 (CEPAL 1991: 39). In this environment, largely stimulated by García's populist policies, no government could expect reelection.

THE RISE OF AN INDEPENDENT CANDIDATE: BELMONT AND OBRAS

The unexpected surge of independent candidate Ricardo Belmont in November 1989 deprived FREDEMO of a victory in Lima. Although a wealthy man, Belmont was an affable person with a common touch who was able to present himself as the candidate of the average person against the political establishment. He controlled a television channel and hosted a talk show called "Habla el Pueblo" ("The People Speak") and an annual charity telethon. Belmont assiduously avoided controversial or ideological language, refused to directly attack opponents, and eschewed identifying himself with the left or right of the political spectrum.[12] He reportedly told Vargas Llosa "my voters are above all in sectors C and D,[13] and the votes I will take will not be those of FREDEMO but rather of the United Left. My own class, the bourgeoisie, despises me, because I speak in slang and because they believe I am uncultured. In contrast, although I am light-skinned, the mestizo indians and blacks in the shantytowns like me a lot and will vote for me" (Vargas Llosa 1993: 135). Belmont's movement, Obras (or Works) stressed the need for public works around Lima. Belmont's rise in 1989 was the first clear indication of the new phenomenon of the "independent" candidate, and a premonition of Fujimori's success.

In the 1989 municipal election Obras drew support from across Lima—in most districts Belmont won over 15 percent more votes than FREDEMO. Only in FREDEMO strongholds like Miraflores and San Isidro did Belmont win less than a plurality of the vote. His support was strongest in working-class districts in the center of Lima, and in the shantytowns in the southern cone. His support in 1989 was very strong with the informal sector and workers.

The phenomenon of the "independent" candidate is an initially puzzling one. Belmont avoided polarization and class conflict, drawing support from across social classes and sectors. Nevertheless, as table 3.3 shows, his support was strongly correlated with the size of the informal sector or working-class population in districts of Lima. The explanation lies in the preponderance of workers and members of the informal sector in Metropolitan Lima. By occupying the center, Belmont was able to assure a plurality of the vote from those groups whose votes count the most while studiously avoiding antagonizing other sectors.

The data in table 3.3 suggests an interesting comparison between Obras and APRA: both demonstrate the same pattern of electoral support. The vote for both APRA and Obras was positively correlated with workers and the informal sector, negatively correlated with white-collar employees, and strongly negatively correlated with employers. In effect, Belmont was able to put together the same multiclass coalition that supported the rise of Alan García in 1985 and APRA's successful 1986 mayoral candidate, Jorge del Castillo.

TABLE 3.3
Ecological Correlations between Percent of Economically Active Population in Occupational Groups and the Informal Sector and Shares of the Vote for Obras in Municipal Election, 1989

	Workers	Employers	White-Collar Employees	Informal Sector
Obras	0.662	-0.814	-0.553	0.715

Pearson's r correlation coefficients: all correlations significant at the 0.005 level.
N = 25 districts.
Sources: See appendix to chapter 3.

THE CENTER AND THE INFORMAL SECTOR

The parties that traditionally occupied the center or center-left of the political spectrum have been those which have been able to construct winning electoral coalitions in Peru. The findings of this chapter suggest that during the 1980s the informal sector became an increasingly important part of those coalitions. The informal sector was not a cohesive collective actor capable of establishing enduring or institutionalized links with political parties. However, evidence from the 1985 election suggests that the informal sector had a center-left orientation in politics. A number of studies have confirmed this finding. They indicate that a high level of individualism, combined with support for social change, tended to coexists in the attitudes of the informal sector, which placed a higher value on individual initiative than on class struggle, but also believed in an interventionist state that would redistributes wealth (Tueros 1984, Chávez O'Brien 1990a).

Other studies find an affinity between the informal sector and populist politics (Franco 1989, 1992). A study by Adams and Valdivia (1991) found members of the informal sector to be supportive of populist and centrist ideas. Class conflict was a less significant part of their vocabulary. This is consistent with Grompone's observation that the informal sector will tend not to support demands for guilds or corporatist groups from which its members feel marginalized (Grompone 1991: 49). There is also comparative evidence for this thesis: Amparo Menéndez-Carrión (1986: 449–50) has shown that the growth of the informal sector strengthened clientelistic parties and populist politicians in Ecuador.

Grompone rejects the idea that the informal sector is a social actor capable of stable linkages with political parties and leaders. He sees the informal sector as a world of "multiple personal ties, some lasting, others that are done and undone in a short period, based on family networks, on neighborhoods (in popular barrios that have been converted into poles of economic activity) and in the extension of subcontracting relations" (1991: 48). The relationship between this world and the political arena is intermittent, fluid, and unstable. In the face of these actors, political parties cannot build lasting ties; they can win temporary adherents, but they rarely know whether their support is solid (Grompone 1991: 49).

CONCLUSION

Whether voters in the informal sector are courted as victims of dependent capitalist industrialization or enemies of "redistributive combines," they are clearly perceived as a major political constituency for politicians seeking office. Political parties across the ideological spectrum have sought to build a social base on informal sector support. "At election time," writes Ray Bromley, "all political parties seek the votes of street vendors, para-transit operators, and squatters, but between elections a policy of selective repression and benign neglect prevails" (1990: 343).

Populist leaders have competed with parties of the Left and the Right. The informal sector has proven an elusive source of electoral support. Successful politicians have been those who presented themselves as independent and oriented toward change. The Left had a mixed record in competing for support from the informal sector; the record of the Right was worse.

Throughout the 1980s the Left won most of its support from the urban poor. The informal sector tended to vote much like the rest of the urban poor. As a result, some groups assumed that the informal sector would provide an enduring base for the Left. Yet in recent elections populist candidates like García (and, as we shall see in chapter 6, Fujimori) built broad-based multiclass electoral coalitions with the support of the informal sector.

The principal winners in recent elections were centrist and populist candidates who represented change without the threat of class conflict and polarization. Alan García personified this new brand of populism in 1985. The strength of candidates like Belaúnde and García reflected the lack of partisan loyalty in the Peruvian electorate. That electorate was increasingly disconnected from formal institutional arrangements—whether the formal economy or the established party system.

The class position of the informal sector is so ambiguous that it is impossible to predict behavioral outcomes on the basis of class position. In the political arena, a floating and independent electorate has refused to accept the traditional party system. These two processes are tightly intertwined. The growth of the Peruvian informal sector has given rise to important institutional changes with powerful ramifications in the political system.

Party competition in Peru since the 1970s has been highly polarized and often based on a deep class cleavage. Although the informal sector did not emerge as a distinct electoral bloc with interests clearly differentiated from the rest of the urban poor, it did contribute to the transformation of the party system. The class cleavage did not disappear, but the opposed poles of the class vote—the Left and the Right—were both debilitated by their inability to build a political relationship with an increasingly elusive urban poor.

APPENDIX TO CHAPTER 3

Table III.1

Vote for AP, 1980-1985

Districts	1980p	1980m	1983m	1985p
Independencia	52.31	28.97	7.01	4.21
Villa El Salvador	53.03	39.11	9.50	4.59
Comas	50.30	32.01	7.52	4.04
Lurigancho	51.17	37.42	12.79	5.95
San Juan de Lurigancho	53.21	34.61	8.85	4.05
Ate	57.72	32.54	8.98	3.56
El Agustino	18.43	29.47	8.52	4.19
San Juan de Miraflores	50.57	35.76	9.20	5.07
Chorrillos	49.39	36.89	10.49	4.69
San Martín de Porres	24.59	31.35	7.81	3.92
Rímac	45.43	33.81	11.25	4.60
Lima	44.50	32.79	11.64	4.53
La Victoria	47.07	35.65	11.35	4.20
San Luis	53.20	35.10	11.51	5.17
Breña	43.79	31.89	11.85	4.09
Surquillo	47.84	36.17	12.20	4.67
Barranco	47.07	35.77	15.95	4.26
San Miguel	46.47	35.89	12.80	3.81
Surco	48.63	37.97	13.06	3.92
Lince	46.00	36.68	14.30	4.30
Magdalena	46.26	34.00	14.90	4.70
Pueblo Libre	46.33	36.55	15.05	4.13
Jesus María	47.38	36.67	15.56	4.61
Miraflores	45.95	39.08	16.68	3.91
San Isidro	44.44	39.26	19.38	3.35

m = Municipal
p = Presidential

Source: Tuesta (1987).

Table III.2

Vote for APRA, 1978-1989

Districts	1978c	1980p	1980m	1983m	1985p	1986m	1989m
Independencia	19.8	20.5	15.5	25.6	53.4	37.6	12.8
Villa El Salvador	21.7	18.2	13.4	24.7	55.1	46.3	13.0
Comas	25.2	22.4	16.0	28.3	54.9	43.9	16.0
Lurigancho	26.9	21.0	19.8	25.2	52.7	47.3	12.3
San Juan de Lurigancho	27.2	20.0	15.9	26.6	52.5	42.5	11.4
Ate	24.6	14.6	14.9	23.3	47.3	36.7	11.0
El Agustino	25.4	18.4	19.3	24.4	50.4	41.8	11.9
San Juan de Miraflores	24.4	21.3	14.2	26.1	52.8	41.6	11.5
Chorrillos	22.6	20.4	14.9	24.2	55.5	46.4	10.7
San Martín de Porres	25.8	24.6	17.5	29.9	55.9	38.4	12.5
Rímac	26.4	26.6	18.2	30.8	55.9	41.4	13.2
Lima	26.0	25.1	17.0	29.0	51.9	35.6	12.5
La Victoria	27.4	24.4	17.3	29.7	53.6	39.5	11.6
San Luis	23.7	19.8	18.4	26.2	50.4	35.7	10.1
Breña	29.6	28.5	22.5	31.8	55.0	39.0	14.4
Surquillo	35.5	23.3	15.5	27.8	53.0	39.1	11.4
Barranco	23.1	22.1	14.2	30.8	50.9	38.7	11.0
San Miguel	26.9	24.4	16.5	29.2	50.5	33.6	10.3
Surco	21.7	18.4	11.6	21.4	42.7	30.2	8.8
Lince	25.5	23.3	17.2	27.1	47.7	33.4	10.8
Magdalena	28.8	22.4	16.3	25.8	46.5	32.3	9.9
Pueblo Libre	23.9	21.8	15.0	26.2	44.8	30.0	10.2
Jesus María	27.7	22.2	16.3	25.4	44.0	29.9	10.2
Miraflores	20.0	17.2	11.2	19.5	36.2	24.4	7.0
San Isidro	18.8	14.9	9.2	17.3	31.6	20.3	5.6

c = Constituent Assembly
m = Municipal
p = Presidential

Sources: Tuesta (1987, 1994a).

Table III.3

Vote for Obras in Municipal Election, 1989

Districts	
Independencia	46.78
Villa El Salvador	47.98
Comas	45.25
Lurigancho	36.12
San Juan de Lurigancho	51.07
Ate	45.53
El Agustino	51.67
San Juan de Miraflores	53.24
Chorrillos	58.46
San Martín de Porres	53.80
Rímac	47.62
Lima	48.99
La Victoria	51.23
San Luis	48.31
Breña	44.32
Surquillo	48.64
Barranco	42.38
San Miguel	43.06
Surco	35.86
Lince	39.76
Magdalena	39.41
Pueblo Libre	36.30
Jesus María	36.10
Miraflores	29.22
San Isidro	24.36

Source: Tuesta (1994a).

PART III

CRISIS IN THE LEFT AND THE RIGHT

*T*his section examines the crisis within the political coalitions that occupied the extreme poles of the class vote in Peru in the 1980s. Whereas previous chapters explored the social bases of political parties in Peru, these chapters are interested in coalition politics. In particular, they seek to explain why parties of the Left and Right in Peru lost viability leading up to the 1990 presidential elections, thus creating an "entry opportunity" for anti-system candidates.

Coalition dynamics surrounding Vargas Llosa's resignation from the candidacy of Fredemo in 1989 provide crucial insights into the internal politics of the Right in chapter 4. Vargas Llosa's decision to remain in an alliance with the traditional parties of the Right undermined his independence and made it impossible for him to occupy the center.

The division of the Left could have provided a center-left candidate with an image of independence and catapulted him into the Palace of Government. However, chapter 5 shows that the way the Left divided confused the electorate, discouraged party activists, and ultimately contributed to the perception that a vote for the Left was a wasted vote. Insights from the internal politics of coalitions from these chapters are applied to understand why class-based parties failed to occupy the center and win the 1990 presidential elections.

.4.

ALLIANCE BARGAINING
IN THE DEMOCRATIC FRONT

hortly after being formally proclaimed the candidate of FREDEMO for the presidential election of April 1990, Mario Vargas Llosa suddenly withdrew from the race. Political elites were thrown into disarray. A complex strategic "game" was initiated; at stake was the leadership and consolidation of the Right before the 1990 elections. Coalition unity was restored to FREDEMO after a period of intense negotiations in which Vargas Llosa forced his partners to bow to his leadership.[1]

Why did Vargas Llosa threaten to resign, and why was his defection from the coalition a successful bargaining strategy? This chapter proposes a model of strategic interaction based on the theory of games. N-person game theory is particularly suitable because it is primarily concerned with the dynamics of coalition formation and disintegration, and the distribution of payoffs within coalitions (Zagare 1984: 64). A major limitation of game theory, however, is that it assumes all actors have the same motivation to play. This is unrealistic: actors may try to influence other actors' perceptions of their willingness to play in order to extract concessions. Such a strategy is only effective where all actors place a high value on unity.

Vargas Llosa took advantage of the need for coalition unity to extract concessions from his partners. This created a new game in which the collapse of the coalition became a feasible outcome. Models of these games are generated by ranking actor preferences and assigning simple decision-rules to strategic interaction. A three-dimensional matrix provides a model of the games that takes into account the various strategies open to the actors. Using the Nash solution concept, the deductive power of game theory can then be employed to explain bargaining outcomes.[2]

Chapter 2 analyzed the social basis for the division between political leaders seeking to build wider coalitions with groups outside the formal sectors and party bosses who aimed to preserve the strength of their party machines and their position in the political elite. This chapter analyzes a short episode of bargaining and leadership struggle that provides a window into larger problems faced by ideological parties in Peru in the decade of crisis. Social scientists have been loath to focus on historically brief, discrete events with few actors and a finite set of possible bargaining outcomes (Riker 1957: 69), yet this is precisely where the analysis of strategic choice is most likely to be profitable.[3]

There have been a number of efforts to apply rational choice models to the analysis of coalitions and regime transitions in Latin America (O'Donnell 1973: ch. 4; Przeworski 1986, 1991; Geddes 1991, 1993; Shugart 1992), but such efforts are unfortunately rare. David Collier and Deborah L. Norden have recently observed that "analysts of Latin America often view these models as an alien tradition of research" (1992: 229). A larger goal of this book is to illustrate the utility of a game-theoretic model of coalition building in Latin America, without presenting a highly technical argument. Readers who are not interested in game theory should, by following the narrative, be able to capture the argument and understand the main findings.

VARGAS LLOSA AND THE DEMOCRATIC FRONT

Actor Preferences

The point of departure for any game-theoretic analysis is the preferences of the players. The often tedious task of defining actor preferences is ignored at great peril in applications of game theory. For example, an analyst might begin by observing noncooperative behavior. Immediately, the situation is defined as a "prisoner's dilemma." It is demonstrated that cooperation is difficult to achieve in a prisoner's dilemma, and this is presented as an explanation for the observed behavior. Unfortunately, the argument is circular. Not surprisingly, such findings inevitably become embroiled in unproductive controversy over whether the situation is really a prisoner's dilemma, or some other game.

The basic mistake in the above approach is in failing to start from a careful description of the actors' preferences. A prisoner's dilemma emerges from a game in which two players have a specific preference ranking (namely, where being a "traitor" is better than being "rewarded" for cooperation, "punished" for non-cooperation, or "suckered"). But non-cooperation can also be caused by "deadlock" (where players actually prefer, say, being "punished" to being "rewarded"), and the difference is not trivial. The analyses in this book are intended to demonstrate how the ranking of preferences among actors results in a game of conflict that helps explain the collapse or unification of a coalition, without resorting to circular reasoning or forcing observed behavior into the procrustean bed of the prisoner's dilemma.

Who were the major players in FREDEMO, and what were their preferences? In 1988 FREDEMO was formed as an electoral coalition to run in the April 1990 presidential elections in Peru (Durand 1989: 2). Three actors within FREDEMO were involved in the bargaining: the Movimiento Libertad, AP, and the PPC. At the time of FREDEMO's founding, no explicit agreement was reached concerning whether the parties in the front should run as a unified slate of candidates or as separate political forces in the November 1989 municipal elections.

The first task confronting Vargas Llosa upon assuming the leadership of FREDEMO in June 1989 was to arrive at an agreement on this sensitive issue. Vargas Llosa sought a solution that would enhance his position relative to the traditional party bosses. He knew that tough austerity measures would fail unless implemented by a team of well-trained technocrats supported by a broad-based social consensus regarding the goals of adjustment. The party bosses would be more interested in jobs and personal benefits than in appointing the best technicians. This negative image of the party bosses was shared by much of the electorate. One commonly expressed view was that "the *pitucos* from AP want to steal from us again."[4] Therefore, it was necessary to keep the party bosses and other special interests in line. Vargas Llosa's publicity managers made it clear that were the old party leaders visibly in control of the campaign, Vargas Llosa's appeals for support for the "great transformation" of Peru would have little credibility.

Three outcomes were considered possible in the bargaining over the municipal elections:

A. A unified slate of FREDEMO candidates.
B. Separate and rival party slates.
C. Division of FREDEMO.

The worst possible outcome for all of the players was C, because it would presumably lead to a defeat in the subsequent presidential election, which all players believed they could not afford to lose. All players within FREDEMO valued victory in the 1990 election (relative to future ones) because of the perceived likelihood that future elections would not be held if the IU came to power. As one of Vargas Llosa's advisers put it, "a triumph of the extreme left could close the doors on democratic renovation in Peru" either "by means of a military golpe, or by the path of the imposition of red totalitarianism from the entrails of the regime."[5]

Vargas Llosa was concerned about the need for the Right to be unified going into the election. Concerning his decision not to run as an independent, he said:

> I was aware of the risks, but I decided that they were outweighed by the benefits of an alliance. Many reforms were needed in Peru, and to see them through, a broad popular base was required. Popular Action and the Christian Popular Party had impeccable democratic credentials and could influence significant sectors of the populace. To present ourselves to voters as separate parties would split support between the center and right and make either United Left or APRA the winner. The negative image of 'old pols' could be effaced with our new programme, reforms that had nothing to do with the populism of Popular Action or the conservatism of the Christian Popular Party but that would be associated with a radical liberalism never before put forward in Peru. Perhaps, most important, *Libertad* consisted mainly of members with no political experience—there was no party apparatus—and we needed help from the established parties merely to compete with both APRA (which in addition to its own organization could also depend on the machinery of the state in its campaign) and a left that had been battle-hardened in a number of elections (1991: 38–39).

The difference between *A* and *B* was that *A* meant running unified slates in both the municipal and the presidential elections. The alternative, *B,* was to allow each party to run as a separate political force in the municipal elections, and then form a grand coalition for the presidential election. The key municipal races were between mayoral candidates in the major cities. The idea of unified slates created conflict over who would be the mayoral candidates, especially in Lima.

Players attached different values to *A* and *B*. AP, the strongest party in the Front, preferred *B* because it was most likely to win votes in a separate slate. A decisive AP victory in the municipal elections would provide an assessment of electoral strength that Belaúnde could use to wield increased influence within FREDEMO. Manuel Ulloa, the former president of the Council of Ministers in the 1980–85 Belaúnde government, argued that without an electoral victory in Lima AP would lose its "strongest card." Moreover, AP leaders wished to reaffirm the identity of their party as a political force. Many feared that AP would lose its integrity as a party when it joined FREDEMO, Belaúnde made it clear that the rank-and-file of his party would not tolerate sharing municipal candidates with the PPC (M. Vargas Llosa 1991: 44).

Libertad preferred *A* over *B* to prevent a dispersion of forces, and also to consolidate the leadership of Vargas Llosa. Vargas Llosa felt he had to consolidate his power prior to the April 1990 elections in order to have a free hand in selecting first-class technicians and in choosing his cabinet. Having stated his preference for *A*, losing out to Belaúnde would have seriously undermined his authority.[6] As Libertad's general secretary, Miguel Cruchaga Belaúnde, put it: FREDEMO needed "a candidate, not a monarch."[7]

On the other hand, *A* was in the interests of the PPC because candidates in a unified FREDEMO slate would surely be selected on the basis of the most recent electoral results. The PPC had many mayors in Lima because AP did not contest the 1986 elections.[8] The PPC also wanted a unified slate because it was strong in rich districts of Lima but weak in the provinces and shanty-towns. Leaders of AP believed Bedoya wanted FREDEMO candidates in the municipalities to disguise the lack of support for the PPC in the provinces.

In sum, the actor's preferences regarding the above outcomes can be ranked as follows:

Libertad (Vargas Llosa) $A > B > C$
AP (Belaúnde Terry) $B > A > C$
PPC (Bedoya Reyes) $A > B > C$

Libertad and the PPC preferred *A* first, *B* second, and *C* third. AP preferred *B* first, *A* second, and *C* third.

The following chronology of events surrounding the resignation of Vargas Llosa provides critical background information.[9]

Chronology of Events

On June 1, 1989, Belaúnde arrived in the southern city of Arequipa for the proclaiming of Vargas Llosa as the presidential candidate of FREDEMO. The enthusiastic reception he received appeared to draw attention to popular support for AP. Other members of FREDEMO complained that AP was trying to showcase its popularity to the detriment of FREDEMO's image as a unified force. Two days later, Vargas Llosa arrived in Arequipa and was driven through the city in an open vehicle, accompanied by Eduardo Orrego, the former mayor of Lima and AP member.

On June 4, 1989, Vargas Llosa was proclaimed the presidential candidate of FREDEMO by Belaúnde in the half-filled Plaza de Armas in Arequipa. In his speech, Vargas Llosa promised a broad-based government, not a government run by party bosses. Bedoya's speech was perceived as critical of Vargas Llosa. In the evening Vargas Llosa expressed to Belaúnde concern over the poor attendance at the rally. Belaúnde responded with a metaphor, saying that bullfighters fill the plaza only at the end of the season. The next day Belaúnde and Bedoya returned to Lima while Vargas Llosa remained in Arequipa for extensive consultations with Orrego about the municipal elections scheduled for November 1989.

On June 6, 1989, Vargas Llosa stated in an interview that he supported the option I have labeled *A:* FREDEMO should run a unified slate of candidates in the municipal elections as well as in the presidential election of April 1990. He asserted that rival lists would be a disaster for FREDEMO, and nominated Eduardo Orrego to be FREDEMO's candidate for the mayor of Lima. Orrego, however, indicated that AP preferred *B,* and that he would only run under AP banners.[10] He further announced that AP and PPC would enter secret conversations to select a candidate both could support. Vargas Llosa supported the idea, but some sources suggested he was privately concerned about the outcome.

As the names of various candidates were discussed, opposition to *A* quickly developed within AP. At the same time the prospect of a left-wing victory in November was ostensibly increased by the election of Henry Pease García, a moderate, as candidate of the United Left in Lima. On June 13, Edmundo del Aguila, secretary of AP, after a meeting with top party leaders, stated that AP would run its own candidates in the municipal elections, and that *B* was nonnegotiable.[11] Leaders of AP reiterated that since Belaúnde had already given up the presidency, he should not also give up AP control over the municipalities. Spokesperson for Libertad, Frederick Cooper, was incensed. He protested that negotiations were underway within FREDEMO to establish a unified slate of candidates both in Lima and in the rest of the country. An equally irritated Vargas Llosa called Belaúnde and insinuated that the ex-president still harbored presidential aspirations.[12] He also informed Belaúnde that he would outline his position in a letter. Miguel Cruchaga Belaúnde, secretary general of Libertad, passed on a letter from Vargas Llosa to Bedoya. In response, a top PPC leader reaffirmed the willingness of the PPC to accept *A.*

The next day Belaúnde learned from the daily papers that Vargas Llosa had written a letter to him. Annoyed by the fact that the media had heard of the letter before he had read it, Belaúnde reiterated his opposition to the idea of a unified slate in Lima and affirmed the candidacy of Orrego. Members of AP had not joined FREDEMO, he said, to give up their municipal obligations. In response, Cruchaga asserted that the obstacle to *A* was the intransigence of AP; he implied that blame for *C* would fall on Belaúnde.

Vargas Llosa traveled to Uruguay on June 15, expressing misgivings about the aggressive position of Belaúnde. The APRA-controlled government media disseminated rumors of Vargas Llosa's resignation and interviewed political leaders who called for Belaúnde to assume the presidential candidacy. AP leaders reiterated that since Belaúnde had given up the presidential candidacy, the rank-and-file members of AP were not willing to give up *B*.

In a meeting on June 19, Belaúnde offered to pick a candidate for the municipality of Lima, leaving the PPC to choose the candidate for the nearby port city of Callao: each candidate would run under separate party banners, but there would be no direct rivalry between members of FREDEMO. Vargas Llosa suggested that Orrego should be the candidate, with Bedoya's son—Luis Bedoya de Vivanco, the mayor of Miraflores—as the first council-member. Subsequently, Vargas Llosa met with Bedoya, whom he perceived to agree with the formula. In the afternoon, Vargas Llosa announced that the other parties had agreed to something close to *A:* "In the upcoming elections FREDEMO will run unified lists based on consensus," he stated.[13]

Bedoya de Vivanco heard about the deal from his father. The younger Bedoya objected to what he perceived as a postponement, without prior consultation, of his aspiration to be mayor of Lima. Late that evening Bedoya told a dismayed Vargas Llosa that there had been a misunderstanding.[14] He announced his intention to hold a press conference the next day to clarify the matter.

The next day Bedoya visited Belaúnde and declared his intention to hold a press conference to clarify the misunderstanding. They discussed alternatives for selecting candidates. Then Bedoya went into the press conference and declared that Vargas Llosa had mistaken his silence as approval for *A;* the "agreement" was based on a misinterpretation. That same day AP leader Carlos Ausejo stated, without consulting the rank-and-file, Orrego would be the AP candidate. Vargas Llosa watched Bedoya's press conference on the television, and then spent the rest of the night considering his position in FREDEMO (M. Vargas Llosa 1991: 46).

Vargas Llosa, having found *A* an elusive goal, chose *C* instead. He wrote his letter of resignation the following day, on the morning of June 21. He secretly made plans to travel abroad "to avoid the initial reaction" (M. Vargas Llosa 1991: 46). His son, Alvaro Vargas Llosa, delivered the letter to both Belaúnde and Bedoya. "The impossibility of reaching an accord to avoid rival lists in the municipal election" was cited as the cause of the resignation. Vargas Llosa made it clear that *B* was inconceivable: without *A*, FREDEMO would not be a "solid and coherent alliance."[15] Belaúnde responded to Vargas Llosa's resignation by saying that he would guard his silence to avoid further controversy. Supporters of FREDEMO, including prominent politicians, journalists and industrialists, gathered around Vargas Llosa's house in the fashionable Barranco district to pressure him not to abandon FREDEMO. Vargas Llosa insulated his household from all communication: "I gave instructions to the security guards not to allow anyone to enter the house, and we unplugged the telephone" (M. Vargas Llosa 1991: 46).

The next day Vargas Llosa left for West Germany and Spain to attend literary and political engagements. Cruchaga asserted that no thought had been given to placing demands on the other parties. Libertad was quietly registered with the National Election Board as an independent political party. The movement claimed 15,000 new adherents had recently joined Libertad as a result of Vargas Llosa's resignation. Leaders of both AP and PPC feared that Vargas Llosa intended to run as an independent. They accused one another of trying to undermine his leadership to advance their own candidate.[16] Bedoya called Vargas Llosa a "novice," and asserted that he had always supported A.[17] However, he subsequently confessed to being confused and he criticized himself for expressing his position poorly and for being inflexible in the negotiations.

After a June 28 meeting between the younger leaders of AP and the PPC, an accord was signed on June 30 that resulted in A. The parties accepted unified lists in provinces that were capitals of departments, and vowed to increase efforts to unify lists elsewhere.[18] On July 2, Vargas Llosa withdrew his letter of resignation, congratulating his coalition partners for agreeing to A.[19]

In the days following the withdrawal of Vargas Llosa's resignation there remained signs of conflict within FREDEMO. Leaders of AP stressed that they had made great sacrifices for the sake of unity. Belaúnde even said A was an "error," and B would have been "more just and democratic." He criticized the growing rejection of political parties in Peru, and emphasized that AP had made "institutional sacrifices" for the sake of unity.[20] However, he also asserted that, with the withdrawal of Vargas Llosa's resignation, FREDEMO returned to the status quo ante of June 4. Bedoya reiterated that he had always supported A, but he also obliquely warned of "a party of the Right about to be born." Finally, on July 15, Vargas Llosa returned to Lima and was greeted at the airport by FREDEMO leaders, but not by the embittered Bedoya or Belaúnde.[21] With his popular support at its zenith, Vargas Llosa asserted that Libertad was "not a party" but rather a "broader" movement.

The Consolidation Game

To construct a payoff matrix of the bargaining, we assign ordinal payoffs to each outcome according to each player's preference ranking. The highest outcome for each player is 3, the lowest outcome is 1.

	A	B	C
Libertad (Vargas Llosa)	3	2	1
AP (Belaúnde Terry)	2	3	1
PPC (Bedoya Reyes)	3	2	1

In addition to the player's preferences, a "decision-rule" allows us to assign values to the game matrix. The decision-rule is that when players disagree or one player defects, the outcome is division. Belaúnde synthesized this rule by comparing FREDEMO to a tripod: "when one of the friends attacks the other, the tripod falls."[22]

Assuming that Libertad always seeks its first preference, A, we can depict the game between AP and the PPC in a two-dimensional outcome matrix (see figure 4.1). The decision-rule stipulates that where actors cannot reach an consensus the outcome is C. According to the preference ranking, the value of C to all actors was 1.

Figure 4.1

The Consolidation Game
(AP and PPC)

AP

		A	B	C
	A	3,2	1,1	1,1
PPC	B	1,1	2,3	1,1
	C	1,1	1,1	1,1

This is a mixed-motive game; one that involves both mutual dependence and conflict (Schelling 1960: 89; see also Snyder and Diesing 1977: 41–48). There are two equilibrium outcomes in this game (3,2 and 2,3). One of the two players must capitulate. The first preference of the PPC is A. However, because disagreement would lead to the breakdown of the coalition, the payoff is (1,1) if the PPC chooses A and AP chooses B. Likewise, the payoff is (1,1) if AP chooses B and the PPC chooses A.

If the assumption that Libertad always pursues A is dropped, the two-dimensional game matrix of figure 4.1 becomes the three-dimensional matrix in figure 4.2. This matrix takes into account three strategies available to Libertad: to pursue A, B, or threaten C. The outcomes in the expanded game are still defined by the same decision-rule.

In the first game, we assume Libertad pursues its sincere preference for *A*. The outcomes are the same as in figure 4.1, namely (3,2) or (2,3). In the unlikely event that the leader of Libertad were to pursue *B* as his first choice, the equilibrium outcome would clearly be *B* (3,3). On the other hand, Vargas Llosa may prefer quitting to one of the outcomes. For example, he may prefer *C* to *B*, though not to *A*. In this game, represented in the third matrix, where the outcome is *C* the payoff to Libertad is 2. The collectively best outcome is *A*, the upper left-hand cell (3,2). If Vargas Llosa pursues *A* and Belaúnde *B*, then Vargas Llosa gets the relatively high score of 2, whereas Belaúnde gets 1. AP can improve its score by choosing *A*.

Figure 4.2

The Consolidation Game
(AP, PPC, and Libertad)

AP

	A	B	C
A	**3,2**	1,1	1,1
B	1,1	**2,3**	1,1
C	1,1	1,1	1,1

AP

	A	B	C
A	2,2	1,1	1,1
B	1,1	**3,3**	1,1
C	1,1	1,1	1,1

AP

	A	B	C
A	**3,2**	2,1	2,1
B	2,1	1,3	2,1
C	2,1	2,1	2,1

Libertad: A, B, C

Assuming complete information—that is, all actors know both the decision-rule and the preferences of the other actors (Zagare 1984:67)—the outcome of the three-person game in figure 4.2 is the same as the two-person game in figure 4.1. That is, if all players pursue their first preference, the outcome is *A* or *B* (3,2 and 2,3). Since there is no unique solution to this game, how can actors promote the outcome most favorable to them? In the first place, actors may try to convince other players of the intensity of their preferences and the strength of their resolve to pursue their first choice. AP pursued the first strategy by saying B was "non-negotiable." A second strategy is to signal a willingness to walk away from the bargaining and accept the collapse of the coalition. Vargas Llosa pursued this option. He did not deny his preference among the two alternatives on the agenda. However, by resigning he indicated C was more tolerable than losing his demand for A. Vargas Llosa sought to convince his partners that his preference order was $A > C > B$, rather than $A > B > C$. By claiming to prefer C to B, Vargas Llosa shifted the bargaining to the third game where he could pursue A—the collectively best outcome (3,2).

Vargas Llosa did not deceive his coalition partners, yet we may be skeptical of supporters who argued that "at no time did he act in a premeditated way; he acted with the same transparency as always, and if anything good comes of this it will not be because he looked for it."[23] Another leader of Libertad told the press that "Vargas Llosa's resignation appeared to be aimed at forcing the coalition to choose him as its undisputed leader."[24] The same leaders of Libertad who emphasized that it would be very difficult to convince Vargas Llosa to reconsider his resignation attempted to mobilize public opinion in favor of his return. Yet Libertad politicians did not have to enter negotiations or make demands. Their strategy was to wait for the other parties to capitulate or accept the consequences.

In response to AP intransigence, Vargas Llosa signalled a low motivation to play. His threat to resign was reinforced by asymmetrical communication, by the use of a bargaining agents, and by pledging his reputation (Schelling 1960: 26). The main instrument Vargas Llosa used to pledge his reputation to $(A > C > B)$ over $(A > B > C)$ was his letter of resignation. He attempted to convince the other players that he preferred C to B for tactical reasons. Thus, he deplored the failure of Bedoya and Belaúnde to reach an agreement, and said that the "impossibility of reaching an accord to avoid rival lists in the municipal election" was the cause of his resignation.[25]

Vargas Llosa needed all his rhetorical powers to convince the other actors that B was worse than C. Without such an accord FREDEMO would not, he argued, be a "solid and coherent alliance." Its forces would be dispersed. Thus, the presidential candidate would be "obliged to be mute or evasive" in order to avoid positions that might "antagonize one of its theoretical bases of support," thereby reaching November "without prestige or authority." Although FREDEMO "could still win the presidential elections," it would not have the "civic and moral force to accomplish the profound transformation that our country will need to pull itself out of the abyss." Vargas Llosa warned that the "collapse of the front could open the doors of our country" to the center-right's worst possible outcome—namely, "retrograde and totalitarian Marxism."

Vargas Llosa closed the letter by stating that if the causes of the division among the members of FREDEMO were to be removed, "I have no doubt that they could count again on the support of the many independents who have become involved in this process with the sole intention of arresting the decadence and barbarism in our unfortunate country."

Vargas Llosa's letter made it clear that FREDEMO should seek to win in the first round of the elections. The system of majority rule with runoff elections tends to encourage a proliferation of candidates hoping to get into a runoff in the second round (see Shugart and Carey 1992: 215–19). A major fear of FREDEMO strategists was that other candidates would perform well enough to deny a first round victory to FREDEMO and force a runoff in which the Left and APRA (which together won over 70 percent of the vote in 1985) would join together against Vargas Llosa. This made it imperative to win in the first round. As the *Latin American Weekly Report* noted in May 1989, Vargas Llosa "has been playing on the assumption that APRA and the Left will pull together, and is campaigning to spread the image of *aprocomunismo* as the threat to overcome."[26]

Moreover, electoral rules enhanced the credibility of Vargas Llosa's threat to resign by showing the need for unity in order to win in the first round. As Matthew S. Shugart and John M. Carey (1992: 215, fn 7) point out, "Because majority runoff opens up the possibility that a candidate finishing second initially can then go on to win, Vargas Llosa was able credibly to point to the possibility that he could win without a coalition with established parties. Indeed, this is precisely how the election was won, but not by Vargas Llosa!"

The letter of resignation left unclear whether an agreement among the parties could induce Vargas Llosa to return, but it offered enough hope to encourage the other players to reach an agreement. Linking the municipal election to the presidential election allowed Vargas Llosa to imply that any concession on this issue would encourage the party leaders to revise their estimate of his strength as a leader: to protect his reputation, he would have to stand firm.

Communication with Vargas Llosa was asymmetrical. The first thing he did after resigning was to insulate himself from communication; he flew to Europe, thereby making himself unavailable to be deceived or deterred by threats or messages from the other parties. Vargas Llosa also made artful use of his supporters as bargaining agents to communicate with the other players. Supporters negotiated for Libertad while Vargas Llosa was in Europe. They registered Libertad with the National Election Board, a move that intensified the climate of uncertainty by making an independent candidacy appear more plausible. Nevertheless, a serious effort was made to avoid C. Libertad leaders subsequently claimed that an independent candidacy was never considered an option.[27]

They knew that Bedoya and Belaúnde were concerned about the formation of a third party in the center-right of the political spectrum. Thus, Libertad leaders insisted that the registration of Libertad as an independent political force did not signal the definitive rupture of FREDEMO.

Vargas Llosa's strategy successfully created uncertainty, not about his preference for A over B, but about the value he placed on C. Political leaders in the other groups within the Front expressed what was apparently sincere doubt about whether Vargas Llosa would return. Expressing disdain for public bargaining, Belaúnde maintained a "cure of silence." However, Bedoya openly acknowledged his genuine bewilderment and confusion; "If anyone has the explanation he should say it. The only thing I can do is express my concern and perplexity," he said in one interview.[28] Bedoya professed his inability to "see the panorama clearly," and said he could not understand the "motivations of this sudden rupture."[29] Likewise, other top leaders of the PPC were disconcerted and perplexed by the rupture, and uncertain whether FREDEMO would reunite.

Given the uncertainty about the value Vargas Llosa placed on C, what was AP's best strategy? Belaúnde had to play against an actor committed in advance to AP's second best outcome. By publicly presenting AP with a *fait accompli* Vargas Llosa enhanced his bargaining position, but also risked a collectively bad outcome.

Belaúnde had the last clear choice. From Belaúnde's point of view, Vargas Llosa's preferences were either $A > B > C$ or $A > C > B$. He could not be sure whether C was Vargas Llosa's second or third preference. However, the ex-president was given no reason to doubt that Vargas Llosa preferred A to both B and C. To keep Vargas Llosa in the game—and therefore avoid being blamed for C—Belaúnde's best reply was to pursue A and thereby avoid the worst outcome, C, represented in the first game as $(1,1)$ and in the third game as $(2,1)$. Thus, the Nash equilibrium is A $(3,2)$ in the third game.

Belaúnde's best reply was to capitulate. Either Belaúnde could stick with B and get the payoff of $(2,1)$ or he could opt for A and get the payoff of $(3,2)$. The agreement reached between the AP and the PPC on June 30, 1989, placed the players in A. It provided a unified slate in Lima and most of the important cities in the provinces. In Lima, 21 district municipalities would be allocated to the candidates of the PPC, and 20 would go to AP. AP would select the candidate for Metropolitan Lima, and Bedoya would choose the candidate for Lima's sister city of Callao. AP would run candidates in 14 provincial capitals, and the PPC would run candidates in 9. Both would make their choices in consultation with the other. This agreement covered 62 percent of the national electorate, leaving the remaining 38 percent provincial and municipal districts to separate slates.

Vargas Llosa accepted the agreement. He had won *A*, his most preferred outcome. Leaders of Libertad expressed the hope that Vargas Llosa's leadership would not be questioned any further; in the event it were, they expected to have established firmer political support through the campaign to collect signatures for the registration of Libertad with the National Elections Board.

Vargas Llosa was at the height of his popularity. "The number of people who were prepared to vote for me rose markedly," he observed.

> The opinion polls had always shown me to be the leading candidate, but I never had support greater than thirty-five percent. After my withdrawal that figure rose to fifty percent, the highest I attained at any point in the campaign. In my absence *Libertad* enrolled thousands of new members, ran out of membership cards and had to print new ones. Local headquarters were filled to overflowing, day and night, by supporters who wanted *Libertad* to break with Popular Action and the Christian Popular Party and go before the voters by itself. I learned later that 4,980 letters had arrived from all over Peru, congratulating me for having broken with the two parties, with Popular Action in particular. (M. Vargas Llosa 1991: 47)

Among those who supported the idea of an independent candidacy for Mario Vargas Llosa was his New York based campaign consultant firm. Consultant Mark Malloch Brown described Vargas Llosa's decision to build a coalition including AP and PPC as "a dreadful mistake" and he now told Vargas Llosa "don't mend the pact you have broken. Let the old politicians run against you. It will restore your political independence and make you unbeatable" (Malloch Brown 1991: 89–90). He perceptively observed that for the voters "Popular Action and the Christian Popular Party stood for all that was worst in the traditional political order. . . . Peruvians held these parties and their leaders responsible, along with García, for the national collapse. . . . Mario failed to see that the anti-political tide that had initially carried him forward was aimed as much at the dinosaurs of the old right as at his nemesis Alan García, the populist left" (1991: 89). However, Vargas Llosa argued that he "would lose an entire grass-roots organization if he cut his band of *Libertad* intellectuals from the political parties" (Malloch Brown 1991: 90).

Another reason to avoid the division of the Right in the 1990 election was that the system of runoff elections made it imperative to win the highest possible percentage of the vote in the first round. The president of Brazil, Fernando Collor de Mello, would subsequently warn Vargas Llosa of the need to avoid a second round. "The second round is the worst experience of my political career," he said to Vargas Llosa. "The best I can wish you, Mario, is that you do not have to go into a second round. How much advantage do you have in the polls?" (A. Vargas Llosa 1991: 90). It is not clear whether Vargas Llosa was aware that he would inevitably face a broad "anyone-but-Vargas Llosa" coalition in a second round. However, it is clear that he intended to win in the first round and for that, division on the Right could be detrimental.

Moreover, Vargas Llosa did not want to appear to be an opportunist. He would resist all efforts to break with his allies, seeing in such factionalism the kind of political opportunism he abhorred (A. Vargas Llosa 1991: 33–34). Thus, said Malloch Brown, Vargas Llosa "bartered away his most precious asset, his independence" (1991: 90).

There are a number of attractive features of the game-theoretic representation of the strategic situation in FREDEMO. First, it draws attention to the importance of incomplete information and tactical self-commitment. The outcome was different from that which would have been expected under conditions of complete information in which all players pursued their "sincere strategy." Thus, once the game was played and actors had retrospective information, it naturally seemed to some that the payoff had been assigned in a manner inconsistent with the distribution of power resources among the players. This led to bitterness within the biggest loser, AP. Belaúnde appeared to have given up much and to have received little in return. Thus, subsequent to the agreement of June 30 he stated it was an error to run a unified slate of FREDEMO candidates. On the other hand, there was a spirit of elation in Libertad captured by the slogan, "Mario changed politics, Mario will change Peru."

The model also draws attention to a fact about which most analysts agree: the obstacle to unity was a faction within AP.[30] Bedoya was the politician most frequently cited in opinion polls as the cause of Vargas Llosa's resignation.[31] However, according to the game matrix, the outcome would have been the same regardless of the strategy pursued by the PPC. PPC leaders stated that they did not believe the resignation happened because Vargas Llosa spoke with Bedoya before he went to the press. They felt, correctly, that Vargas Llosa's problems were essentially with Belaúnde. As the novelist observed: "Belaúnde always conveyed the sense that the alliance was there to serve his Popular Action, and Bedoya and I were merely two bit players. Beneath his elegant manners, there was a vanity and stubbornness and a touch of the *caudillo* accustomed to doing and undoing whatever he pleased without anybody in his party daring to contradict him" (M. Vargas Llosa 1991: 40).[32] Thus: "Belaúnde had placed the greatest obstacles in the way of an agreement concerning the municipal elections, but it was Bedoya who brought on the crisis" (1991: 44).

It is not clear to what extent Belaúnde and other leaders of AP fully understood their strategic predicament. There is reason to believe that many AP leaders were genuinely uncertain of the motivation behind Vargas Llosa's strategy. Having pursued a strategy of intransigence, they were confronted with a partner who was apparently not strongly committed to playing. Even if they suspected Vargas Llosa was bluffing, he forced them to act in a perturbed game by precommitting himself to the other players' worst outcome unless they capitulated. As the daily newspaper *La República* succinctly put it, Vargas Llosa was like a player who, "losing the game, shakes the chess board to reaccommodate the pieces in a more favorable position."[33]

Did Vargas Llosa write anything after the 1990 elections to contradict the "rational resignation" thesis? In a 1991 essay, entitled "A Fish Out of Water," Vargas Llosa provides a brief and ambiguous account of his own motivation. He outlined his reason for resigning and then used the views of his wife to confirm the possibility of another, very different, interpretation of his motives:

> In fact most people ultimately viewed my withdrawal as proof that I wasn't such a bad politician after all. The truth is that it was not planned, but was a genuine expression of my loathing for the political manoeuvering in which I found myself submerged. This is disputed by Patricia, who lets me get away with nothing. I did not, she says, announce that my resignation was irrevocable, and she thinks that in some secret place I harboured the illusion, the desire, that my letter would settle the differences among the allies. (1991: 47)

Patricia de Vargas Llosa is used as Mario Vargas Llosa's alter ego in another place in the same text. His decision to run for office, he says, was motivated by "a moral reason"—the desire to implement changes that Peru needed. "It appeared that, supported by a majority of Peruvians, there was an opportunity to accomplish the liberal reforms which I had defended in articles and polemical exchanges since the early 1970s" (1991: 33). However, according to Vargas Llosa,

> Patricia doesn't see it that way. "The moral obligation wasn't the decisive factor," she says. "It was the adventure, the illusion of an experience full of excitement and risk. Of writing the great novel in real life."

Here again, Vargas Llosa concedes to the reader that this

> may be the truth. If the presidency had not been, as I said jokingly to a journalist, "the most dangerous job in the world," I might not have become a candidate. If the decadence, impoverishment, terrorism and constant crises had not made governing the country an almost impossible challenge, it would never have entered my heart to take on the task. (1991: 33)

In both passages Vargas Llosa uses his wife to express what he regards in retrospect as illusions: writing the great novel in real life, and settling the differences among his allies. He does not deny that he hoped to settle the differences among his allies, indeed he implies that such a denial would be less than candid. But he also offers an interpretation that is more consistent with the position taken by his supporters—that his resignation was prompted by a genuine loathing for the maneuvering of partisan politicians. Perhaps these views are not inconsistent: through his own maneuvering Vargas Llosa was able to assert his leadership and force the partisan politicians to bow to his authority.

CONCLUSION

The theory of N-person games has been used to explain the strategies behind the resignation of Vargas Llosa from FREDEMO, as well as the bargaining stimulated by this event. The game model illustrates how a resignation may be used to bargain for leadership and the distribution of payoffs within a coalition. It provides a fine-grained account of the interaction between the preferences of actors in highly uncertain environments. This episode was a complex strategic game that merits microscopic analysis.

Games can be generated by ranking the preferences of the players and using decision-rules to assign values to payoff matrices. We can then use the deductive power of game theory to explain bargaining outcomes. The results allow us to identify the strategic logic behind the choices of the players. The results also highlight the important analytical distinction between a strategy of signalling an intense preference for an outcome in a mixed-motive game, and influencing other actors' perceptions of one's motivation to play. Game theorists often assume all players are equally motivated to play. However, where the need for unity is reflected in the preferences of the players, a willingness to risk the breakdown of a coalition is a powerful source of bargaining leverage.

Obstacles to unity in FREDEMO came from sectors of AP that feared a loss of influence in the coalition. Vargas Llosa resigned to assert his leadership. He forced Belaúnde to choose between a unified slate of FREDEMO candidates or the division of the coalition. This strategy broke the impasse created by the unstable game in which each player pursued his sincere strategy. The strategy was successful because AP was unwilling to disrupt the coalition.[34] The analysis highlights the inevitable tension between an independent leader and established politicians who are anxious to preserve their power base within the larger electoral front. Exactly the same tensions plagued the United Left, as we shall see in the next chapter.

Game theory is valuable when its deductive power is "used to generate new findings and understandings rather than to reconstruct individual situations"

(Snidal 1986: 27). In this analysis, preference rankings and decision-rules taken from observation are used to derive games. The deductive power of game theory can then be used to explain the bargaining outcomes. In the process, behavior is seen in a new light. What appeared to be an irrevocable decision to resign by Vargas Llosa was in fact a strategic ploy.

Actors do not always confine themselves to playing within a given "game." Rather, they may attempt to manipulate other actors' perceptions of their willingness to play in order to promote a new game. Their success in this effort crucially depends on the value attached to unity by the other players. Once we correctly assign such values, the games derived allow us to accurately predict the outcome of the bargaining.

·5·

DIVISION OF THE UNITED LEFT

I n the early 1980s the United Left (IU) was widely regarded as one of the largest legal Marxist coalitions in Latin America, with a good chance of winning a presidential election in 1990 or beyond (Taylor 1990: 108; on the history and evolution of the Left see also Cotler 1988; Rochabrún 1988; Ballón 1986b, 1991; Nieto 1983). In 1983 Alfonso Barrantes won the mayoral race in Metropolitan Lima and immediately became the Left's most credible candidate for president. Affectionately nicknamed Uncle *Frejolito* (little bean) for his short stature and dark complexion, Barrantes fashioned an image for himself as a leader able to unify the fractious IU coalition and design policies—like the campaign to provide a glass of milk every day for each poor child in Lima—capable of eliciting an enduring identification with Peru's impoverished masses. "I am the engine that pulls this train," Barrantes once said of his leadership role in IU.[1]

By the end of the decade the IU faced internal disarray and electoral decline. Barrantes lost the mayoral race for reelection in 1986. He came under fire within IU for his reluctance to criticize the government of Alan García Pérez (1985–1990) and for acting like a traditional *caudillo*. In May 1987, after criticism for being outside the country during a major national strike, Barrantes withdrew from the leadership of the IU. In June 1989 he declined to participate in internal IU elections to select a candidate for the Lima municipal election of November 1989. His coalition placed an annulment on the registration of the IU with the National Election Board.[2] The United Left remained divided past the deadline required for registration as a unified front.

The rupture of IU led to its weak performance in the November municipal elections and the subsequent presidential election in April 1990. As a result, the Peruvian Left was reduced to a nearly insignificant electoral force with only 11 percent of the vote in the presidential election (Taylor 1990: 106, 116). From the point of view of electoral competition, the rupture of the Left seemed to be a suboptimal choice.

According to George Tsebelis, suboptimal choices often turn out to be disagreements between actor and observer: "either the actor actually does choose a nonoptimal strategy or the observer is mistaken" (1990: 7). I assume that the leaders of the Left were rational, and that they chose optimally. This does not mean that actors always choose the course of action that leads to the best outcome for them; rather, actors choose what they believe is the strategy that will best serve their interests. The outcome, however, often depends on the choices of other actors. Unintended consequence of choices abound in situations of strategic interdependence. The usefulness of the assumption that actors are rational depends not on whether it accurately describes the actors—often such an assumption is dubious—but on whether it generates hypotheses that help explain situations of strategic choice (Tsebelis 1990: 31).

Barrantes, for example, may have believed that he could win an election without the support of IU. In retrospect, that belief was clearly wrong. The electoral performance of the Left in the 1989 municipal elections demonstrated that unity was required for strong electoral performance.[3] Nevertheless, this chapter suggests that Barrantes's choices were rational in light of his beliefs and preferences. The rationality assumption implies that actors' strategies will reflect their beliefs about what is in their interests, not that the actors have complete information.

The division of the IU was collectively suboptimal; for each faction there was a superior outcome. Division was particularly devastating to the prospects of the IU in electoral competition. The electorate that routinely voted for the Left was divided in halves. By running two slates with similar ideological profiles, the Left confused the electorate and made voting for either faction tantamount to wasting a vote (Taylor 1990: 116). However, for part of the Left, mass struggle outside the parliament was more important than winning elections. For the "revolutionary bloc," winning elections was secondary to controlling the United Left coalition and turning it into a "genuine mass front" to seize power through class struggle. Divisions within the Left were intensified by the issue of how to respond to the existence of armed groups—mainly the Shining Path and the Túpac Amaru Revolutionary Movement (Movimiento Revolucionario Túpac Amaru, or MRTA) (McClintock 1989: 131–32).

Thus there was a deep tension in the Left between advocates of revolutionary and reformist strategies. These two blocs competed for the support of a third faction which held the balance of power within IU—the independent bloc. The independent bloc had greater ideological affinity for the reformists. But its members were also committed to playing a leadership role in the IU, strengthening internal democracy, and avoiding division. Bargaining among these three groups is the subject of this analysis.

A model of coalition bargaining in the United Left is generated by ranking actor preferences and assigning simple "rules of the game" to strategic interaction.[4] The bargaining is modeled using N-person game theory.

BARRANTES AND THE UNITED LEFT

Actor Preferences

The United Left was an electoral coalition formally composed of six registered political parties (on factions in the IU see Taylor 1990; Letts 1981; Bernales 1987: 128–132). Within the United Left there were three major factions: the "revolutionary bloc," the "reformist bloc," and the "independent bloc."[5] The principal conflict within the United Left was between the revolutionary and reformist blocs, and concerned Barrantes's leadership. There were three possible outcomes:

A. A moderate coalition in support of Barrantes as presidential candidate.
B. Internal IU election to select a presidential candidate.
C. Division of the IU, with Barrantes running on a separate slate.

The leaders of the reformist bloc wanted A. They wanted to maximize electoral support for the Left and minimize disruptive internal tensions within the coalition. Barrantes, the leader of the reformist bloc, preferred to run with the support of the independent bloc and without the revolutionary bloc. He did not want to repeat the tragic history of Salvador Allende's government in Chile. Allende was, according to Barrantes, undermined by internal tensions (Barrantes 1985: 236–37). "I need 10 years to convince the military that a United Left government is not the end of the world" he once said.[6] To do so, Barrantes needed to show that a future government of the United Left would not be undermined by the revolutionary bloc, which he likened to a "Trojan Horse."[7] Thus, a minimum condition for Barrantes's candidacy was the subordination or exclusion of the revolutionary bloc. This option implied a rupture in the IU.

The problem Barrantes faced was that the revolutionary bloc controlled the strongest party machines, and this allowed them to dominate the internal organization of the United Left even though their popularity with the broader electorate was limited. By demanding his candidacy be accepted without an internal election, Barrantes hoped to force his leadership on the coalition, avoid elections, and even provoke the revolutionary bloc to split away.

Thus, the best outcome for the reformist bloc was A, to build a winning coalition of moderates around Barrantes candidacy in which the revolutionary bloc would be subordinated or excluded. The second best outcome, C, would be to leave the United Left and run an independent presidential candidacy. The reformists would not be hindered by internal tensions. However, in this option they would not have the support of other moderates in the independent bloc. Barrantes would have no claim to be the candidate of the United Left, nor would he be able to use its symbols and name. Without the support of the independent bloc he would have to compete against former allies.

The worst outcome was B—to submit to an internal electoral process. In this option, the organized parties held all the strongest cards. Barrantes feared that such an outcome would allow the revolutionary bloc to wage an "anybody-but-Barrantes" campaign to thwart his candidacy and consolidate their leadership. Having lost the nomination, Barrantes would no longer be able to run as a credible candidate on a separate slate, and the independent bloc would not follow him if he split away after an internal defeat.

The leaders of the revolutionary bloc wanted B. They placed a lower priority on participation in "bourgeois democratic institutions." They were less interested in building the widest possible electoral base for the United Left than in building an organized, revolutionary alternative to existing power structures. As Javier Diez Canseco said, "The Left should not even be contemplating trying to be the government if it lacks a power base. . . . He [Barrantes] should realize that sitting in a palace can be a very frustrating experience. . . . Just getting there could do a disservice to the Left. It would be political suicide. One does not get to the government in order to fail. One goes there with a strategy for victory, which means with the intention and the means to transform the country."[8]

The existence of the Shining Path further diminished the value attached to electoral competition by the revolutionary bloc. Although they recognized that Barrantes was the leader with the widest popular appeal—and that the withdrawal of Barrantes could weaken the electoral prospects of the Left—they preferred a rupture in the United Left, C, to the consolidation of the leadership of the reformist bloc, A.

The revolutionary bloc placed a high priority on electoral competition *within* the United Left—option B—where it controlled the party machinery. According to Taylor (1990: 114), "the pro-Barrantes faction remained weak vis-à-vis the party organizations inside IU, a weakness that was highlighted at the first national congress of IU held in January 1989" in Huampaní. Having successfully captured the leadership of the IU at that congress, the revolutionary bloc saw Barrantes's effort to avoid an election as a challenge to the results of Huampaní, and to their leadership in the National Leadership Committee. Thus, the condition for their acceptance of Barrantes was that he abide by the norms of the congress and submit to an internal election, B. Moreover, by insisting on B over C, the revolutionary bloc hoped to prevent the formation of an alliance between the reformist and independent blocs.

The third group, the independent bloc, tended to strongly support the leadership and candidacy of Barrantes. He was the candidate closest to their ideological preferences. However, they were committed to the democratization of the United Left, which they also sought to control through a membership drive and by establishing democratic procedures for leadership selection. The independent bloc felt that Barrantes represented the widest possible constituency and had the best chances of winning in the elections. However, although they liked Barrantes and wanted to win elections, they disliked his autocratic and personalist style, and his contempt for the political process within the United Left. Independents demanded unity and discipline within the IU in accordance with its statutes and norms. In 1988 IU senator Rolando Ames stated:

> We have . . . decided to transform the front from a multiparty alliance into a political organization that will allow people to participate directly even if they are not active in one of the parties per se. . . . In theory we have a winning candidate—the political indicators are very favorable to Alfonso Barrantes—but there is a certain amount of tension between Barrantes and some sectors of the left. . . . We expect that once the front has been constituted, there will be negotiations with Barrantes to convince him to accept our guidelines and program. We do not want him to be the candidate unconditionally; we want him to be the candidate through political negotiations with the front. (Farnsworth 1988b: 775–6)

Unlike the reformists, the independents did not support C over B. In their view the purpose of the IU was not merely to serve as a vehicle to launch Barrantes's candidacy, but to provide a strong and democratic organization that would give the Left the force needed at the national level to form a government.

In summary, the actors' preferences were:

The reformist bloc	$A > C > B$
The independent bloc	$B > A > C$
The revolutionary bloc	$B > C > A$

The following chronology of events surrounding the division of the United Left provides critical background information.

Chronology of Events

Internal elections for mayoral candidates of the United Left were scheduled for June 11, 1989. Henry Pease García, an independent, ran against Michel Azcueta, a member of the revolutionary bloc and local mayor of Villa El Salvador, a populous shantytown district of Lima.[9]

The reformist bloc rejected what they called the "undemocratic imposition" of elections for mayoral candidates by the National Leadership Committee and demanded elections "with full guarantees" for their candidates.[10] Barrantes asked the veteran secretary general of the Partido Comunista del Perú (Communist Party of Peru, or PCP), Jorge del Prado, to postpone the June elections. However, neither Azcueta nor Pease were willing to suspend the elections at Barrantes's behest, and the elections were held as scheduled. On June 11, 1989, Pease was elected United Left's candidate to the municipality of Lima.

Barrantes, in retaliation, placed an annulment on the registration of the IU as an electoral front with the National Election Board. In a presentation before the National Election Board the reformist bloc argued that "ultra-militarist" groups had taken over the IU and were appropriating its name and symbols. The revolutionary bloc countered that electoral fronts, unlike political parties, have to be registered before each electoral process. The composition of the front can change every time it is registered. Moreover, the doors were open for the PCR and the PSR to sign the registry of the National Election Board as part of IU; no person or party within the reformist bloc was excluded from joining.[11]

On June 20, 1989, the National Election Board indefinitely postponed the decision regarding the annulment at the request of both sides, in order to allow time for a settlement without legal intervention. The IU's National Leadership Committee offered Barrantes full guarantees of participation in the internal electoral process for the selection of presidential candidates, and dialogue based on respect for the accords of the Congress of Huampaní. A series of meetings occurred between Jorge del Prado and Barrantes, aimed at laying the foundations for subsequent talks that would include the rest of the IU. The talks were then expanded to include other groups in the independents' camp. The compromise that was hammered out—that the reformist bloc would withdraw its annulment and the rest of the IU would withdraw its registration—was vetoed by the revolutionary bloc.[12]

The reformist bloc went ahead with its own plans for an internal election of candidates for the municipal elections, scheduled for July 9, 1989. The election would also subject the presidential candidacy of Barrantes to an internal test. On July 2, 1989, Barrantes asked the Coordinating Committee of Acuerdo Socialista to withdraw the annulment in the National Election Board. He argued that political considerations and the need for unity should take precedence over legal problems.[13] However, on Monday, July 3, the reformist bloc rejected Barrantes's last-minute efforts after a discussion of a letter he wrote outlining his views. Barrantes did not press the matter.

On July 4, members of the reformist bloc and the rest of the IU met with the National Election Board to present their arguments for and against the annulment. The spokesperson for the reformist bloc argued that the rights to IU— its symbols, name, and legal personality—belonged to all six of the founding parties; the PSR and PCR had been unilaterally excluded when the PUM, UNIR, FOCEP and the PCP registered as IU. "By so doing, they violated the rights of the citizens who belong to the political parties to participate in the electoral process through political alliances. . . . Parties as juridical subjects, once registered in the registry, acquire and hold a set of rights. One of those is to participate in the electoral process through party alliances."[14] In this view, IU was the property of all six parties, each of which "had ratified its willingness to participate in the IU in four electoral processes." The reformist bloc emphasized that the intention behind their annulment was to encourage unity in IU, "for it points out that the IU continues to be composed of the six" parties. The reformist's spokesperson asked the jury to accept the annulment, because there was still time to register IU with all six parties before the August 12 deadline.

The spokesperson for the rest of the IU said that the reformist bloc was trying to destroy the Peruvian Left. The claims of the reformist bloc had no foundation; alliances were registered for nothing more than specific electoral processes. After each election, the National Election Board declares all alliances dissolved. Thus, the rights to an alliance are not like commercial rights. IU had never excluded any group from participating. Both the PSR and the PCR were invited, in writing, by the National Leadership Committee to participate in the IU. The doors remained open to participation. The leaders of IU also threatened that "the masses would take to the streets to safeguard the identity of the front," and they warned ominously that a decision in favor of annulment would close the electoral arena to the Left: Guillermo Herrera Montesinos, a member of the National Leadership Committee, said, "If the National Election Board decides to accept the appeal, it could be excluding the Left from the scene of political struggle."

On July 7, 1989, the National Election Board decided against the appeal of the Acuerdo Socialista and confirmed the legality of the registration of the IU. The decision was largely based on the fact that the members of Acuerdo Socialista were free to integrate into the IU and join the other parties registered as part of IU. The IU's National Leadership Committee stated that they would welcome the PSR and PCR with open arms. The declarations of the revolutionary bloc were more aggressive; they called on the reformist bloc to suspend parallel elections scheduled for the next day and said that the reformist bloc should not use the logotype of IU in the elections under penalty of incarceration. Leaders of the reformist bloc deplored the decision and confirmed the elections as scheduled.[15] They declared that the resolution was contradictory, that it did not resolve the problem, that it postponed the necessary political solution, and that it favored both the Right and the revolutionary bloc, which were "against [the Left] being in government."[16]

Following the decision of the National Election Board, the PCP intensified efforts to support the candidacy of Barrantes for internal elections within IU. Barrantes was given until July 31, 1989 to decide whether to run, after which the PCP would consider sponsoring the candidacy of Pease. Del Prado resumed talks with Barrantes. These talks were supported by the independents and opposed by the revolutionary bloc.

The reformist bloc's internal elections complicated the talks. On July 9, 1989, roughly 150,000 members of the reformist bloc elected candidates for the municipal election and ratified virtually unanimous (98 percent) support for the candidacy of Barrantes.[17] On July 15, 1989, Pease was proclaimed candidate of the IU in the Plaza de Acho in Rimac, and he called on the reformist bloc to reincorporate into the IU.

In a last-ditch effort to achieve the unity of IU under Barrantes leadership, a movement was organized by supporters of Barrantes to collect 200,000 signatures among the members of the IU unaffiliated with any political party, and register them as a separate political force with the National Election Board. The Movimiento Socialista No-Partidarizado (MSNP), as it was called, would be the vehicle for the reincorporation of Barrantes in the IU as a powerful electoral contender. One independent observed that Barrantes was trying to establish a new "correlation of forces" favorable to his candidacy.[18] Barrantes claimed that the unaffiliated members of IU were the majority in IU.

The independent bloc found Barrantes's initiative an encouraging sign for unity and a hopeful contribution to the vitality of internal democracy in the IU. However, the MSNP faced opposition from the revolutionary bloc, which did not want a challenge to its power within IU.

Once the new movement was registered with the National Election Board, another round of bargaining, under the auspices of PCP, was announced in the last week of July. This round followed informal talks between Barrantes and Del Prado in Nicaragua during the tenth anniversary of the Sandinista revolution. In the first meeting, seven parties participated. In the second round of talks, it became increasingly clear that unity would not be achieved before the municipal elections. As a result, leaders of the reformist bloc took the decision to register as a separate political force for the municipal election.

However, a framework agreement was sought as a foundation for broader talks leading to unity.

On August 2, 1989, a framework agreement was signed and published by leaders of the independent and reformist blocs. The declaration supported Barrantes's candidacy within the IU, creating "the necessary conditions for the impartiality of the process . . . there will not be problems in discussing all the norms and procedures necessary for this end." The authors of the framework agreement also saluted the registration of the MSNP, and ratified their commitment to the reconstruction of IU in the terms defined by the Congress at Huampaní.[19]

The next day, in a press conference, the leaders of the revolutionary bloc flatly rejected the candidacy of Barrantes in the terms outlined. They suggested that the agreement amounted to an attempt to impose Barrantes's candidacy from outside the IU, without respect for the "internal norms" of IU approved in the Congress of Huampaní.[20] Strong criticisms were also directed at the leadership of Del Prado. The registration of Barrantes's Acuerdo Socialista as a separate political force with the National Election Board that morning was noted as a sign of the definitive rupture of IU. As a result, no negotiation was possible with parties in Acuerdo Socialista: "There is nothing left to do but end all possibility of an agreement."[21] Finally, the revolutionary bloc called on the independent bloc to not allow themselves to continue to be mistreated by Barrantes: ". . . enough slaps in the face for those who have turned all possible cheeks in search of unity."

The talks between the reformist and independent blocs had been premised on the hope that such a confrontation between Barrantes and the revolutionary bloc would not occur. When the internecine dispute reached this rhetorical pitch it sounded the death knell of unity talks. Barrantes had once said it was harder to govern the Left than to fight imperialism.[22] The acrimonious press conference marked the end of all efforts to achieve unity. As one insider put it, "People were just tired of fighting."[23]

The Division Game

To construct the game, we assign ordinal payoffs to each outcome according to the player's preference ranking. The higher numbers represent a higher payoff.

	A	B	C
The reformist bloc	3	1	2
The independent bloc	2	3	1
The revolutionary bloc	1	3	2

The preference ranking immediately suggests the possibility of an alliance between the revolutionary and independent blocs. Such an alliance seemed counterintuitive because of ideological differences between the independents and the revolutionaries. Many observers expected an alliance between the reformist and independent blocs to be formed because the leaders of both were close personal friends and long-time allies. However, the expected alliance never materialized. Friendships that went back to university days were destroyed in the factional conflict. The two groups, whose ideological affinity was reflected in their common support for the candidacy of Barrantes, found themselves on opposite sides of the fence when the United Left divided. The logic of coalition-building prevailed over ideological factors. The alliance expected on the basis of the players' preferences did occur, but not in an optimal way. Analysis of the bargaining helps explain why, but first, we must specify the choices available, sequence of moves, rules of the game, and information conditions.

In the first place, strategies and outcomes are distinguished. Strategies are given with small case letters *(a, b, c)*, outcomes with upper-case letters *(A, B, C)*. The bargaining is modeled as a sequential game with perfect information; all players know where they are in the game, and the choices of the previous players. However, the players have incomplete information—they do not know the other players' preferences until the other players have moved. This creates a situation of asymmetrical information in the game, since the earlier players have revealed their preferences but subsequent players can conceal theirs.

The reformist bloc moves first. It must choose among strategies *a, b,* and *c.* Strategy *a* is the pursuit of a moderate coalition in support of Barrantes candidacy. Strategy *b* is to demand an internal election to select a candidate for IU. Strategy *c* is the exit option, and it implies withdrawal from the IU coalition.

The reformist bloc's choice partly depends on the preferences of the two other players—which it does not know for sure. The independent bloc responds to the reformist bloc's choice, again choosing *a, b,* or *c.* Their decision is made in light of the choice of the reformist bloc and based on expectations about the likely response to their own choice by the revolutionary bloc. Finally, the revolutionaries choose between *a, b,* or *c* and payoffs are assigned to outcomes after their choice.

There are rules of the game that allow us to determine the outcome of any sequence of decisions and assign payoffs to the outcomes. We start with the premise that unity is based on mutual consensus between all of the players. As journalist José María Salcedo observed, "none of the factions, by itself, was in a position to impose itself on the rest" (Salcedo 1989: 30). Candidates may be chosen by agreement if all parties concur on a single candidate. Such candidates are referred to as "candidates of consensus," and this is how Barrantes was chosen to lead the IU in 1980 (Barrantes 1985: 229). Otherwise, the candidate must be chosen through internal elections. In other words, A occurs only if all players choose a. If some players choose a and others choose b, the outcome is B.

The second aspect of the rules of the game stipulates what happens if any player chooses the exit option, c. Here the sequence of moves is important. If the reformists choose c, then the outcome is C regardless of the other players' moves. The reformist bloc, by unilaterally breaking away from IU, would almost certainly alienate the independent bloc. However, if the independent bloc chooses c after the reformists have first chosen a or b, then the outcome is A. That is, the IU is divided and there is an alliance between the reformist and independent blocs which spares Barrantes the necessity of an internal election. Likewise, if the revolutionary bloc chooses c, it leaves IU to form a separate slate and the reformist and independent blocs are left in control of IU—again, outcome A.

Figure 5.1 presents the game tree. There are nine nodes at which the revolutionary bloc chooses among actions (represented by branches). Each choice leads to a terminal node with a payoff. There are also three nodes at which the independent bloc makes choices. Each leads to a self-contained set of nodes, or subgame. And there is one initial node, the decision point at which the reformist bloc chooses among its actions, that leads to all the other nodes in the game. This too may be thought of as a subgame, one that is coextensive with the entire game tree.

The terminal node at the top of the subgame that follows the choice of a by both the reformist and the independent blocs represents the payoff for the outcome A which occurs if all players pursue a—a moderate consensus in favor or Barrantes's candidacy. This is the best outcome for Barrantes because it implies the avoidance of internal elections and the submission of the revolutionaries to his leadership. However, it is the second-best outcome for the reformists, who like Barrantes candidacy but prefer internal elections. It is the worst outcome for the revolutionaries because it implies submission to Barrantes.

The second outcome in the same subgame reflects the payoff to each player if Barrantes chooses to remain in the IU (plays a) but at least one player, in this case the revolutionary bloc, refuses to accept Barrantes's candidacy except through internal elections (plays b). This is the worst outcome for Barrantes because he risks a major political defeat at the hands of the revolutionary bloc. It is the best outcome for the independents because it implies the consolidation of internal democracy, and they think Barrantes can win an internal election. It is the best outcome for the revolutionaries, who control the party machinery and think they can beat Barrantes in internal elections.

Figure 5.1

The Division Game

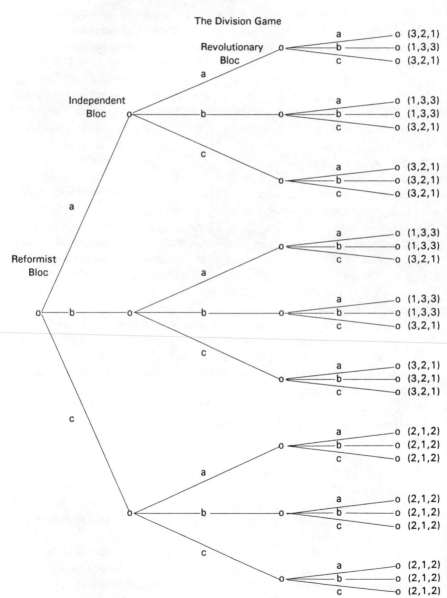

The third outcome in the subgame occurs when Barrantes seeks to be the "candidate of consensus" with the support of the independent bloc (both play *a*), and the revolutionaries force an independent candidacy by Barrantes by refusing to support his candidacy even in internal elections (plays *c*). The outcome is *A*, an alliance between reformists and independents, which is what Barrantes wanted. The revolutionaries avoided open confrontation with Barrantes because they did not want to force such an alliance between the independent and reformist blocs.

Moving down to the subgame that follows the decision by the independent bloc to play *b* after the reformist bloc has played *a*, the revolutionaries again choose between *a* or *b*, which leads to internal elections (*B*), or they play *c* which leads to an alliance between the reformists and independents (*A*).

The third subgame results in the choice of *c* by the independent bloc after the reformist bloc has chosen *a*. The outcome is an alliance between reformist and independent blocs that divides the IU (*A*). The payoff is the same regardless of the choices of the revolutionaries, as stipulated by the rules of the game.

Through backward induction we can solve the subgame beginning at the decision node that follows the choice by the reformist bloc to play *a*. If the independents choose *c* the payoff is 3, 2, 1 regardless of the choices of the revolutionary bloc. This is the best outcome for the reformist bloc, the second best for the independent bloc, and the worst outcome for the revolutionary bloc. If, on the other hand, the independent bloc chooses *b* the payoff is 1, 3, 3 unless the revolutionaries choose *c*, which is unlikely because it would lead to a payoff of 3, 2, 1 which is the worst the revolutionary bloc can expect. The best reply of the revolutionary bloc would be *b*. Similarly, if the independent bloc chooses *a*, the revolutionaries will choose *b*, which results in their best payoff and the best payoff for the independent bloc. In short, the independent bloc will choose their first choice, *a*, knowing that the revolutionaries will choose *b*. This leads to the reformist bloc's worst outcome, *B*.

Can Barrantes do better in the subgame following his decision to play *b*? Here again, by backward induction, we can arrive at the most likely payoff for the reformist bloc. In this subgame, if one of the other players chooses *c*, then the outcome is—according to the rules of the game—*A*. This is because even if Barrantes decides he is willing to submit to an internal election he would always prefer to be accepted by agreement. If the independents promote him as their candidate, Barrantes would prefer to leave IU with the support of the independents rather than go ahead with an internal election. This provides Barrantes with the best outcome—agreement on his candidacy by a majority of the Left. Similarly, if the revolutionary bloc attempts to force Barrantes into a separate candidacy this aggressive attitude will alienate the independents and force them into alliance with Barrantes. Here again, this is the outcome Barrantes would prefer. However, both the independent and the revolutionary blocs are best off pursuing their best outcome as long as the reformist bloc has chosen this option—namely, b. A payoff of 1, 3, 3 would result from any of the following strategies: (b, a, a) (b, a, b) (b, b, a) (b, b, b).

The outcome of the subgames that follow the decision by the reformist bloc to play a or b is thus always the worst outcome for the reformists. Rather than choose a, knowing the outcome will inevitably be b, the reformists prefer to choose c in which they unilaterally separate from the IU, alienate the independent bloc, and run an independent campaign. This gives the reformists their second-best payoff—a separate candidacy, which is better than accepting an internal election in which Barrantes could be defeated at the hands of the revolutionaries—but is less attractive than an outcome that wins the support of the independents. Thus, we can deduce that the reformist bloc will play c rather than a or b, leading to the payoff 2, 1, 2. This outcome is subgame perfect.[24]

The preferences of the players was not initially common knowledge. In particular, neither the reformists nor the revolutionaries knew whether the independents preferred to be in alliance with the reformists outside the IU, or remain inside the IU in alliance with the revolutionaries. In short, the preference of the independents across A, B, and C was private information. Likewise, the independents did not know whether Barrantes would accept B over C.

By fighting over the registration of IU, Barrantes sought information about the independent bloc's preferences. Were they holding out for B while secretly willing to accept A? Surely they would find C intolerable for ideological reasons, many of the leaders of the reformist bloc thought. Such speculations by Barrantes and others underestimated the commitment of the independents to the institutionalization and democratization of the IU. The failure of the independent bloc to understand that the reformists preferred C to B also contributed to the outcome. The independent bloc did not know whether the reformists were willing to risk running on a separate slate. The revolutionary bloc was, similarly, uncertain whether the independents were willing pawns of Barrantes's political machinations or genuinely committed to the unity of the coalition.

The Bargaining

The game captures the strategic logic behind the bargaining within the IU. It allows us to generate new interpretations for behavior that seemed incomprehensible to outside observers. The reformist bloc refused to play a for fear of being exploited by the independent and revolutionary blocs. The bargaining only lasted as long as the players were uncertain of each others' preferences. The bargaining ended with Barrantes playing c once it became clear that the independent bloc would not form an alliance with the reformist bloc.

Barrantes initially sought to unilaterally impose his leadership on the IU and divide the independent and revolutionary blocs in order to bring the independent bloc into his fold. Pease described the strategy of the reformist bloc as an effort to use the strength of Barrantes's candidacy to subordinate the rest of the Left by threatening to divide the IU.[25] To achieve this goal, Barrantes tried to build an alliance with the independents and the PCP, while undermining the IU as an institution. Barrantes hoped to drive a wedge between the revolutionary and independent blocs. By annulling the registration of the United Left, all factions would be denied the right to the name and symbols of the front. Thus deprived of an institutionalized coalition, the independent bloc would be forced to choose the alliance partner closest to its ideological persuasion.

Barrantes sought an alliance with the independent bloc without exposing himself to the risk of a political defeat at the hands of his opponents in the IU. He tried to show willingness to negotiate with the independent bloc without making himself vulnerable to exploitation. For example, Barrantes tried to convince other members of the reformist bloc to withdraw their annulment of IU in the National Election Board. This was meant to be interpreted—and was by Del Prado—as evidence of willingness to bargain on the part of Barrantes. Barrantes was careful to argue that the reason why the rest of the reformist bloc should "ratify [its] willingness to be united, unilaterally withdrawing the appeal" was that "the boundaries with vanguardist militarism have been flatly marked."[26] But rather than make concessions to Barrantes that would result in the imposition of a moderate consensus in IU over the opposition of the revolutionary bloc, the independents continued to insist that Barrantes play by the rules established in Huampaní and expose himself to attacks by opponents.

The independents did not offer to play c (thus creating a moderate coalition, A) in return for evidence that the reformist bloc would remain in the IU. This is because Del Prado and others clearly believed Barrantes would recognize the National Leadership Committee and accept internal elections. According to Del Prado, Barrantes initially demanded modification of the composition of the National Leadership Committee to subordinate the revolutionary bloc and pave the way for acceptance of his candidacy without an internal election.[27] This would open up the possibility of the unification of the IU around A. However, Barrantes "was not sure that all the members of the National Leadership Committee had overcome their resistance to him, and did not want to expose himself to mistreatment."[28] Thus, Barrantes was willing to work toward a moderate coalition in the IU but was afraid of being exploited by the revolutionary bloc. The leaders of the independent bloc did not realize that Barrantes would choose c rather than "expose himself to mistreatment."

The independent bloc argued that the revolutionary bloc could be neutralized more effectively working within the National Leadership Committee, as long as Barrantes accepted the rules of the Congress at Huampaní. The reformist bloc did not accept this argument. Indeed, a major obstacle in the negotiations was deliberately created by Barrantes to signal his commitment to running without IU support if necessary—he called for separate elections within the reformist bloc in disregard for the norms and principles established by the First National Congress.[29] The purpose of calling for elections in Acuerdo Socialista was to threaten to play c if the independent bloc did not work with Barrantes to subordinate the revolutionary bloc within IU (that is, play c after Barrantes played a). The threat was not credible. The independent bloc believed that Barrantes would suspend these elections. As long as they doubted Barrantes willingness to play c they were always better off playing b.

Over time, as the bargaining dragged on, players acquired information about each others' preferences. It became clear that the positions within the IU were irreconcilable. The revolutionary bloc saw the annulment and constant delays as a desperate attempt by Barrantes to avoid B. Members of the reformist bloc emphasized, in increasingly harsh terms, that the only understanding possible was with the PCP and the independents; there could be no agreement with the revolutionary bloc. As one spokesperson for the reformist bloc bluntly put it: "In no way could there be an agreement with vanguardist and militarist sectors. The forces of APS, MAS, the Communist Party of Peru and the Acuerdo Socialista were the overwhelming majority in the Congress of the IU. Those forces routed the vanguardist, militarist postulates of that contest. They must continue united."[30]

The reformist bloc heaped contempt on the revolutionaries. One member of the reformist bloc said: "The IU was only united for the purpose of opposition. . . . For the purpose of government it was never united." It was united "to defend popular conquests, to strike . . . this defensive vision is completely different from the vision of achieving government, of leading and administering a country."[31] Another leader of the reformist bloc claimed that the independents and the PPC were "being taken advantage of . . . in practice it has been demonstrated that it is the vanguardist-militarist sector that is taking control [of IU]."[32] Such statements were more than desperate rhetoric. They were intended to convey to the independent bloc that the reformists would rather accept a second-best solution (C) than play a and be exploited.

The independent bloc made the mistake of thinking that in the end Barrantes would prefer B to C. After the National Election Board decided against the reformist bloc's appeal, the general feeling among the independent bloc was still that the best decision by the reformist bloc would be to return to IU. Del Prado assumed that Barrantes would ultimately accept the internal elections in IU rather than "risk his political future."[33] Jorge del Prado lamented that Acuerdo Socialist had to suffer the misfortune of having its appeal rejected, but felt the possibility of cooperation remained. Henry Pease declared the result a victory for the consolidation of internal democracy initiated in the Congress of Huampaní. Gustavo Mohme, a devoted supporter of Barrantes among the independents, said, "the internal differences should be discussed within the front and should not be attacked from outside." Ames said the event should be forgotten and unity reestablished.[34]

Barrantes did not share the view that he had no alternative but to return to IU *(B)* or risk his political future *(C)*. Where *A* seemed elusive, Barrantes opted for *C*. Barrantes was encouraged by electoral rules that forced a second round of elections if the winner failed to gain an absolute majority. As long as the leading candidate did not win an absolute majority in the first round Barrantes felt he had the popularity to become the runner-up and then attract votes from both the Left and the governing American Popular Revolutionary Alliance (APRA), which Vargas Llosa had alienated.[35] The results of the polls in early 1989 encouraged this view. Barrantes was running at 27 percent against Vargas Llosa's 31 percent in February, with APRA's Luis Alva Castro trailing at 7 percent.[36] By May, Barrantes's odds had improved; he was preferred by 32 percent of those polled against 36 percent for Vargas Llosa and 16 percent for Alva Castro. "On the strength of these figures," wrote the *Latin American Weekly Report,* "it seemed safe to assume that, even if Vargas Llosa were assured an easy first-round victory, APRA voters could be persuaded to throw their weight behind Barrantes in the second round."[37] As divisions within the Left continued through June, the lead for Vargas Llosa increased, yet the reformists were "still gambling that his margin will remain insufficient for a first-round victory. With Barrantes a clear contender for second place, they reckon that he will end up attracting all left-wing votes, plus a large share of the APRA vote, and win comfortably in the second round."[38]

The reformist bloc refused to return to IU because Barrantes would not submit to internal elections as long as he felt he had a chance to win national elections without IU. The independent bloc made a miscalculation by underestimating the willingness of Barrantes to play *c*. The leaders of the revolutionary bloc were not making a miscalculation by rejecting the separate electoral process sponsored by the reformist bloc and agreeing to support Barrantes only if he won an internal election within IU. Their position was based on the view that "the elections should not be the top priority; it is necessary to mobilize the struggle of the workers."[39]

In the end the negotiations came down to whether Barrantes could play *a* without ending in *B*. For the reformist bloc to avoid *B,* the independents would have to play *c*. Agustín Haya de la Torre, a member of the PUM who competed with Pease for the leadership of IU, said, "what has not yet been defined is whether the possible candidacy of Barrantes will be the product of internal elections of the IU or not."[40] But he insisted on rules that gave the revolutionary bloc an advantage in any confrontation with Barrantes. As a condition for their acceptance of Barrantes candidacy, leaders of the revolutionary bloc said that Barrantes would have to fight internal elections: "It is not a question of the caprice of anyone; it is a question of the Congress of Huampaní."[41] They knew Barrantes feared that he might not win internal elections because of opposition from the revolutionary bloc, and taunted him for his obvious reluctance.

In explaining the vitriolic press conference that prompted the final rupture of the IU, one revolutionary-bloc leader said, "we thought that we could perceive that a bloc had formed" between the PCP and the independents "to push for the candidacy of Alfonso Barrantes from outside the IU. Under these terms, we considered that they had not fulfilled what was agreed in the Congress of Huampaní in which it was decided that all political positions would be granted through internal election."[42] Thus, the revolutionary bloc forced the independents to play their cards—be loyal to the IU or leave and join Barrantes. The independent bloc, predictably, chose to remain in IU.

The compromise between the revolutionary bloc and the independents was an IU slate lead by presidential candidate Henry Pease and vice-presidential candidate Agustín Haya de la Torre. These candidates were imposed by the leaders of the United Left, after negotiations behind closed doors, despite the intense demands for unity and internal democracy from the rank-and-file. This caused "intense frustration among the rank and file whose hopes for a united Left had been first raised by the congress and then shattered by the leadership" (Poole and Rénique 1992: 137).

CONCLUSION

A major objective of this chapter has been is to illustrate the utility of research that "combines rational-choice theory's use of deductive reasoning with the case study literature's emphasis on accurate description of historical events" (Wagner 1989: 178). A game-theoretic model of coalition bargaining provides insight into why groups in the Peruvian Left made choices that seem suboptimal. The explanation lies in strategic interaction among actors with very different preferences across the set of feasible outcomes.

Obstacles to unity came mainly from the profound antagonism between the reformist and revolutionary blocs. Neither was willing to submit to the dominance of the other faction within the front. Barrantes attempted to lure the independent bloc to his camp in order to isolate the revolutionary bloc. However, the independents were unwilling to split from the IU because they were more committed to the rules and norms of the IU established in Huampaní than to the candidacy of their preferred leader.

Barrantes wanted to build an alliance with the reformist and independent blocs. However, he was unwilling to risk political defeat and humiliation at the hands of the revolutionary bloc that controlled the strongest political machines in the front. Barrantes sought to drive a wedge between the independent and the revolutionary blocs and undermine the institutional integrity of the IU by questioning its legality. In the process he hoped to avoid abandoning IU to run a separate slate and to entice the independents to join him in abandoning the alliance with the revolutionaries. He was unwilling to make any concessions that would leave him vulnerable to attacks by the revolutionaries. Yet the concessions Barrantes could offer were not attractive as long as the independents remained convinced that the reformist would not play c. Moreover, as long as they thought Barrantes would play a they were unilaterally better off playing b rather than c.

Another objective of this chapter has been to suggest an interpretation of the Peruvian Left in which the struggle for leadership and the distribution of payoffs within the coalition is prominent. Ideological disagreements existed within the IU from the time of its formation in 1980, and they alone cannot account for the division of the Left. To understand the precise dynamics of IU's disintegration requires a careful reconstruction of the choices and perceptions of the players at the time of the rupture. It is in such periods of bargaining, in which a relatively small number of players negotiate over a finite set of outcomes, that rational-choice models are most useful. What game theory reveals is that fear of exploitation can be a powerful disincentive to collaborate in a coalition that has not institutionalized mechanisms for resolving leadership disputes. It also accounts for the why divisions with IU seemed to have more to do with disagreements among the leaders than ideological differences.

The experience of the IU suggests a powerful lesson for the Latin American Left generally. Ambivalence about democracy in IU was deeply implanted in the minds of contending players. Yet because the IU had no institutional mechanism for resolving internal tensions, each faction sought to impose its will on the others and each was afraid of being exploited by the others. The result was, for the Left, a collectively suboptimal outcome.

Institutionalized democracy in IU would have required that political factions accept restrictions on their power in the interest of achieving a solid and powerful coalition. The breakdown of IU in 1989 demonstrated that this was impossible because the underlying strategies and beliefs of each bloc remained so radically different.

PART IV

INSTABILITY OF DEMOCRACY

The chapters in this section examine the disintegration of the Peruvian party system in the two rounds of the 1990 presidential election and the subsequent erosion of Peruvian democracy. Chapters 6 and 7 integrate the findings from the previous two sections to explain the phenomenal rise of an anti-system candidate. They show how extremist parties were undermined by their inability to occupy the center and appeal to the new electorate, especially the informal sector. Independent candidates, however, were more successful.

Chapter 8 addresses the stability of the new political system based on a hybrid of democracy and authoritarianism (a soft dictatorship or dictablanda). Results of elections leading to a new Congress and municipalities, as well as a referendum to legitimize the new constitution, are examined for evidence of the consolidation of a new political system. It argues that the weakness of political parties is an obstacle to the consolidation of any representative political system in Peru.

.6.

A SPATIAL ANALYSIS
OF MULTIPARTY COMPETITION

he results of the 1990 election provide compelling evidence of the pertinence of the median-voter theorem to the dynamics of party competition in Peru. The theorem states that candidates will move toward the electorate's median preference if voter preferences are single-peaked (Ordeshook 1992: 104–105). Most Peruvians located themselves at the center of the political spectrum. By the late 1980s the two main parties of the center—AP and APRA—were discredited by their performance in government. Yet extremist parties were unable to construct winning coalitions by moving from the ideological hinterlands toward the center. Rather than vote for extremist candidates of the Left or Right, a majority of Peruvians turned to a virtually unknown candidate who astutely located his movement in the center of the political spectrum. In short, a new entrant to the political system was able to emerge and "steal" the election from the traditional political parties by locating himself near the median voter.

The astonishing results of the 1990 election, and the victory of Alberto Fujimori, raise many important questions about voters and political parties in Peru; questions critical to the stability of Peru's fragile democratic institutions. How many voters were located in the center, and how many at the periphery? What tradeoffs did extremist parties face in shifting from the ideological hinterlands to the center? Why were the extremist parties unable to deter entry of anti-system candidates? What constrained their mobility? Did party activists force their leaders to remain faithful to extremist positions? What opportunities did the electoral system offer to new entrants, and how did it weaken established parties?

To address these diverse questions within a single framework, this chapter develops a set of hypotheses drawn from the literature on spatial models of electoral competition. The hypotheses are followed by a brief chronology of the events leading up to the April 1990 election, and are then checked against the evidence.

MULTIPARTY COMPETITION IN PERU

Spatial models provide a way of analyzing problems in electoral competition such as entry, entry deterrence, abstention, factionalism, the role of party activists, and the limits of each candidate's programmatic mobility (see Downs 1957; Barry 1978; Enelow and Hinich 1990b; Shepsle and Cohen 1990; Shepsle 1991; Wittman 1990). This chapter uses these models to analyze a specific empirical problem: the unexpected outcome of the 1990 election in Peru.[1]

Review of Spatial Models

The seminal work in this tradition is Anthony Downs's 1957 book, *An Economic Theory of Democracy*. Downs assumed that parties are coalitions that seek office; that they can be ordered from left to right; and that they cannot leap over each other. He then examined the effects of various distributions of voter preferences along a left-right political scale on (1) the number of parties, (2) the conditions under which new parties are formed, and (3) whether parties seek to resemble one another or try to remain ideologically distinct.

Downs found that two-party systems provide stable and effective government to the extent that there is ideological consensus. If most voters cluster around the median voter, parties will converge rapidly on the center. In a bimodal distribution of preferences, balancing center parties are less likely, and democracy is more likely to produce chaos. A polymodal distribution of preferences encourages a multiparty system, and parties tend to distinguish themselves ideologically. Downs also assumed that parties tend to merge to capture a combined total of votes larger than their opponents share. However, as they move away from their constituency they face a tradeoff between losing the support of loyalists through abstention and winning new adherents.

New parties form, according to Downs, "immediately after some significant change in the distribution of ideological views among eligible voters." The distribution of voters is "a crucial determinant molding a nation's political life" according to Downs. Moreover, "major changes" in this distribution "are among the most important political events possible." Yet Downs is silent about how such changes occur. He suggests that "though parties will move ideologically to adjust to the distribution under some circumstances, they will also attempt to move voters toward their own locations, thus altering it." (Downs 1957: 140).

Since Downs's original contribution, much effort has been devoted to refining and modifying spatial theories of voting.[2] Many of Downs's assumptions about voters, candidates, parties, and party systems have been questioned or modified. Analysts have questioned the idea that candidates are strategic but voters choose sincerely on the basis of their preferences (Enelow and Hinich 1990b). Candidates may be unable to adopt policies that maximize votes—there may be costs involved in changing policy positions. As Shepsle and Cohen (1990: 40) suggest: "In many circumstances, politicians and parties come to a contest with reputations that can be altered only marginally during the course of a campaign. In contrast, lesser known candidates may be endowed with considerably more spatial mobility" (see also Shepsle 1991: 33–39).

Downs characterizes parties as teams seeking to win elections. However, as Wittman (1990) notes, parties may not be teams and they may have objectives other than to win elections. For some members of a party, policies are not just vehicles to attract voters—voters are sought in order to win office to implement policies. Treating parties as teams may ignore agent-principal problems. The tension between seeking office and seeking to implement policies may undermine the cohesion of a party. Even if parties seek only to win elections, the need to win a place on a party's slate will force candidates to be sensitive to the median voter within their party. Another constraint on parties is their fear of alienating core supporters: "Established candidates will hesitate to desert their respective bases for fear of alienating core constituents in the ideological hinterlands" (Shepsle and Cohen 1990). This may undermine the ability of parties to maximize votes and deter entry.

The party system itself may constrain parties more than was initially understood by Downs. Much of the work in the spatial theories of voting have concentrated on two-party systems. In multiparty systems, equilibria are harder to find. Runoff elections may encourage candidates to seek to rank among the top candidates even though under alternative arrangements they would have no chance of winning. Thus, "rank maximization" replaces "vote maximization." Finally, uncertainty plays a larger role in multiparty systems. Candidates may lack information about voters, other candidates, what is "common knowledge," or the costs of entry versus benefits of victory. As a consequence, beliefs and conjectures may be crucial.

A Spatial Model of Multiparty Competition for Peru

Spatial models assume all parties can be located on a spectrum from left to right. To make the model relevant to the Peruvian case, we must assume voters are located across the spectrum in a polymodal distribution. Most voters are located in the center. However, a substantial minority are located close to the extreme left and extreme right. A party on the left will locate itself closest to the largest number of leftist voters, and the party on the right will locate itself as close as possible to the largest number of right-wing voters. What prevents parties from moving toward the center in such a polymodal distribution is the fear of losing the support of extremist voters—through abstention or support for another candidate—faster than new adherents at the center can be attracted. This fear is reinforced by the constant possibility of new entrants who may occupy the abandoned space in the ideological hinterlands if an extremist party moves too far toward the center.

We know from previous chapters that parties in Peru are characterized by factionalism. For the purpose of the present analysis, both left- and right-wing parties can be assumed to have two factions, moderates and extremists. Moderates are highly mobile, extremists have limited mobility. Suppose that a moderate faction within the Left decided to move toward the center and compete with the centrist party for center-left votes. By locating itself slightly to the left of the center party, the new center-left party could capture new voters in the center-left. A faction will do this, however, only if the new voters attracted through such a strategy are expected to be more numerous than the number of voters lost (those who remain loyal to the extremist faction). This is most likely when there is a major redistribution of voters away from the ideological hinterlands toward the center, when there is a vacancy at the center caused by the decline in support for a centrist party, or when both occur simultaneously.

What factors account for the limited mobility of extremists? The role of party activists is the key here. The ideological hinterlands are the terrain in which activists thrive. Activists constrain candidates through their power of nomination, contributions, and by being the "raw material" from which leadership emerges (thus creating candidates with preferences close to the median activist). Extremist candidates linked to party machinery may share the policy preferences of the party's activists. Indeed, some party leaders, particularly those tied to powerful party machines, may be more concerned with the median activist than the median voter. Electoral performance may be a means to achieving more activist support, rather than vice versa.

The notion of core supporters gives a class dimension to the model. Data from previous elections indicated that there is a bias in favor of the working class in the Left, and toward the upper-middle class and employers in the Right. Party activists are drawn from these sectors of society. The Left cannot move beyond a certain point without alienating activists drawn from within the area to the left of that point; the same is true of the Right (Przeworski and Sprague 1986).

Activists may not be distributed the same way as voters. In fact, there are good reasons for assuming they are not. It is possible that under certain conditions divergence between activists and voters is great, and that activists become radicalized while the electorate becomes more moderate. Relations between supporters and activists may determine whether the party is able to move toward the median voter. Voters may like the candidate but not the activists: indeed, a candidate may change programmatic positions without the electorate noticing a difference because it perceives more clearly the statements, positions, and rhetoric of the party's activists.

Finally, the rules of electoral competition may influence candidates' strategies. Runoff elections encourage candidates to seek to place in a second round, even though they have no prospect of winning a plurality of the vote in the first round. Voters may also take the electoral system into account in their response to the spatial location of parties (Shepsle and Cohen 1990: 27). Voters may cast their ballot in the first-round election with an eye to improving the choices available in the runoff election, rather than voting sincerely for their first preference. Thus, depending on the electoral system, some voters may not support the candidate closest to them (Shepsle and Cohen 1990: 28; Greenberg and Shepsle 1987).

To summarize, the decisions of extremist candidates or factions to move toward the center will depend on:

1. the number of voters they can attract in the center;
2. the number of voters they will lose to abstention or
   competitors in the periphery;
3. the severity of the tradeoff between voters in the center
   and the periphery;
4. the mobility of the candidates;
5. the role of the activists; and
6. the rules of the electoral system.

We now turn to a discussion of the Peruvian case to check these hypotheses against the evidence from the 1990 election.

Center versus Periphery

Polls and election data show that most Peruvians located themselves at the center of the political spectrum. It is unclear to what extent the number of voters in the center of the electorate was growing. However, there is evidence of a sharp increase in the number of voters who would not locate themselves on a left-right scale. This suggests a growing volatility of the electorate.[3]

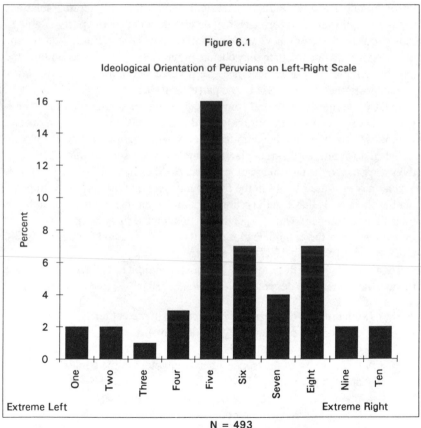

Figure 6.1

Ideological Orientation of Peruvians on Left-Right Scale

N = 493
Average response: 5.8
Does not know the term "left" or "right" in politics: 53%
Source: APOYO Lima, November 1991.

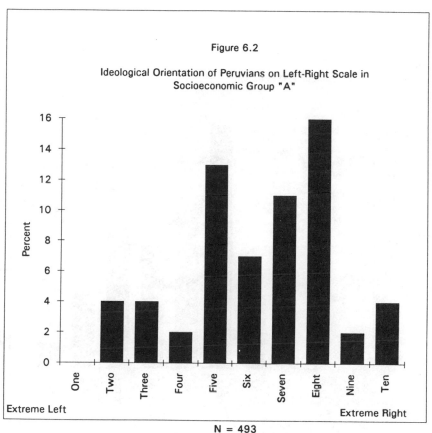

Figure 6.2

Ideological Orientation of Peruvians on Left-Right Scale in Socioeconomic Group "A"

N = 493
Average Rsponse: 6.3
Does not know the term "left" or "right" in politics: 31%
Source: APOYO Lima, November 1991

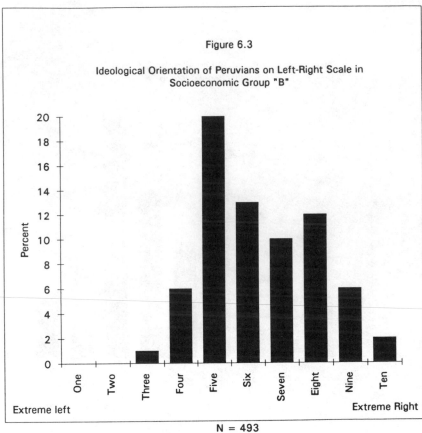

Figure 6.3

Ideological Orientation of Peruvians on Left-Right Scale in
Socioeconomic Group "B"

N = 493
Average Response: 6.4
Does not know the term "left" or "right" in politics: 28%
Source: APOYO Lima, November 1991.

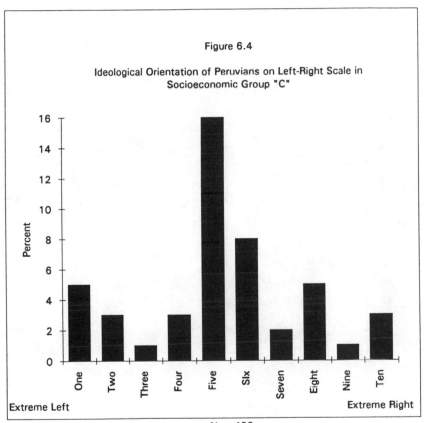

Figure 6.4

Ideological Orientation of Peruvians on Left-Right Scale in
Socioeconomic Group "C"

N = 493
Average Response: 5.3
Does not know the term "left" or "right" in politics: 50%
Source: APOYO Lima, November 1991

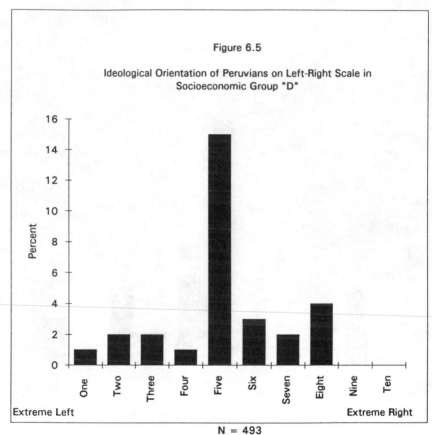

Figure 6.5

Ideological Orientation of Peruvians on Left-Right Scale in Socioeconomic Group "D"

N = 493
Average Response: 5.1
Does not know the term "left" or "right" in politics: 71%
Source: APOYO Lima, November 1991.

A distribution of the electorate is graphically displayed in figure 6.1. Most voters were located in the center; a smaller but significant number of voters were located at the extremes. However, an astonishing number of voters refused to locate themselves on the ideological spectrum at all. Over half of the respondents refused to identify their position on a left-right spectrum. The number was even higher among the lowest socioeconomic groups. Figures 6.2–6.5 show the results from figure 6.1 broken down by socioeconomic status. Among the poorest groups, those in the socioeconomic bracket "D," 71 percent of the respondents claimed to not know the terms "left" or "right" in politics; the same claim was made by 50 percent of those in group "C"; 28 percent of group "B"; and 31 percent of group "A."

The results of this survey suggest a dramatic decline in the level of ideological commitment among working-class voters.[4] Indeed, in a similar survey conducted by APOYO in February 1988, only four percent of the respondents refuse to locate themselves on a left-right continuum, and there was no consistent variation across social class in the strength of such ideological definition (APOYO 1988: 24).

A number of important, although tentative, observations can be made about the findings in figures 6.1–6.5. The data are consistent with the argument that a dramatic process of ideological reorientation was occurring in the Peruvian electorate in the late 1980s, especially among working-class groups. This process apparently involved a sharp decline in the level of identification with the Left among working class voters. At the same time, much of the electorate appeared unable or unwilling to find a new location on the ideological spectrum. A further implication is that the refusal of the electorate to reveal its political preferences—or even to formulate clear preferences—meant that politicians were forced to operate in an incomplete information environment.

Figures 6.1 through 6.5 must be interpreted with caution. The sample size is extremely small, and probably unrepresentative. Moreover, individuals in lower socioeconomic groups might have been uncomfortable responding to the question. Choosing the center, or refusing to recognize the distinction between left and right, may have been ruses to avoid revealing true preferences.

It is probably not a coincidence that half of those polled refused to locate themselves on an ideological spectrum in a period when roughly half of the electorate was consistently voting for independent candidates. Figures 6.1–6.5 may reinforce the claim that, to the extent that voters saw themselves on a left-right spectrum at all, they tended to converge at the center. Yet, as previous chapters have shown, the parties that traditionally occupied the center were largely discredited due to their performance in government between 1980 and 1990. Degregori and Grompone report data from the public-opinion firm

DATUM that show the dramatic decline of support for Belaúnde between 1980 and 1985, and for García between 1985 and 1990 (see figures 1 and 2 in Degregori and Grompone 1991: 139–140), and they suggest that the triumph of Ricardo Belmont in the 1989 municipal elections in Lima was the first major signal of public scepticism and disenchantment with existing electoral options in the center. Candidates like Belmont and Fujimori were able to win by attracting the volatile electorate that refused to locate itself on the left-right spectrum, that was disenchanted with the performance of centrist parties, and that was alienated by ideological extremes.

The large number of voters at the center—and floating voters without clear preferences—was partly due to a process of migration from the periphery of the political spectrum, especially from the extreme left, as working-class and other voters reacted against violence and the polarization of the country caused by the seemingly relentless growth of the Shining Path. Undecided voters wanted an option between polarizing extremes.[5] Attractive candidates were few; the gap between parties and society grew, and the search for new, independent candidates began.

The growth of the informal sector also strengthened the center and contributed to a floating electorate without clear ideological commitments. As previously noted (see chapter 3), the informal sector tended to be composed of people who were highly individualistic, yet supportive of social change, and favorable to a redistributive role for the government (Tueros 1984, Chávez O'Brien 1990a). This observation held true for the 1990 election. Asked to locate themselves on a scale from one (extreme left) to ten (extreme right), most respondents in the informal sector in a study by Adams and Valdivia (1991: 165) located themselves in the center-left, ranging from two to six. In short, the informal sector and the median voter became nearly synonymous.

Few people in the informal sector seemed eager to support the free-market prescriptions of FREDEMO (Adams and Valdivia 1991: 155). De Soto reported to the Chamber of Commerce that "these people do not identify with us, they do not identify with the private sector. In all our surveys . . . we have asked two questions: 'are you a member of the private sector?' and the answer is 'no' . . . so we asked: 'who is in the private sector?' and the answer is 'they are the big shots.'"[6]

Tradeoffs Between Center and Periphery

The voting patterns for the Right remained consistent with those of previous elections, providing evidence of a sharp tradeoff between its core supporters on the Right and the voters at the center. Support for the Right was negatively correlated with the presence of the informal sector in districts of Lima in all elections from the time the Constituent Assembly initiated the transition to democracy (see chapter 2).[7]

In the municipal elections, FREDEMO's candidate for Lima, Juan Incháustegui, failed to win support among voters in the shantytowns. Instead, they voted for an independent candidate, Ricardo Belmont. Whereas FREDEMO won an absolute majority of the vote in districts with the smallest percent of the population in the informal sector (under 30 percent), it captured just under a quarter of the vote in districts with over 50 percent of the work force in the informal sector. Overall, FREDEMO won roughly 40 percent of the vote in Lima, far short of the absolute majority that would be needed to avoid a runoff in the presidential race, because it failed to overcome the traditional social isolation of the Right.

There was little evidence that the informal sector was different from manual workers in their political orientation in the 1990 election (Grompone 1991: 51), a result that is consistent with the findings in chapter 2. Thus, the Left faced a minimal tradeoff in moving toward the center. The existence of a large floating electorate without clear ideological preferences obscured the consistent patterns of class-based voting in previous elections and may have contributed to the perception among the political elites that there were few sharp tradeoffs in the way Peruvians voted. The volatility of the electorate encouraged candidates to aspire to broad support from nontraditional constituencies. Such strategies failed to recognize that the volatility of the electorate was a manifestation of a profound rejection of the political class among Peruvian voters.

Candidates Mobility and Activists

Hernando de Soto's Instituto Libertad y Democracia (ILD) feared that by forming an alliance with AP and PPC, Vargas Llosa would lose the mobility necessary to win the support of the center. Data from chapter 2 were presented to researchers in the ILD before the elections in 1989 and 1990; the researchers predicted that Vargas Llosa would not be elected unless he was able to change these voting patterns. They acknowledged that if the Peruvian Right was to win it could not be perceived to be associated with AP and the PPC, and would have to make an effort to attract the support of the urban poor. As long as Vargas Llosa was tied to the traditional parties of the Right, he would have trouble gaining the trust and support of the informal sector.[8]

What was less clear was the extent to which candidates of the Left were also identified with the political establishment. Barrantes, for example, was seen as a close ally of the APRA government, and suffered some contagious effects due to that association—a point repeatedly driven home in FREDEMO propaganda.

The Electoral System

Schmidt (1994) has noted that two aspects of Peru's electoral rules decisively affected the outcome of the 1990 presidential campaign: the majority runoff format and the preferential vote for congressional candidates. Peru's 1979 Constitution established a majority runoff system in which there were two rounds of voting if no candidate captured an absolute majority of the valid votes cast in the first round. As Shugart and Carey have demonstrated, this system encouraged the proliferation of candidates. In their words,

> Peru is an example of a party system in which the use of majority runoff for presidential elections may be blamed for the proliferation of candidates. What had been a two-bloc party system before military intervention in 1968 led to two consecutive presidential elections in the 1980s that were won by first-round majorities of valid votes cast. However, by 1990 the majority runoff rules encouraged two 'outsiders' to enter the first round as challengers to the established party system. With a decisive plurality election, such a proliferation would have been far less likely. An "outsider" like Alberto Fujimori, the eventual winner, could not have appeared as a viable candidate under plurality rule. (1992: 214–15)

The preferential vote allows voters to select candidates from party lists; in Peru, they could choose four candidates, two for the senate and two for the lower house. Under Peru's proportional representation system, each party gets a number of seats that corresponds to the total number of votes it receives; seats are assigned according to the rank of candidates on the list and the preferential vote.[9] The preferential vote was designed to give the electorate more choice and weaken the power of party insiders, but it also weakened established parties. The preferential vote provided an incentive for individual campaigns as candidates compete with other candidates on their own list for preferential votes (Schmidt 1994: 36–41).

THE DYNAMICS OF THE CAMPAIGN

Vargas Llosa critically needed to locate himself near the median voter. He faced opponents dedicated to painting him into a corner as an extreme right-wing ideologue. Even before the campaign began, most voters perceived FREDEMO to be an extreme right-wing coalition. A poll taken by APOYO in February

1988 showed that whereas most voters located themselves at 5.4 on a scale of 1 to 10, where 1 represents the extreme left and 10 represents the extreme right, FREDEMO was located on average at 7.8 on the same scale (APOYO 1988: 23–5). Unfortunately for FREDEMO, Vargas Llosa's tendency to take extremist positions made his opponent's job easier and contributed to the public perception that FREDEMO was an extreme-right coalition.

Vargas Llosa's campaign for the presidency involved three stages: the first stage, prior to the municipal election in November 1989, aimed to create an image of Vargas Llosa that the electorate could identify with; the second stage, which lasted until February 1990, involved the diffusion of the liberal ideas behind his program; and the final stage was the creation of "momentum," with the slogan, "Lets Go Peru, In The First Round" (A. Vargas Llosa 1991: 34–37).

An example of Vargas Llosa's tendency to take extremist positions came in the second stage of the campaign, in December 1989, when Vargas Llosa outlined his political program at a forum for presidential candidates sponsored by the Annual Conference of Executives (Conferencia Anual de Ejecutivos, or CADE), a key business association. His program involved harsh, anti-inflationary stabilization measures followed by trade liberalization, encouragements for private enterprise and foreign investment, privatization of state-owned enterprises, elimination of price controls and subsidies, reform of the taxation structure, and elimination of job-security legislation. The proposed reforms would be bitter medicine for trade unions and inefficient businesses accustomed to operating in a highly protected environment.

Vargas Llosa appealed for a "clear and unequivocal mandate" for his program, rejecting the idea of a "national pact" (acuerdo nacional) among major interest associations and political parties. Vargas Llosa did not want to be a prisoner of "mercantilist" pressures or constraints from within his own coalition. Without a broad mandate, he would be forced to make concessions and compromises that would dilute the "great transformation" that he proposed. "Although someone might come knocking on my door to tell me that he is going bankrupt," he said, "I would not change the program because it forms part of a [comprehensive] system" (cited in Schmidt 1991: 29–30). Needless to say, such a position made many business leaders, as well as organized workers, extremely uncomfortable. Vargas Llosa seemed almost to take pleasure in emphasizing the costs of his program: "The cost will be very high," he said, "but if the people decide to pay this cost, they will back me with their vote" (Schmidt 1991: 30). Not surprisingly, few voters warmed to this vision.

Making the CADE speech was a critical mistake because it made Vargas Llosa look too radical, even to members of his own core constituency and coalition partners.[10] As one AP leader put it, the speech was "one of the greatest blunders in the country's political history. . . . Mario Vargas Llosa was not going to win the election after the CADE speech" (Daeschner 1993: 167).

In addition to creating a deep schism within FREDEMO, Vargas Llosa's inflexible position was easily attacked by his opponents. President García deliberately sought to draw Vargas Llosa into a public fight that would polarize the election and eliminate FREDEMO's chances of occupying the center of the political spectrum. García warned of the loss of half a million public-sector jobs, and promptly certified the Interunion Confederation of State Workers (Confederación Intersectorial de Trabajadores Estatales or CITE), the largest single union in the country. APRA also devised a very effective propaganda "spot" for television that emphasized the social cost of Vargas Llosa's "shock" measures, thus tapping into a deep reservoir of fear of orthodox economic medicine among Peruvian workers, shantytown dwellers, and other lower-income groups.

Vargas Llosa responded to García's attacks as if the incumbent president were running for reelection. The result was that Vargas Llosa boxed himself into a right-wing campaign. The candidate's advisors pointed out that the polarization of the electorate along class lines could result in a second-round election in which Vargas Llosa would be unlikely to pick up Aprista votes.[11]

Vargas Llosa needed to pick up the swing voters who had given García his ample majority in 1985. These groups were identified by Sawyer/Miller as low-income groups, center and "soft" left voters, and young voters. By attacking Vargas Llosa, García hoped to deprive him of precisely these voters in the center of the spectrum. Vargas Llosa's advisors warned him that his message was failing to resonate with the urban poor (Daeschner 1993: 113–14).

Throughout the campaign FREDEMO was plagued by its inability to win solid support from the centrist swing groups. FREDEMO's surveys distinguished between four income groups; A and B were the upper- and middle-class groups, C and D were the lower-middle- and lower-class groups. The support of lower-income groups was soft and vulnerable. "We are not making a breakthrough in the C/D class" claimed Mark Malloch Brown in January 1990 (A. Vargas Llosa 1991: 47). Although the weak adhesion of the poor was evident to campaign strategists, none of the FREDEMO team saw any clear rival until the final weeks of the campaign.

The weakness of the Left—and his substantial but soft lead in the polls—may have emboldened Vargas Llosa and lulled him into a false sense of security. The campaigns by the two leftist candidates never seemed to awaken much enthusiasm. Prior to the division of the Left, Barrantes was the leading candidate. In a poll conducted in 1988 he had the support of 34 percent of those surveyed; Vargas Llosa had 24 percent and Alva Castro 17 percent. The votes for APRA and the Left combined added up to 51 percent, suggesting the possibility of a second round victory for Barrantes even if all the undecided votes went to FREDEMO.[12] Already in 1988 members of the Left began drawing up lists of cabinet appointments in a Barrantes government. The 1989 division of the Left permanently damaged its image among voters.

Still hoping for a second-round victory in 1990, the Izquierda Socialista (IS), the successor to Acuerdo Socialista, relied too much on Barrantes's charisma and leadership. Pease's more collegial style was apparent in the campaign for IU.[13] The candidates avoided attacking each other. However, the division between the IS and the IU clearly dampened the excitement of activists and supporters alike. The spectacle of Pease's and Barrantes's running against each other confused and frustrated the electorate. Popular images of the candidates confounded the messages that each attempted to project. Barrantes sought to locate his candidacy at the center of the spectrum, in order to take second place and win in a runoff election. His slogan was "Peru united, Barrantes for President."[14] Yet Barrantes was seen as a leftist, a candidate of popular extraction, closely identified with the radicalism of the urban poor. Pease, who had remained in alliance with the revolutionary bloc within IU, was seen as a technocrat and a centrist. This exacerbated the inevitable problems created by any division, and resulted in a lower lever of support for both candidates.[15]

Despite the weakness of the Left, surveys done by FREDEMO under the supervision of Sawyer/Miller revealed that Vargas Llosa was having difficulty winning adherents among subordinate groups. There was a perception in the electorate that Vargas Llosa was the "candidate of the rich" (A. Vargas Llosa 1991: 32). FREDEMO's strategists recognized that their challenge was to "avoid a polarization that would impede the attraction of the masses situated in the center . . ." (A. Vargas Llosa 1991: 33). They knew that the fundamental problem FREDEMO faced in appealing to the electorate as "independent" and "apolitical" was the alliance with the traditional political parties, AP and PPC. "At first [the alliance] had seemed necessary," said Alvaro Vargas Llosa, "given that we believed that it was impossible to mount a party structure from point zero that could compete efficiently in every locality with more powerful machines and which would be able to defend the vote in every one of the 50,000 electoral booths in the country. On the other hand, we had the mistaken impression that the two parties [AP and PPC] had a more or less solid structure; we discovered in time that their national presence was more of an entelechy than a real base" (A. Vargas Llosa 1991: 34).

Moreover, even the foreign consultants appeared to recognize the social changes that had taken place in Peru; "The political know-how [of the traditional political parties] appears threadbare and based on political and demographic circumstances that no longer exist: Belaúnde's former deferential rural voter is today's angry, ruthless peasant of the Sierra or lumpen proletariat," according to a Sawyer/Miller memorandum to the candidate (Daeschner 1993: 108). However, their solution to Vargas Llosa's alliance was unfortunate. The consultants had initially supported a clean break with the parties. When Vargas Llosa refused to break with the parties, Vargas Llosa's advisors insisted that he marginalize them within the coalition. They proposed "a deceit intended to get you off the hook with FREDEMO for organizational purposes." An "organizational divide" would be created in the coalition. A "loyal battalion" of coalition activists would have operational control of the campaign, and the parties would be eliminated from the day-to-day management of the campaign (Daeschner 1993: 106–8).

The result was a disaster for FREDEMO. Vargas Llosa cut the traditional political parties out of the loop, yet was widely seen as their ally. The leaders of the traditional parties figured prominently on the FREDEMO slate, yet Vargas Llosa refused to benefit from their experience and resources. "Vargas Llosa suffered the cons—the rejection of the *pueblo* toward them—and failed to benefit from the pros—their experience and provincial organization" said one AP leader (Daeschener 1993: 129). Indeed, Vargas Llosa antagonized his coalition partners to such a degree that he lost control over the party activists. For example, he was unable to control their campaign spending.

In March 1990 FREDEMO conducted a survey and found that its support was around 40 percent of the electorate, and Alva Castro of APRA had risen to about 20 percent. In view of these results, the advisors from Sawyer/Miller began to doubt whether Vargas Llosa could win in the first round. Another survey of voter preferences conducted in late March showed that Fujimori had overtaken Alva Castro in Lima, with 20 percent of the voters declaring their intention to vote for Fujimori's Cambio 90. FREDEMO strategists were stunned (A. Vargas Llosa 1991: 128). The polls showed that Fujimori was growing precisely in the "C/D class" where FREDEMO was most vulnerable (A. Vargas Llosa 1991: 129).

As soon as it became likely that Vargas Llosa would not win in the first round, and that Fujimori was moving into second place, panic hit FREDEMO. Recognizing that electoral rules were having an influence on voters' calculations, Belaúnde nervously suggested that the 50 percent required to win the election on the first round should be changed to 36 percent of valid votes cast.[16] However, the other candidates expressed no support for this proposal. Vargas Llosa and his supporters had no other option but to continue their strenuous efforts to convince voters that a second round would be unnecessary and damaging to the country. With less than two weeks before the election, the campaign for Vargas Llosa had to develop an emergency strategy.

Vargas Llosa recognized that excessive propaganda and constant repetition of FREDEMO's musical jingle was irritating voters. He demanded that FREDEMO candidates for the House of Deputies and the Senate reduce their spending on media campaigns. Not all candidates were willing to comply, however, because media exposure was critical to winning preferential votes. Fujimori was clearly taking more votes from FREDEMO than from the Left or APRA, and was cutting into areas of weak support in the urban shantytowns and the provinces. Thus, the overall share of the vote going to FREDEMO was shrinking in the final days of the race. Under these circumstances, it was hard to control the campaign spending of candidates; those who had spent heavily wanted to recover their investment with a tangible return. Those who had not yet spent all their resources wanted to exploit the final days of the campaign. The cumulative effect of lavish spending by FREDEMO (especially candidates on the Libertad ticket) was a campaign bonanza that was inconsistent with the liberal austerity measures FREDEMO candidates ostensibly espoused. This contributed to the impression that, once in power, Vargas Llosa would be unable to control the opportunists in his coalition. Unrestrained spending by FREDEMO candidates, caused in part by competition for the preferential vote, became a central issue in the campaign and a major cause of the erosion of support for Vargas Llosa (Schmidt 1994: 97–107).

The sudden resurgence of support for APRA in the final weeks of the campaign was another key factor in shifting voters to Fujimori.[17] It became conceivable that Alva Castro would emerge as the runner-up to contest the second round against Vargas Llosa. Alva Castro assiduously sought the support of the center-left of the political spectrum, including voters without strong party affiliations, as well as the working-class electorate in the shantytowns and the provinces. "The poor will never vote for the rich" he argued, seeking to consolidate the class patterns of voting that had led to García's victory in 1985 (Schmidt 1994: 111).

Schmidt has argued that "the imminent elimination from the race of the moderate, reassuring Barrantes, prompted many Peruvians to look at the first round with fresh eyes. They now confronted the prospect of a runoff between Vargas Llosa—an increasingly abrasive and aloof candidate who candidly advocated very severe economic polices—and Alva Castro—a colorless politician who represented a failed government. This very unpleasant choice led many voters to consider new alternatives" (1991: 47). Voters, taking the electoral system into account in their choices, began to look for a new candidate. That is when Fujimori began to emerge as a contender.

After Alva Castro surpassed Barrantes in mid-March, polls showed a dramatic increase in the number of the voters intending to vote for Cambio 90.

Fujimori's share of the electorate started at 3 percent in surveys conducted on March 8 to 11, grew to 6 percent on March 16 to 18, then to 9 percent on March 24 to 26. Finally it climbed to 21 percent, overtaking that of Alva Castro in the final week of the campaign, and Fujimori placed second to Vargas Llosa in the election on April 8.[18]

The rise of independent candidate Alberto Fujimori in the last weeks of the campaign robbed FREDEMO of crucial support in the poor areas of Lima and the provinces. Moreover, Vargas Llosa did not improve his image with Peru's mestizo majority by offering to "Europeanize" Peru.[19] In a public debate with Fujimori on June 3, 1990, after the first round, Fujimori said "It seems that you would like to make Peru into Switzerland, Doctor Vargas Llosa." When Vargas Llosa conceded the point, he saw Fujimori smirk; "He had won a point. Wanting to see Peru made into 'a Switzerland' came to be, for a considerable number of my compatriots, a grotesque goal" (M. Vargas Llosa 1991: 37). Thus, Fujimori made Vargas Llosa appear to be the "foreign" candidate. As Mark Malloch Brown (1991: 93) observed:

> Fujimori became a dark-skinned Peruvian who had taken on the light skinned and aristocratic Vargas Llosa. He may have been first-generation Peruvian, but in the war of images he represented the polyglot Peru that had been exploited and marginalized by the European interlopers that Vargas Llosa symbolized. I remember cringing when Vargas Llosa sought to defend his long years of exile by saying he had nothing to be ashamed of because Europe was the future Peru should be striving for. He surrendered to Fujimori's definition of alternative role models for Peru: Japan versus Europe.

The members of Vargas Llosa's ticket were nearly exclusively upper class Peruvians. Malloch Brown noted in his first meeting with FREDEMO leaders that "several of them had, like [Vargas Llosa] spent long periods out of the country: all were visibly upper-class. Enrique Ghersi was the darkest-skinned but nobody would have mistaken the well groomed lawyer for a representative of the cholos, Peru's Indian majority" (Malloch Brown 1991: 88).

Fujimori, a candidate of Japanese descent and previously rector of the Agrarian University, rejected economic shock measures and avoided any political affiliation with traditional political parties or politicians.[20] His slogan, "honesty, technology and work," captured positive images associated with the Japanese in Peru.[21] More importantly, Fujimori recognized that traditional political parties had failed to understand the phenomenon of the informal sector, which he decided to make his social base. He reportedly said, "the truly marginal ones in Peru are the *informales,* this great popular sector that

Hernando de Soto studied in his book *The Other Path,* which I had read. I realized that this had to be my social base, that this was the great phenomenon of the new Peru. And also that the political parties had not understood it, that their leaders did not understand what was going on in the country" (Salcedo 1990: 18). Fujimori also understood that if he placed second he had a strong chance of winning in a runoff election—he had lost his bid for rector of the Agrarian University in 1977 in a runoff election (Jochamowitz 1993: 216).

One of the first allies Fujimori sought was Maximo San Román, the president of Peru's most important association of small and medium-sized businesses. San Roman agreed to run for office in Fujimori's movement, Cambio 90, as a candidate for senator and vice-president. Fujimori then began to campaign around the country, often driving with San Román through shantytowns on a tractor called the "Fujimobile." He focused on the provincial and urban areas where the informal sector was concentrated. "My entire campaign was organized," said Fujimori, "so that my message would reach my social base: the informal sector and the marginalized" (Salcedo 1990: 45).

Fujimori promised a decentralized bank to provide loans to the informal sector and a law that would legalize street hawking. He offered to simplify administrative procedures. Above all, Fujimori promised to modernize the Peruvian economy without IMF-sponsored "shock" treatment, just as García had done in 1985. By contrast, Vargas Llosa proposed monetarist and recessionary medicine, deregulation and liberalization of the economy, and privatization of the state-owned enterprises. Yet he failed to offer any tangible, immediate benefits to the poor. Nor did he campaign heavily in the poor districts or the provinces.

The urban poor voted their pocket books. The final results of the first round of the election gave Vargas Llosa a slim 2.99 percent lead over Fujimori (see figure 6.6). Vargas Llosa won 27.61 percent of the vote to Fujimori's 24.62 percent, and APRA won 19.17 percent. The Left trailed with 11.04 percent between two candidates.[22] Falling short of an absolute majority, the two strongest candidates were forced into a runoff election in June. FREDEMO won a plurality of seats in both the Chamber of Deputies and the Senate.

One of the few studies of how the informal sector voted in 1990 suggests that it overwhelmingly supported Fujimori because Cambio 90 was seen as a more representative vehicle for its interests. Eliana Chávez O'Brien asked 100 people in the informal sector "For whom did you vote in the election?" 56 said Cambio 90; 16 voted for FREDEMO; 10 for APRA; 8 for IU; 7 for IS; 3 said none (Chávez O'Brien 1990a: 37). When asked "Why did you vote for Cambio 90?" the most common response was "Because their leaders know our problems" (18); followed by "Because with them we will be represented" (13);

"Because they are working people like us" (11); "Because the parties never keep their promises" (8); "Because only independents can be believed" (6) (N = 56, Chávez O'Brien 1990a: 38). Only a minority (11) gave an answer that could be interpreted as a reflection of class consciousness.

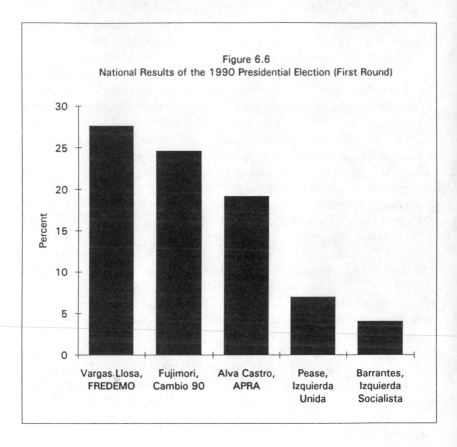

Figure 6.6
National Results of the 1990 Presidential Election (First Round)

Source: Schmidt (1991): 53-54

Chávez O'Brien attributes the success of Cambio 90 to the fact that it was the only slate that included prominent members of the informal sector (1990: 38); to the perception that FREDEMO was a "party of the rich," or a "party of the whites" (1990: 39); and to the belief that the Left "does not represent us;" "they only represent the personal interests of politicians and intellectuals;"

"they divide and they do not explain the division" (1990: 39–40). She also found that the better-off members of the informal sector supported FREDEMO.

THE CLASS CLEAVAGE IN THE 1990 ELECTION

The first round of the 1990 election confirmed the enduring strength of the class cleavage established in previous elections. However, the center-left was no longer occupied by APRA, and the Left was too divided and discredited to mount a serious challenge. As a result, Cambio 90 was able to capture the center-left majority, with support that was strongly correlated with workers and the informal sector in districts of Metropolitan Lima. These results confirmed the worst fears of members of De Soto's Instituto Libertad y Democracia who supported Libertad: that Vargas Llosa would be unable to change the class-based polarization of Peruvian voting.

TABLE 6.1
Ecological Correlations between Percent of Economically Active Population in Occupational Groups and the Informal Sector and Shares of the Vote for Political Parties in the Presidential Election in Metropolitan Lima (First Round), 1990

	Left	Cambio 90	APRA	Right
Workers	0.862**	0.963**	0.522*	-0.962**
Informal Sector	0.847**	0.841**	0.583**	-0.880**
White Collar	-0.806**	-0.917**	-0.320	0.891**
Employers	-0.724**	-0.807**	-0.744**	0.848**

Pearson's r correlation coefficients:
**significant at the 0.005 level; *significant at the 0.05 level.
N = 25 districts.   Sources: See appendix to chapter 6.

FREDEMO failed to break away from the ideological hinterlands, winning massive support in elite districts of Lima (FREDEMO won 77.7 percent of the vote in San Isidro and 70.9 percent in Miraflores [see table VI.1 in the appendix]), but confronting indifference in the shantytowns and working-class neighborhoods. For example, Vargas Llosa won only 19.2 and 19.8 percent of the vote in the populous districts of Independencia and Villa María del Triunfo/Villa El Salvador respectively. FREDEMO won only 39.5 percent of the vote in all of Lima, to Fujimori's 34.4 percent. Cambio 90 won a clear plurality of the vote in the poorer districts of Lima; for example, Fujimori captured 46.3 percent in Independencia and 46.5 percent in Villa María del Triunfo/Villa El Salvador.

Cambio 90 was able to occupy the center-left and capture the kind of majority that had catapulted APRA's García into power in 1985. One young woman said of Fujimori, "His position is in the center, not on the left, nor on the right; he represents change."[23] The center was—as is suggested by figures 6.1–6.5—the most fertile ground for cultivating popular sector support.

Correlation coefficients in table 6.1 show a powerful correlation between support for Cambio 90 and the size of the working class and the informal sector in districts of Lima. Cambio 90 clearly drew its strongest support from working-class neighborhoods and shantytowns, coming close to an absolute majority in a number of these districts. The data in the appendix show that Cambio 90 also won about 20 percent of the vote in a number of middle-class districts. Thus, by positioning itself at the center-left of the ideological spectrum, Cambio 90 was able to win a plurality of the vote in the populous poor districts while picking up a significant number of votes in middle-class districts. Only in the elite districts was Cambio 90's support as low as APRA's.

The traditional parties of the Left were reduced to 11.0 percent, slightly less than APRA's 13.8 percent. Table 6.1 shows a weaker correlation between workers and the informal sector and shares of the vote for APRA. This reflects the continuing erosion of APRA's hold over the center-left, a return to its core constituency of supporters, and a continuation of the trend in patterns of support starting after 1986: moderately strong correlations with workers and the informal sector, no correlation with white-collar workers, and strongly negative correlations with employers.

Although class-based parties had suffered a major setback, the class cleavage remained a defining feature of Peruvian elections. Cambio 90 eschewed polarization and confrontation in the first round of the 1990 presidential election, but the pattern of support for Fujimori illustrated the deep class divisions in the Peruvian electorate.

EVALUATION OF THE SPATIAL MODEL

The Right

Vargas Llosa lost the election because he ignored the median voter, overestimated the barriers to entry in electoral competition, and underestimated the tradeoffs created by class cleavage in Peruvian elections. At one level it might have been easy to explain the inability of the Right to respond to the challenge of the growth of the informal economy and the resulting uncertainty and volatility of the Peruvian electorate. To the extent that the Right moderated its position it stood to lose support from its core constituency without picking up support until it approached the center (that is, the center-right is weak). Thus, parties of the Right were constrained from moderating their policies by their core constituency. Any effort to win support from manual workers or the informal sector would come at a cost in terms of the Right's traditional constituency. Hernando de Soto's proposal for a "coalition of the formal and informal sectors" ultimately floundered on the mutual suspicion that exists between Peru's white mercantilist elite and the mestizo population in the informal economy. However, this does not entirely explain the failure of FREDEMO.

Vargas Llosa's decision to form an alliance with the traditional conservative parties undermined his mobility. Vargas Llosa knew that in order to win the presidential election in 1990 he would have to build a broader base of support—including the undecided voters, the floating electorate, workers and people in the informal sector. The alliance made it very difficult for Vargas Llosa to present himself as an "outsider," an "independent," someone untarnished by links with the established political class. His mobility was restricted by his allies. More importantly, however, Vargas Llosa chose to deliberately defy the well-known preference of Peruvians for centrist candidates and pursue instead what William Riker calls a "heresthetic" strategy; rather than appeal to the voters preferences he sought to change their tastes, to alter the shape of their indifference curves.[24] He treated the campaign as a process of "moral education" as much as an electoral competition. Among his themes was the need for a new kind of capitalism that would break the oligarchies and restore competition. This, presumably, would create opportunities for the informal sector. Vargas Llosa was more interested in implementing neoliberal policies than in winning the election. He claimed to want a decisive first round victory to have the "moral authority" to implement radical policy changes. Vargas Llosa also failed to position himself at the center of the spectrum because he allowed himself to be drawn into a futile and counterproductive conflict with Alan García. This conflict undermined Vargas Llosa's image as an independent who could stand above partisan conflicts, and it strengthened the perception that he was a right-wing candidate.

Belaúnde and the leaders of AP were distressed by Vargas Llosa's failure to position himself at the center. Vargas Llosa's efforts to bypass the parties was intended to consolidate his image as an independent. However, it also eliminated any constraints that the traditional parties might have placed on the extreme liberal message of the campaign. The politicians of AP and the PPC stepped aside, partly out of fear that Vargas Llosa would resign again unless they permitted him to run the campaign with a free hand. However, activists from the traditional parties were never able to generate much enthusiasm for the FREDEMO campaign since their leaders were not used.

The party system also had an effect on candidate strategies. Peru had an open-list system with runoffs. Vargas Llosa wanted to win in the first round of the presidential election. A runoff would have been—as Brazil's Collor de Mello pointed out to Vargas Llosa—a disaster for FREDEMO. That is because it would be relatively easy to build an "anybody-but-Vargas Llosa" campaign in the second round. The runoff election system encourages candidates who, under alternative institutional rules, would have no chance of winning an election. All Fujimori had to do was rank second among the candidates and thus place in a runoff. This he was able to do with a mere 24.6 percent of the vote.

Vargas Llosa could hardly have expected the "Fujimori phenomenon." Few people took Fujimori seriously until the last three weeks of the campaign, and Barrantes was widely seen as the most serious threat to FREDEMO. Libertad was not plugged into the network of communication that spread the word of Fujimori's candidacy. Thus, Vargas Llosa lacked crucial information about the candidate who turned out to be his main rival. Even in the runoff FREDEMO was crippled by its inability to comprehend the Fujimori phenomenon. The volatility in the rankings of the leading candidates in the final weeks of the election illustrates that many voters were unable to make up their minds until the final days of the campaign.

Degregori and Grompone (1991) argue that ethnicity was also a barrier to Vargas Llosa's ability to win broad support. Class and ethnicity reinforce each other in Peru. Employers tend to be white and workers tend to be mestizo. When a prominent member of FREDEMO was asked whether there were any common problems facing the Left and Right; she replied, "of course, we're all white."[25]

In short, Vargas Llosa allowed himself to be perceived as a "traditional politician," not an "independent." The reputation of his members constrained party mobility and undermined his chances of winning broader support, but the responsibility also rests with Vargas Llosa's political strategy. His extreme liberal message did not locate the candidate so as to maximize votes and deter entry. Vargas Llosa undermined his own ability to occupy the center through his political alliances, which ignored the low barriers to entry into electoral competition; and he failed to acknowledge the tradeoffs created by the class cleavage.

The Left

The Left clearly could have picked up more votes by moderating its position. There is no evidence of a tradeoff between support from manual workers and the informal sector. The Left would only have improved its performance by moving toward the center. With the decline in leftist voting (evident in the 1989 municipal elections, and demonstrated consistently by the polls) the IU should have been able to recognize the need to move toward the center-left where García had located his candidacy so successfully in 1985. And, indeed, part of the Left—the politicians associated with Barrantes—clearly attempted to occupy that center-left position. However, Barrantes proved to be no more mobile than Vargas Llosa.

The basic problem for the Left was that it did not act as a team with the single-minded purpose of getting elected. A faction of the Left—the revolutionary bloc—was not interested in electoral competition at all, and frankly did not want to win the 1990 election. The members of the revolutionary bloc were more interested in creating the conditions for a social revolution than in winning elections within bourgeois democratic institutions. As a result, the leaders of the revolutionary bloc were not particularly concerned with winning support from the informal sector, which they did not regard as a force for revolutionary change in Peru. Voters, both in the informal sector and in other groups that historically supported the Left, did not want to waste a vote on a coalition that had no chance of forming a government and which was not genuinely interested in their support.

The party system encouraged the division of the Left, because it promoted "rank" rather than "vote maximization." Barrantes, for example, hoped to do exactly what Fujimori did: place in the runoff contest, then win with the support of APRA. Moreover, the uncertainty in the elections made it possible to believe that Barrantes could have been successful. In other words, Barrantes did not himself know how much mobility he had but it seemed like a reasonable conjecture that he could get into a second round. This conjecture was wrong; neither Barrantes nor Vargas Llosa took seriously the idea of a new entrant emerging to displace them in the final weeks of the campaign. Opinion polls contributed to their misperceptions about voters, other candidates, and the costs of entry.

Finally, party militants constrained the Left from moderating its position. As the electoral incentives shifted to encourage the Left to moderate its position to retain electoral support, the party militants became even more radical and thus forced the Left to remain locked into its ghetto. The median voter of the Left was far to the left of the median voter in general. The 1989 division of the Left did not give either faction greater mobility because it happened in such a way that the two front-running candidates were nearly identical. Given this uncertainty about which was the stronger candidate, a vote for the Left was a wasted vote.

In short, the Left was less constrained than the Right by the structure of incentives created by the distribution of electoral preferences. It would not have to abandon core constituents in the ideological hinterlands in order to win new supporters—on the contrary, its core constituents were flooding to the center. Unequivocally, the Left would have captured more votes by moving to the center. The problem was that the informal sector is not represented within the Left, and it was difficult to build channels between the informal sector and political parties. The Left failed to locate near the median voter because of internal politics rather than strategic obstacles.

CONCLUSION

The results of the 1990 election provide evidence of the impact of the median voter, but it also shows how difficult it can be to formulate electoral strategies in an environment in which a significant share of the electorate does not have clear or fixed preferences. The growth of the center, and the lack of a credible centrist party, provided incentives for extremist parties to move toward the center. However, the size of the floating or "independent" electorate would have disrupted even the best-laid electoral strategies.

Ideological political parties demonstrated that they were far from perfectly mobile. The Right had little mobility due to the conservative composition of its alliance partners. However, the candidate decisively contributed to its failure by making no effort to appeal to the median voter. Instead, he tried to move the median voter to the right. Internal factionalism and coalition breakdown in the Left undermined the chances of one of its factions' successfully moving to the center. Jointly, the failure of Left and Right to occupy the center created a powerful incentive to entry that attracted new outside candidates.

Ultimately, the loss of influence and support for the parties was due to their tenuous linkages with society. The power of the Left, for example, was largely based on its ties with trade unions that were increasingly unrepresentative of a working class-population that was overwhelmingly engaged in informal and highly precarious forms of employment. The economic crisis also weakened mass social movements and encouraged the search for individual survival strategies rather than collective action aimed at social objectives.

Grompone notes that as the informal sector became a majoritarian segment of the work force, it began to have an impact on elections. Although the informal sector was large enough to determine electoral outcomes, "the parties of the Left and Right, nevertheless, committed errors and omissions that did not place them in a position of being able to confront this reality" (1991: 44). Thus, there was "no party or candidate in condition to occupy the center or center-left space" (Grompone 1991: 34). When the party system fails to reflect the preferences of the voters, the decline of political parties is inevitable. In the Peruvian case, this resulted in the rise of an anti-system candidate who would relentlessly attack the political parties.

APPENDIX TO CHAPTER 6

Table VI.1

Results of the Presidential Election in Metropolitan Lima (First Round), 1990

Districts	Left	Cambio 90	APRA	Right
Independencia	18.36	46.29	14.67	19.17
Villa El Salvador	14.98	46.49	16.46	19.75
Comas	16.23	43.62	17.27	21.12
Lurigancho	8.93	48.96	11.54	29.42
San Juan de Lurigancho	13.97	46.01	13.43	24.80
Ate	12.23	44.20	11.51	30.32
El Agustino	13.98	49.72	12.06	21.95
San Juan de Miraflores	12.26	42.18	14.91	28.81
Chorrillos	8.84	39.04	12.41	37.69
San Martín de Porres	12.52	40.91	15.51	30.04
Rímac	10.11	35.41	15.16	38.30
Lima	12.17	33.02	15.21	38.64
La Victoria	9.46	35.81	14.26	39.15
San Luis	9.74	36.43	11.81	40.63
Breña	9.38	28.36	17.25	44.31
Surquillo	9.30	32.03	14.89	42.89
Barranco	7.47	25.92	12.88	52.88
San Miguel	7.48	24.11	13.06	54.86
Surco	6.83	21.55	9.92	60.64
Lince	7.51	20.73	13.23	57.86
Magdalena	7.33	21.48	12.28	58.22
Pueblo Libre	7.85	18.11	12.27	61.23
Jesus María	8.51	18.34	12.26	60.33
Miraflores	5.95	13.83	8.83	70.86
San Isidro	4.69	9.92	7.12	77.71

Source: Tuesta (1994a).

.7.

THE RISE OF AN ANTI-SYSTEM CANDIDATE

The second round of the 1990 presidential election eliminated APRA and the Left as contenders. This forced Cambio 90 and FREDEMO into a confrontation that intensified the polarization of the electorate. A pact between Cambio 90 and FREDEMO would have assured a government with a parliamentary majority. Fujimori rejected the idea of a political alliance with FREDEMO, believing he could win in a second round.

Fujimori's optimism was well-founded; his best strategy was to seek to capture support that had gone to the Left and APRA in the first round, while retaining the broad base of voters he had attracted in the first round. Fujimori received support from the Left because the Left saw the anti-system candidate as less threatening to its interests than the Right.

FREDEMO had been boxed into a right-wing campaign by Vargas Llosa's first-round strategy. As a result, FREDEMO had few new votes to pick up from the Right. FREDEMO was unlikely to attract many of the voters who had opted for the Left or APRA in the first round, especially after his aggressive attacks on what he called *aprocommunism*. To win in the second round, FREDEMO had to attract voters who had opted for Fujimori in the first round. Thus, it faced a two-fold challenge: to attack Fujimori while shifting the image of its own candidate toward the center.

The outcome of the runoff system was to propel a candidate into office with a minimal coalition in the legislature. Peruvian voters had been forced to choose the composition of Congress before they knew who would be the next president. In the end, they elected a candidate with 14 seats in the 60 seat Senate and 49 seats in the 180 seat Chamber of Deputies. Such an outcome made institutional gridlock inevitable.

FROM FIRST TO SECOND ROUND

On Sunday, April 8, Vargas Llosa and his family occupied the 19th floor of the posh Sheraton Hotel in downtown Lima to await the results from the polls. Early results gave Vargas Llosa about 35 percent to Fujimori's 30 percent, without counting the blank and null notes. The voters "have not conceded us the mandate that we asked for," (A. Vargas Llosa 1991: 146) said Vargas Llosa. "I cannot govern under these conditions." He decided to withdraw from the race, and "publicly invite Fujimori to talk and . . . give him the presidency" (A. Vargas Llosa 1991: 148).

When Vargas Llosa addressed a crowd assembled in the ballroom of the hotel, he noted that the majority of the Peruvian electorate had rejected the "statism" and "collectivism" represented by APRA and the Left. Vargas Llosa then appealed to Fujimori's patriotism to prevent a second round. Promising an "open dialogue," he said: "We should talk immediately, without a mediator, to find the quickest formula to save Peru the inconvenience of a second round," and to work together against the grave economic crisis that confronts the country in order to open the doors to its reinsertion in the international community. "I invite him to dialogue where he wants and when he wants, in order to arrive at a formula that obviates a second round."[1]

Vargas Llosa's intention was to hand over the presidency to Fujimori, so that FREDEMO and Cambio 90 could form a coalition government, and he would withdraw from politics. Before Vargas Llosa had concluded his speech, the assembled crowd was distracted by the impromptu appearance of Fujimori at the back of the ballroom. In the midst of pandemonium, he strode to the podium and greeted a surprised Vargas Llosa, who congratulated him on winning second place in the electoral contest. Fujimori then made a statement that reflected what would later be seen as a defining feature of his political style: contempt for traditional political parties and a lack of enthusiasm for political compromises. There would be "no pact or alliance with any political party," he said. The second round would decide the presidency. Fujimori was still unaware that Vargas Llosa was willing to decline the presidency to avoid a second round.

The next day Vargas Llosa phoned Fujimori and asked for a secret meeting. The two candidates met for forty minutes in the house of Fujimori's father-in-law on the outskirts of Lima. Vargas Llosa argued that two thirds of the electorate had voted against APRA and the Left. He did not want to see Cambio 90 pushed into the camp of APRA and the Left in a second round. Moreover, he had no vocation to be president and was willing to give up the presidency so that FREDEMO and Cambio 90 could work together to form a government.

Thus, a second round could be avoided. Vargas Llosa offered to turn over plans and projects for government developed over a year by a team of nearly two hundred professionals, and proposed to write a parliamentary agreement that would give the executive an ample majority in Congress.

Surprised, Fujimori asked when Vargas Llosa planned to make his position public. Vargas Llosa said he would make the announcement public the next day. He asked Fujimori to be present with him, so that they would be seen together. This would symbolize the stability of the system and avoid any attempt by the military to suspend Peru's democracy. Fujimori agreed to think about Vargas Llosa's offer and then meet with him the next day (A. Vargas Llosa 1991: 152).

Fujimori worried that a suspension of the second round would be unconstitutional, and would provide an excuse for sectors of the armed forces unhappy with the results of the election to attempt a coup d'etat. Rumors of a coup d'etat in the event of a resignation by Vargas Llosa spread rapidly across Lima. After Vargas Llosa left the house of his father-in-law, Fujimori immediately called President García to inform him of Vargas Llosa's decision, and to ask for his intervention. There should definitely be a second round, he argued: "It is best that the winner take power with the majority vote of the population."[2] García phoned Belaúnde, who had been invited to Moscow, to ask him to use his influence to prevent Vargas Llosa from resigning in the second round.[3] "I called him," said García, "because, as the president of the republic, I was unsettled by the rumors circulating in Lima, since a resignation would not have been good for democracy."[4] Meanwhile, Vargas Llosa had decided to compose a letter of resignation to read at a press conference. The letter would be followed by an interview with journalist Jaime Bayly, an enthusiastic supporter of Vargas Llosa.

Many groups in FREDEMO initially saw a coalition government as an obvious solution and openly proposed a pact with Fujimori. The initial post-election consensus within FREDEMO was that the support for Vargas Llosa and Fujimori reflected a rejection of APRA and the Left, and that the two shared the goal of transforming the Peruvian state and reinserting Peru in the international economy.[5] Manuel Ulloa, a prominent member of AP, described the election as a triumph of the "most serious forces" in the country—AP, PPC, Libertad, Cambio 90—and called for a political and parliamentary alliance with Cambio 90.[6] Likewise, Enrique Ghersi proposed a coalition with Cambio 90. In Ghersi's scheme, Fujimori would be president, his cabinet ministers would be chosen from FREDEMO, and a pact would give the government control of the Congress. Such pacts had worked well before in countries like Colombia, Bolivia, and Venezuela.

The next day, Tuesday, April 10, Vargas Llosa met in the early morning with Eduardo Orrego (AP) and Ernesto Alayza (PPC), candidates for the first and second vice-presidential slots, respectively. Their meeting with Vargas Llosa was tense. Vargas Llosa indicated his determination to resign and abstain from a second round. They indicated that García had told Belaúnde of Vargas Llosa's decision to resign and argued that Fujimori was an instrument of APRA. They also said the military would never accept Fujimori as their commander-in-chief. Ernesto Alayza argued that the presidential ticket could not be renounced or purchased or negotiated. No candidate could make the decision on his own without considering the opinions of the other members of the ticket. Were the candidate to resign, there would have to be a second round led by the second and the third candidates on the ticket.[7] "You have no right to resign" they told Vargas Llosa (A. Vargas Llosa 1991: 153). The leaders of AP and the PPC then met separately to evaluate Vargas Llosa's position.

Fujimori spoke briefly with Vargas Llosa at Vargas Llosa's house, and pointed out that the constitution did not permit a candidate to resign. There would be no guarantees that the rest of FREDEMO would comply with an agreement between the two leaders. Vargas Llosa could resign, said Fujimori, but without conditions. This response tested the patience and pride of the writer, and contributed to his decision to run in the second round.

The meeting between Fujimori and Vargas Llosa had taken place in the absence of the FREDEMO kitchen cabinet.[8] "Nobody knows what themes they dealt with" said Enrique Chirinos Soto.[9] All leaders of Libertad either refused to say anything or did not know the nature of the discussion between the two leaders.

Vargas Llosa then met with the political committee of Libertad. Cruchaga insisted that any decision would have to be made by the political commission of FREDEMO, not by a single individual.[10] Raúl Ferrero Costa said it was necessary to go to a second round. Although he did not comment on the legality of a possible resignation, he affirmed the need for a parliamentary agreement: "No group has a majority, and whoever is the next president of the republic should have the support of parliament. We want to give the Peruvian people a stable government so that we do not have what happens in other regimes, that the president of the republic is unable to govern for lack of majority."[11]

In the afternoon hours the pressure from the parties in the front convinced Vargas Llosa to postpone his decision, which he had initially intended to announce in the afternoon. He would decide on the coming Monday, and would think about his decision over the Easter holiday.[12] Vargas Llosa then suspended further discussion. He left Lima for a few days to consider his next move.[13] Orrego, upon leaving Vargas Llosa's house by the back door, said "We will go to the second round."[14]

Vargas Llosa did not resign on April 10, 1992, as he had initially wished to do. Among the voices that convinced him to remain in the race was that of Monseñor Augusto Vargas Alzamora, a member of the hierarchy of the Catholic Church.[15] The Navy also expressed its fears of the consequences of a resignation.[16] The argument was invoked that it was necessary for the next president to have an impeccable legal mandate. Vargas Llosa's resignation could lead to political instability.

Fujimori issued a press release stating that he had met with Vargas Llosa on April 10, 1990 to discuss the possible resignation of the candidate of FREDEMO from the second round. This, the Fujimori release pointed out, ran against article 203 of the constitution.[17] Asked by a journalist from *La República* about the meeting with Vargas Llosa, Fujimori answered "I will not speak. The communique tells everything."[18] He would later say: "I will not resign under any circumstances. . . . I want to be president of Peru, let him say whether he is willing to be the prime minister." Presumably Vargas Llosa made it clear he did not want a position in Fujimori's cabinet.

Vargas Llosa was clearly a player less committed to political life than most politicians. His penchant for resigning in the face of political obstacles was sharply criticized. However, his decision not to resign in spite of his distaste for a fight with Fujimori suggests that the decision was not based entirely on personal considerations. Vargas Llosa was a liberal and a democrat. He did not want merely to win the 1990 election. He wanted to win convincingly enough to be able to implement a program of radical changes. FREDEMO had not won the majority that Vargas Llosa desired. Without a legislative majority FREDEMO would be forced to rule by decree or by coalition, without the "authority or prestige" Vargas Llosa sought for his mandate. Rule by decree was repugnant to some of the liberals in Libertad, and coalition-building was what Vargas Llosa had sought to avoid by winning a strong mandate in the first round.

The lack of sufficient popular support to implement the "revolutionary" changes proposed by Vargas Llosa meant that his program would be diluted and compromised. Vargas Llosa, who admired Margaret Thatcher's style of leadership, had no heart for governing under such circumstances. He had said in his June 1989 letter of resignation and at CADE that he wanted to govern with a broad mandate, which would give him bargaining leverage with traditional "mercantilist" interests. His failure to win in the first round meant falling short of a key goal of his candidacy.

Moreover, it was clear that Vargas Llosa would have difficulty winning in the second round. He was aware that the parties that were eliminated would seek to swing their voters in favor of the runner-up. Thus, the runner-up in the first round had a good chance of winning in the second. The hostility between

FREDEMO and both the Left and APRA indicated that the last two would seek to swing their voters behind the lesser-known candidate.

Vargas Llosa did not resign because he did not want to be responsible for the breakdown of Peruvian democracy.[19] It was not clear whether it was even constitutional for Vargas Llosa to resign.[20] One option was that Orrego could run as presidential candidate for FREDEMO if Vargas Llosa resigned. However, constitutional lawyers rejected this possibility.[21] The dean of the College of Lawyers of Lima said there was no alternative to a second round; any government that was not elected by such a process would be illegitimate. While García had been able to avoid a second round after he won only 47.5 percent of the vote and United Left candidate Alfonso Barrantes backed down; this created no constitutional crisis because García actually won 53 percent of the vote if blank and null votes were not counted.[22]

The article of the constitution that made it impossible for Vargas Llosa to become president with a plurality of the vote also obliged him to run in a futile second round, or else contribute to the breakdown of democracy by depriving his opponent of a clear constitutional mandate. Vargas Llosa was a prisoner of electoral rules modeled on the French system, which were designed, ironically, to strengthen presidential authority.[23]

Constitutional lawyer Javier Ortiz de Zevallos, a member of the Constitutional Assembly of 1978 who helped write article 203, said:

> I was practically the political arm of President Prado and in 1962 there was a military golpe ten days before we were to terminate our mandate. Haya de la Torre had won by a slim margin, but two-thirds of the electorate was opposed to him, because there were three major political blocs which had just about the same vote. Those who supported Belaúnde and Odría were against Haya de la Torre. So, the main banner of the coup, in 1962, was that there could not be a president who had two-thirds of the country against him. And that remained recorded in my mind. . . . There is one more example, Allende, who won by a slim margin against the Christian Democrats and the Right.[24]

Although article 203 of the constitution was designed to strengthen presidential authority, it makes it possible to win the presidency with minimal representation in the legislature. A second round of balloting would assure Fujimori over 50 percent of the vote, but it would not change the fact that he had few seats in Congress.

The second round forced both candidates to change their strategies. Since Vargas Llosa could not win votes from supporters of APRA and the Left, he could only hope to win back potential supporters who had fled to Cambio 90 in the first round by moderating his message. Fujimori, in search of supporters at the left of the spectrum, deliberately polarized the election by emphasizing class and ethnic themes that divide Peruvians.

Fujimori had no intention of entering into a pact with other political parties. Encouraged by the rapid rise in his share of support over the previous weeks, the candidate hoped that his share of the vote would be correspondingly higher in the second round.[25] By refusing to negotiate he won public support from a citizenry suspicious of all parties, alliances, and pacts. Instead of a political solution negotiated between FREDEMO and Cambio 90, Fujimori insisted on offering a government of technocrats without party allegiance.[26]

The Campaign for the Second Round

FREDEMO got off to a bad start in the campaign for the second round. The initial days after the first round were spent trying to decide who would replace Vargas Llosa if he insisted on resigning.[27] Fujimori also got off to a rough start. He was expected to hold a press conference in the Hotel Crillón in which he would outline his program of government.[28] However, he did not appear due, he claimed, to food poisoning. In reality, he had no plans to unveil.

In a meeting of FREDEMO hosted by Vega Alvear in the locale of Asociación Pro Desarrollo with top leaders of AP, PPC, Libertad and Solidaridad y Democracia (SODE), Vargas Llosa finally announced that he would lead the FREDEMO ticket in the second round of the election. However, the meeting was gloomy. The latest surveys showed 60 percent support for Fujimori, and only 30 percent for Vargas Llosa (10 percent remained undecided or planned to cast blank ballots).

Vargas Llosa railed against racism in FREDEMO, especially declarations by political veteran Enrique Chirinos Soto. Chirinos Soto had argued that the presidency should be denied to first-generation Peruvians. Chirinos Soto showed his contempt for the electorate, saying they had "done mischief," in his view, and the results were "a joke." In politics "there is much psychology and little logic. Proof of this is that they have supported Fujimori for his mysterious attraction."[29] A press release by Alvaro Vargas Llosa said Chirinos Soto was not speaking for FREDEMO in his statements to the press on Fujimori.[30] Racism also came from FREDEMO supporters outside the inner circle of the campaign. Openly racist insults had been hurled against Fujimori by FREDEMO supporters who gathered around Vargas Llosa's house in the elite district of Barranco after the results of the first round became known. Vargas Llosa had appeared before the crowd and lamented what he called "unacceptable cries" against his opponent for being from the Japanese community in Peru; "Fujimori is as Peruvian as I," he said.[31]

The main debate within FREDEMO was between the liberals, who wanted to remain true to their principles and the conservatives who wanted to "learn" from the electoral debacle and alter the program before the second round."[32] Federico Salazar Bustamante, in a thinly veiled attack on AP and PPC, argued that Fujimori projected a more radical image than FREDEMO by not accepting anyone on his ticket tied to "popular mercantilism."[33] Vega Alvear, another liberal, expressed frustration with the inefficiency of party apparatuses.

Supporters of Vargas Llosa's FREDEMO lamented that their candidate's free-market ideology had apparently not reached—or had been rejected by—the masses. Enrique Ghersi, who coauthored *The Other Path* with Hernando de Soto (see De Soto 1989) and was a prominent member of Vargas Llosa's movement Libertad, was dismayed that Vargas Llosa had treated the informal sector with the same paternalistic attitude as the rest of the traditional conservative leaders of the Right. Jaime de Althaus, columnist for the liberal daily newspaper *Expreso,* called what happened a tragedy in which informal entrepreneurs turned their backs on the program of popular capitalism that was designed to benefit them, and instead voted for an unknown candidate.

When Ghersi criticized Vargas Llosa for making the traditional mistake of paternalism, this was a thinly-veiled criticism of the traditional political parties in FREDEMO. Vargas Llosa, a new leader untainted by the corruption and scandals of previous administrations, had allowed himself to be associated with the old paternalistic party bosses. In the second round of elections the traditional leaders disappeared from view, however, the damage was already done. FREDEMO could not shake the image of being little more than an alliance among the old parties with a new leader drawn from the urban intelligentsia. By failing to get across the message that FREDEMO was more than a collection of traditional party oligarchs and rich parvenus, Vargas Llosa lost the opportunity to build support among the broad masses of workers, peasants, the unemployed, domestic employees, and above all, the informal sector.

Leaders of AP and PPC criticized the direction taken by FREDEMO. In their view, the election had demonstrated that Peruvians opposed the idea of a "shock program." AP was the party with the most experience in government and electoral competition—it would have to be a key player in the second round.[34] AP leaders felt that FREDEMO's candidate should not have said he would fire public employees.[35] They argued that it was necessary to emphasize the more positive aspects of the FREDEMO program of government.[36] Fernando Belaúnde Terry said AP would provide Vargas Llosa with "disciplined and fervent support" in the second round. He reminded the media that

AP had "been an example of absolute self-sacrifice, notwithstanding having presided over demonstrations in many regions of the country."[37]

In a meeting a week later, on April 23, the Executive Committee of FREDEMO, after mutual criticisms and recriminations were finished, decided to redouble efforts to popularize Vargas Llosa's message, and to reach out to the "C and D" strata where Fujimori had gouged into FREDEMO's vote. FREDEMO would have to work more in the shantytowns and marginal zones of Lima and Peru's other principle cities. Ghersi was given the responsibility of ties with the informal sector.[38] The campaign command was made up of members of all the parties in FREDEMO; however, it was decided that only Vargas Llosa would speak for FREDEMO.[39] This meeting was very different from that of the previous week in which Vargas Llosa's doubts had dominated the discussion. Vargas Llosa had to be careful about attacking Fujimori after hurriedly proposing an alliance and identifying Cambio 90 with liberal doctrine.

The strategy of APRA and the Left quickly became apparent. Alan García could hardly disguise his glee. The president had kept a low profile while Vargas Llosa deliberated his resignation, even cancelling a press conference.[40] Once Vargas Llosa announced he was back in the race, however, García made it clear he supported Fujimori as the candidate of the informal sector. García presented himself as someone who had fought with the Right over the past few years and could not deny the satisfaction caused by Fujimori's success. He said the aggression directed against the government and against his leadership had not paid off. The Peruvian people had been "wise" in their choice of candidates. He rejected the idea that Cambio 90 did not have a technical team, saying he had seen San Román and Bustamante work in small industry: "when people say they have no technical support they ignore a type of entrepreneurs who are not the big ones in our country, because the team is not composed only of those whose qualifications include studies in Harvard and Paris."[41]

Representatives from APRA and the United Left said their supporters should vote for Cambio 90 because Fujimori opposed the application of shock measures. There were obvious political motives for supporting Fujimori as well. Reports that Fujimori was strong in the "C and D" class endeared him greatly to the Left and APRA.[42] Azcueta argued that voters, having punished the United Left for its division by ignoring them at the ballot box, should "close ranks against the Right."[43]

The Left and APRA also attacked FREDEMO for taking advantage of its enormous financial resources, and an electoral system that placed no limits on campaign spending, to spend an inordinate sum of money to get elected. The Senate approved a motion by the Left to investigate campaign spending by FREDEMO. FREDEMO spent 12.8 million dollars in the presidential and parliamentary campaign in 1990, a sum that amounted to 61.7 percent of total campaign spending. According to Senator Diez Canseco, the expenses of FREDEMO candidates could not be recovered in four consecutive legislative periods.[44] Cambio 90 spent only $222,641, or 1.1 percent of the total (Tuesta 1994b).

Alberto Fujimori had not made the mistake of ignoring or patronizing the informal sector, urban shantytown dwellers, and other groups outside of traditional institutional arrangements. He realized that the informal sector had to be his social base and astutely sensed that traditional political parties were vulnerable because of their lack of strong ties to growing sectors of the electorate outside the formal sector. Fujimori organized his campaign to draw informal-sector support away from FREDEMO to his own coalition. He encouraged representatives of the informal sector to run on his ticket, ultimately bringing some of them into the chambers of the Senate and the House of Deputies. He also encouraged candidates from evangelical groups, prominent mestizos, and other people untarnished by affiliation with the traditional political elite. Federico Salazar Bustamante, another close associate of Vargas Llosa's in FREDEMO, argued—in a strange twist on the view of liberals within FREDEMO—that Fujimori's Cambio 90 projected a more radical image than FREDEMO because Fujimori did not accept anyone on his list tied to "mercantilist" interests.[45]

In the mandatory second round of the presidential race between Fujimori and Vargas Llosa, the United Left coalition threw its support behind Fujimori. Yet the Left clearly had trouble understanding the new multiclass political force that had emerged under the leadership of Fujimori.

Divided between orthodox revolutionaries with an iron grip on the most powerful party machines, and more reformist groups that sought to build a broader, more heterogeneous alliance that would include the strata of society not organized in the formal sector, the Left had nearly exhausted itself as a political force. In a televised interview, one prominent leader of the revolutionary wing of the United Left described the informal sector as "vacillating, because of its class position, and incapable of a national project." Therefore, he said, the Fujimori government would be a "vacillating government." The logic of this position was outlined in a document issued by the Asamblea Nacional Popular (National Popular Assembly, or ANP [1990]). According to the ANP, the political failure of the Left was due to its inability to comprehend social changes in Peru over the previous 15 years, especially the emergence, as a result of the crisis, of new social actors such as the underemployed, the unemployed, and the informal sector. The Left had failed to represent these groups in its programs and policies. None of the organizations that make up the Left, according to the ANP, represented these groups—including the ANP itself. These groups, which previously voted for the Left, were now moving toward Cambio 90 and needed to be "reoriented."

In analyzing Cambio 90, the Asamblea Nacional Popular (1990: 9) suggested it was a movement led by sectors of the petty bourgeoisie, and thus a vacillating and contradictory group capable of swinging in either a reactionary or popular direction. However, since the main objective of the Left was to prevent FREDEMO from reaching power, the ANP called for its members to vote for Cambio 90.

When asked in private whether such a description was not likely to offend the very people the Left obviously needed for votes, the answer of a leader of the ANP was extremely revealing: not only did he acknowledge that such language was likely to scare away the informal sector, he said it also discouraged workers and peasants who might otherwise support the Left. They could see that the Left was incapable of building a coalition broad enough to win a national election. A vote for the Left would be a "wasted vote." Yet anyone who openly espoused support for small business interests within the party that this leader represented would be in for "five years of hassles" with more orthodox sectors of the Left.[46] The answer revealed the extent to which the reorientation of the Left was hindered by the power of activists within the coalition able to block any ideological "deviations."

The Left supported Fujimori in the second round because, in the words of one activist, Vargas Llosa was the "dragon" that had to be slain, even if that meant installing a renegade politician who would be accountable to no organized force, nor any party, and who had no chance of controlling Congress. Vargas Llosa's democratic credentials—he explicitly rejected any departure from democratic rule in Peru—meant little in the struggle for power between Left and Right.

Luis Alva Castro said APRA would continue to combat the shock measures espoused by FREDEMO. APRA was not interested in a pact or national accord; it would look for convergence without overlooking differences in their programs. Regarding the resignation of Vargas Llosa, Alva Castro maintained that "he cannot escape the mandate of the constitution; it is very clear that he should continue in the competition. . . . With barely 29 percent, after such an expensive electoral campaign, it is clear that the candidate lacks the support to do what he said he would do. . . . [We] will maintain a severe and vigilant watch to be sure that the second round is realized." Alva Castro said APRA was the most powerful single force in Peruvian parliament, representing roughly 20 percent of the electorate. The other candidates, by contrast, represented alliances.[47]

Predictably, Fujimori took a more combative stance in the second round. He wanted to solidify the votes of the poorer segments of the electorate that voted for him in the first round, while attracting votes from the Left and APRA. "The *chino* has us in his hands, it is that simple" said an AP leader. Apathy pervaded the organization of the campaign, and pessimism cast a shadow over the outcome of the second round.[48]

The polarization of the electorate could only help Fujimori and reduce Vargas Llosa's chances, as the candidates well knew. Vargas Llosa was widely perceived to be far from the center of the political spectrum, where most voters situated themselves. In one poll he was defined as 8.5 on a scale of 1 to 10, where 1 represented the extreme left and 10 the extreme right.[49] Vargas Llosa obviously had to moderate his image in order to win votes, but any effort to moderate his image, by emphasizing social programs for example, seemed like an effort to buy votes, or hide his initial program.

Vargas Llosa was unable to recover the image of an "independent" in the second round of the election. Comments by politicians like Chirinos Soto had reminded voters that Vargas Llosa was tied to traditional politicians. Vargas Llosa's earlier aggressiveness toward APRA and the Left made FREDEMO anathema to the electorate that had supported Alva Castro, Barrantes, and Pease. Attacks on APRA and the Left, and use of the reactionary term *aprocomunismo,* were uncalled for and guaranteed that wide sectors of the electorate would not support him in the second round.[50] In a curious reversal of Downs's model, which assumes that candidates act strategically but voting is sincere, Vargas Llosa was less strategic than much of the electorate in preparing for the second round.

Fujimori, on the other hand, was able to capitalize on his unwillingness to enter into an alliance with the old political class. In one survey, prospective voters were asked about their reasons for voting for Fujimori: 28.4 percent said it was because he was "independent," 19.4 percent said they were "tired of old politics," 17.4 percent liked Fujimori because he was a "new candidate." In contrast, 52.3 percent of voters who did not support Vargas Llosa disliked his ties with the established political parties, of the rest, 35.6 percent complained about excessive propaganda, 27.3 percent rejected his economic policies, and 9.1 percent perceived him as defending the upper classes.[51]

The results of the second round are presented in table 7.1. It was widely observed that the sum of votes for Cambio 90, APRA, and the Left equalled over half the electorate. In fact, the sum of the votes for these forces in the first round fell within 2 percent of the final vote for Fujimori in the second round. In Lima, Cambio 90 won by a narrow margin of 53 percent to 47 percent for FREDEMO. A massive increase in support for Fujimori in shantytown districts was registered between the first and second rounds.

TABLE 7.1
National Results of the Presidential Election
(Second Round), 1990

	Votes	Percent
Fujimori	4,522,563	56.5
Vargas Llosa	2,713,442	33.9

Source: *Resumen Semanal,* Año XIII – no. 576
Lima, 28 June – 5 July, 1990, p. 3.

The 1990 election was perhaps the most polarized election in Peruvian history. Table 7.2 shows that the race was certainly the most polarized since the transition to democracy in 1978–80. Cambio 90 and FREDEMO were mirror opposites in the second round of the election as they competed for opposed poles of the class vote. While FREDEMO desperately sought to move toward the center by emphasizing the emergency social program and moderating Vargas Llosa's harsh message of economic austerity, Fujimori was able to maintain the level of class polarization to his advantage.

TABLE 7.2
Ecological Correlations between Percent of Economically Active Population
in Occupational Groups and the Informal Sector and Shares of the Vote for Political
Parties in the Presidential Election in Metropolitan Lima (Second Round),1990

	Workers	Employers	White-Collar Employees	Informal Sector
Cambio 90	0.967	-0.827	-0.904	0.880
FREDEMO	-0.967	0.827	0.904	-0.880

Pearson's r correlation coefficients: all correlations significant at the 0.005 level.
N = 25 districts.
Sources: See appendix to chapter 7.

On the night of the election two distinct and antagonistic worlds could be observed in Peru. Downtown, around the Crillón Hotel where Fujimori watched the returns on television, and in front of the Cambio 90 headquarters on Avenida Grau a few blocks away, a crowd of working-class *mestizo* youth congregated expectantly, awaiting the appearance of the president-elect. On the other side of town, elegantly-dressed FREDEMO supporters, some with groomed poodles, others speaking to their children in English, gathered around

Vargas Llosa's house. Calls for a coup d'etat could be overheard. Within two years a coup d'etat would occur, and although its supporters would include members of FREDEMO, its architect would be Fujimori.

CONCLUSION

The 1990 election demonstrated the importance of class in Peruvian elections. Yet the ultimate winner was a candidate without firm links to either business or the workers. Political coalitions with ties to business and labor were unable to exploit the polarization of politics because they were divided along factional lines. This created an opportunity that was vigorously exploited by Alberto Fujimori. He knew he had only to place well in the first round and then build an alliance with APRA and the Left to ensure his victory. Vargas Llosa failed to achieve the mandate he sought in the first round. Under prevailing electoral rules he was obliged to compete in a second round. Yet Vargas Llosa had made it clear he was unwilling to govern without a broad mandate. He was forced to run nevertheless in order to avoid becoming an agent of the breakdown of democracy in Peru. Even after deciding to run in the second round he remained depressed and sceptical about the final outcome. The campaign in the second round resulted in the kind of extreme polarization of the electorate that Vargas Llosa had hoped to avoid. Having formed an alliance with representatives of the traditional political elite, he could not benefit from such a divisive process in a country where the majority of the electorate are workers, *informales* or impoverished shantytown-dwellers.

Enrique Ghersi has argued that it was an error for liberals to ally with the conservative parties, AP and PPC: "We think that they are the grandparents of nothing, the mercantilists, the ones responsible for the electoral failure. It is the mercantilists who did the most damage to FREDEMO, contributing to the failure of the campaign." Fujimori seemed to agree, saying, "If Vargas Llosa had run as an independent, with proposals a little more in tune with the social reality of the country, less arrogant, perhaps he would have been able to carry out the alliance he proposes with me now, and we would have swept everyone."[52] The larger lesson is that the requirements of coalition-building and of electioneering are different. A logical choice in one arena may be counterproductive in another.

APPENDIX TO CHAPTER 7

Table VII.1

Results of the Presidential Election in Metropolitan
Lima (Second Round), 1990

Districts	Cambio 90	FREDEMO
Independencia	73.30	26.70
Villa El Salvador	71.85	28.15
Comas	72.02	27.98
Lurigancho	63.70	36.30
San Juan de Lurigancho	67.34	32.66
Ate	63.32	36.68
El Agustino	70.15	29.85
San Juan de Miraflores	62.46	37.54
Chorrillos	52.80	47.20
San Martín de Porres	61.95	38.05
Rímac	53.48	46.52
Lima	53.66	46.34
La Victoria	52.63	47.37
San Luis	51.37	48.63
Breña	47.13	52.87
Surquillo	48.51	51.49
Barranco	38.76	61.24
San Miguel	37.57	62.43
Surco	33.73	66.27
Lince	35.27	64.73
Magdalena	34.84	65.16
Pueblo Libre	31.85	68.15
Jesus María	33.06	66.94
Miraflores	23.99	76.01
San Isidro	17.76	88.24

Source: Tuesta (1994a).

·8·

EXPLAINING AUTOGOLPES: A COMPARATIVE ANALYSIS

An *autogolpe* ("self-coup") was announced in Peru on the evening of April 5, 1992 by President Alberto Fujimori. The constitution was suspended, Congress was closed, and a number of leading senators and deputies were placed under house arrest. In an address to the nation Fujimori denounced Congress for blocking necessary economic and counter-insurgency measures, and accused its members of corruption. Congress had recently rejected a package of economic and counterinsurgency measures presented by the government. Fujimori's announcement was followed by a statement of support from the joint command of the armed forces.

Opinion polls demonstrated that while most Peruvians preferred to live in a democracy, over 80 percent approved of the emergency measures.[1] Anecdotal evidence suggested support for the coup throughout society. Fujimori was able to walk through the streets of downtown Lima and was greeted enthusiastically by apparently spontaneous crowds. People interviewed on the streets argued that Peru needed stronger government to deal with the chaos, insecurity, and corruption that had become a part of daily life. For many, all Fujimori did by closing Congress was to take 240 bickering politicians off the government payroll.

Leading business representatives also gave their blessing to the coup, despite the fact that it temporarily placed the economic program in jeopardy as a result of the suspension of economic assistance from multilateral and bilateral sources. Business began to support Fujimori when he implemented neoliberal economic policies shortly after being elected.[2] The success of the new government in slashing inflation from 7,650 percent in 1990 to 57 percent in 1992, and its commitment to the "reinsertion" of Peru in the international financial community, consolidated business approval. That support did not waver during the Fujimori coup. On the contrary, Fujimori's popularity grew with his image as a strong authoritarian leader.

Popular support for the coup demonstrated beyond doubt that Peru's democratic institutions were no longer in equilibrium. Indeed, one of the striking features of the post–April 5 debate in Peru was that no politically relevant actor supported the *status quo ante*.[3] No political leader of consequence advocated a return to the previous system; and few calls for repudiation of the Fujimori coup elicited more than a mild reaction from the public. The consensus for change was overwhelming. However, there was intense disagreement over the shape that new political institutions should take, and who should be entrusted with reforming the constitution. Were the new political arrangements that were created after the April 5, 1992 coup more democratic and more stable? This chapter argues that they were neither.

The implications of this analysis extend well beyond Peru's borders. Autogolpes have been widely discussed by journalists and policy analysts interested in current events in Latin America, Eastern Europe, and Russia.[4] However, the discussion has been limited to description and speculation. No systematic effort has been made to rigorously define and analyze the phenomenon of the autogolpe, and to introduce it into the discussion of forms of democratic and authoritarian rule. The objectives of this chapter are to define autogolpes, develop and test a number of hypotheses about their causes, and situate autogolpes within a comparative framework encompassing democratic countries undergoing market-oriented economic reforms.

CAUSES OF AUTOGOLPES

What causes autogolpes? The term "autogolpe" refers to a temporary suspension of constitutional guarantees and closure of Congress by the executive, which rules by decree and uses referenda and new legislative elections to ratify a regime with broader executive powers. This chapter explores three sets of explanatory factors: economic determinants, institutional gridlock, and political calculations.

Economic Determinants

The success of market reforms requires the temporary suspension of democratic institutions in order to give the reforms time to take hold. Economic reforms involve harsh austerity measures (reduction in public spending, declining wages, high unemployment). In a democracy, politicians rarely get elected promising such measures, and when such measures are implemented they often lead to political opposition. Economic causes rarely determine political outcomes mechanically. Harsh austerity measures are a necessary but not sufficient condition for an autogolpe. There are many countries undergoing harsh austerity measures that have not implemented autogolpes. However, there is evidence of serious tensions between market reform and democratization in Eastern Europe, Russia, and Latin America. Short-term adjustment can cause political consequences that lead either to the abandonment of reform or the abrogation of democratic rule (Przeworski 1991). Market reforms require long time frames, yet electoral cycles are short. Opposition to reform can be exploited by politicians seeking to topple the incumbent government. A major objective of an autogolpe is to curtail political opposition to market reform that threatens to undermine the reform process. This is a key element of an autogolpe because it guarantees support from the international financial community.

Institutional Gridlock

Entrenched politicians must be removed through measures that are unconstitutional (but that enjoy the support of broad segments of the public, business, and the military) in order to solve the problem of institutional gridlock. Entrenched political leaders have a vested interest in an inefficient system. The dilemma of institutional change is: How can you create more efficient economic and political institutions when existing institutions serve the interest of entrenched politicians (Geddes 1991)?

A standoff between executive and legislature—often deliberately provoked by the executive—is a critical precondition for an autogolpe. However, for the autogolpe to be supported, this standoff must be widely perceived as a key element in the inability of the government to achieve political results—whether in the area of security or economic growth. Since a successful autogolpe requires widespread support in order to be ratified in a referendum, there must be a virtual consensus that the existing system is not viable. The argument is that existing politicians and political parties have entrenched interests and are thus unable to support positive institutional change. Moreover, they seek to undermine the current government for partisan political gain. The discredit of political parties is crucial to the success of any autogolpe. The perception of a major security threat can also strengthen demands for strong, authoritarian leadership.

Political calculations

The calculations of ambitious presidents lead them to further their own political careers by using widespread dissatisfaction with existing political arrangements to create a new regime in which they have greater opportunities to consolidate their own power.

If entrenched politicians are unwilling to support change that is widely recognized to be necessary because they have entrenched interests in the existing political system, why does the president (who presumably has similar interests) want change? The institutional-gridlock hypothesis would be naïve unless we acknowledge the machinations of presidents seeking to advance their own political careers by changing aspects of the constitution that undermine their chances of consolidating power. An autogolpe will not occur unless a president believes that it is the most efficient means of consolidating executive power.

THE PERUVIAN AUTOGOLPE

Opposition to the Economic Program

A major reason given for the autogolpe was the need to implement economic austerity measures blocked by Congress. Fujimori also sought to eliminate Alan García as a political rival. García represented the threat of a seasoned populist capable of exploiting the discontent created by Fujimori's neoliberal economic policies to build a coalition to block those policies, and then propel himself back into the Palace of Government in 1995.

Neoliberal economic policies sponsored by the International Monetary Fund and the World Bank were crucial to the reinsertion of Peru in the international financial system. The social and economic cost of these measures, however, was very high. According to José María Salcedo (1992), after two years of orthodox economic policies, only 15.6 percent of the economically active work force was employed full-time at the minimum wage or above. Eliana Chávez O'Brien (1990b) found that "severe unemployment"—defined as earning one-third of the minimum wage—afflicted 20 percent of the public sector, 29 percent of the private sector, and 44 percent of the informal sector. Half of Peru's population fell below the poverty line. A study in mid-1992 found that the minimum wage was only 72 *soles,* yet the cost of a family basket was estimated at 654 *soles,* and the cost of covering the basic needs of a family was 258 *soles* (Salcedo 1992: 11-23). To add to the distress, 320,000 cases of cholera were reported in 1991.

Opposition to the economic program had begun to develop under the leadership of Alan García. In 1991 legal channels for charging García with corruption were blocked after the Senate refused to strip García of his status as Senator-for-life, a position guaranteed to all ex-presidents by the constitution, thereby upholding his immunity from prosecution. Freed from legal entanglements, and reelected to the post of secretary general of the APRA party, García was able to pursue his bid for reelection in 1995 without constraints.

On April 5, soldiers surrounded the home of García, who nevertheless managed to escape by hiding in a nearby abandoned lot. After allegedly discovering an arms cache in the headquarters of his party, the government announced it would prosecute García. The official newspaper, *El Peruano,* published an Interior Ministry resolution approving judicial action against García for possession and use of illegal weapons. Ex-interior minister under APRA, Agustín Mantilla, was detained for possession of a similar arms cache in his home, for allegedly defrauding the Peruvian police, and for involvement in a paramilitary organization (the Commando Rodrigo Franco).

Institutional Gridlock

Fujimori took advantage of provisions in the 1979 constitution that "provided for the delegation of decree authority by Congress to the president" (Carey and Shugart 1994: 24). In the first two years of his government the Congress cooperated with the executive. By the end of 1991, however, tensions began to emerge; in November 1991 Fujimori attempted to enact 120 laws to reduce state intervention in the economy. The decree laws represented a significant restructuring of the Peruvian state (Mauceri 1994). The president proposed changes that would modify the 1969 land reform, eliminating restrictions on the sale of land as well as on the management of agricultural enterprises. The decrees also introduced sweeping changes in labor laws, the right to organize and strike, and job security (Mauceri 1994).

Fujimori also sought to expand the powers of the armed forces. "Arguing that the military needed new expanded powers over society to combat insurgency, Fujimori proposed to give the armed forces authority to tighten restrictions on journalists, to confiscate property on grounds of national security, to create special military courts to try terrorist suspects, and to ensure that no military officials could be tried in civilian courts for human-rights violations" (Mauceri 1994: 27–8). Although the legislature modified or repealed 22 percent of the November decrees, mainly those dealing with counterinsurgency measures, in the end it passed 78 percent of them (McClintock 1994: 10).

The dispute between the executive and the legislature came to a head two months before the autogolpe, when Congress passed Decree Law 25397, which restricted the legislative authority of the president (Bernales 1993: 62). The objective of this law was to restrict the power of the president to introduce the sort of legislation Fujimori had introduced in November 1991, and to send a clear signal that Congress would oppose excessive centralization of power in the hands of the presidency. However, Fujimori used this law as a pretext for closing Congress (see Torres y Torres Lara in Acurio et al. 1992: 18–21).[5]

Was institutional gridlock a cause of the autogolpe? Cynthia McClintock argues that Fujimori implemented policies without significant legislative obstruction (1994: 8). Nevertheless, she notes that tensions between the legislature and executive were increasing, and Fujimori "feared the emergence of greater legislative opposition in the future" (1994: 10). She correctly stresses that Fujimori's authoritarian personality and desire for greater power were more important than institutional gridlock. However, in provoking a confrontation with the Congress, Fujimori was able to win public support because of the perception that congressional opposition would undermine the inability of the government to achieve political results in the area of security and the economy.

Closing Congress was an illegal act, as even government officials recognized.[6] However, Fujimori argued that he could not work with "a noisy parliament which sabotaged basic measures."[7] Thus, the autogolpe was an attack by the executive against a legislature it could not control, or with which it was unwilling to compromise. As demonstrated in the last chapter, Fujimori had little interest in building legislative coalitions; he preferred to rule by decree with the support of the armed forces.[8]

In explaining his decision in a speech before the Organization of American States (OAS) in Nassau on May 18, 1992, Fujimori devoted special attention to an analysis of the role of political parties in Peru.[9] His analysis demonstrates a contempt for Peru's established parties. Fujimori began his appraisal of Peru's parties with the observation that there was a "divorce between the people and the peak party leaders" due to the "frustration felt over decades, frustration that threatened to continue because of the political and constitutional blockade of an extremist party opposition. . . ." According to Fujimori:

> In Peru regulations and legislation are not the result of a democratic process but rather of the give-and-take among a few privileged groups, the leaders of the political parties and some legislators. The results are contradictory norms . . . an incoherent and excessively complex legal system which, logically, is a source of corruption. . . . I want to be emphatic: we're not against the political parties but rather against the elitist system within which they operate, which does not permit them to perform their democratic function. It is not a question of choosing between having parties or not, but rather of deciding whether the ones that we will count on will be good or bad promoters of democracy . . . political parties can destroy democracy. . . .

Despite insisting that he was not opposed to parties as long as they were democratic and responsible, Fujimori's assessment of what was wrong with political parties in Peru included standard features of most democratic political systems:

> in Peru the political parties monopolize the electoral process, dominate the legislative process, and penetrate all the politically relevant organizations to such an extent that the spirit of democracy is violated, politicizing the society according to their doctrines. . . .

It would be hard to imagine a electoral system or legislature that was not monopolized by political parties. However, Fujimori's criticisms clearly resonated with his domestic audience. He emphasized the tenuous linkages between parties and society, the lack of internal democracy, and the tendency of parties to promote an excessive politicization of society:

> In Peru parties have turned into mere electoral machinery, into efficient organizations that penetrate other organizations to politicize them unnecessarily, violating the spirit of democracy. In reality, what was at stake in Peru was not the existence of democracy but a dictatorship of parties. . . . [Under the rule of parties] the channels of political participation are narrow, and citizen, regional, or sectoral interests are forced through the filter of party interests. In this manner, every union, housing association, business organization, whether formal or informal . . . must conform to the interest of the party. . . .

Finally, Fujimori related his election in 1990 to the April 5, 1992 self-coup, stressing the lack of identification of Peruvians with the existing parties and his own position in the center of a violently polarized political system:

> What is happening in Peru, gentlemen, did not start on April 5. It happened when I was elected, overcoming a powerful electoral and party machinery and all sorts of propaganda. They thought it would be easy to eliminate an independent candidate, almost with the stroke of a pen. Later they realized that stopping the so-called Fujimori phenomenon was impossible, because the modest candidate was supported by all the people. With the popular "tsunami" the political class in the country was given notice so that they would understand that it was necessary to reform our society before the real enemies finish devouring it. . . . The democracy that today is defended by the peak leaders of the traditional parties, of the extreme Right and extreme Left, is what feeds the most ferocious and inhuman terrorist movement in the world.

A major security reason given for the autogolpe, and linked to the problem of institutional gridlock, was the need to "efficiently struggle against terrorism."[10] Fujimori argued that the armed forces needed greater latitude in the fight against the Shining Path, a fight that had cost 25,000 lives between 1980 and 1992. In December 1990 Fujimori attempted to implement legislation that would have established impunity for human-rights violators by placing all criminal acts committed by members of the armed forces in areas under a state of emergency within the jurisdiction of secret military tribunals.[11]

Events prior to April 1992 created the perception that the insurgency was a growing threat. Data on forced disappearances suggest that the level of violence was constant in the period between 1988–92 (Roberts and Peceny 1993: 9). However, the change in the Shining Path's strategy from rural recruitment and organization to a greater emphasis on the urban struggle brought the war into the cities and closer to the majority of Peru's politically relevant actors.

In Villa El Salvador, the Shining Path took over the CUAVES, the women's federation, and the industrial park. Members of the Left-dominated municipality were forced to be heavily armed and place themselves under the protection of body guards. María Elena Mollano, a popular municipal leader, spoke out against the Shining Path and organized a small demonstration. She was later brutally killed during a party. A massacre of suspected Shining Path sympathizers by the military in San Martín de Porres highlighted the deteriorating human-rights situation and the government's apparent loss of control over the counterinsurgency struggle. The military organized self-defense militias (*rondas urbanas* in Lima and *rondas campesinas* in the countryside) but was unable to stop the expansion of the Shining Path. This critical urban situation provided a key rationale for the authoritarian measures.[12]

Fujimori singled out the judicial wing of government for a particularly bitter attack. In 1992 civilian courts tried over 1,100 cases for terrorism but got only 37 convictions (Roberts and Peceny 1993: 15). The president argued that it was notoriously corrupt and ineffective in prosecuting accused members of the Shining Path and drug traffickers. Moreover, the courts failed to protect human rights. The military tended to be reluctant to hand suspected terrorists over to the courts because they did not expect convictions. After the autogolpe, the government fired 13 members of the Supreme Court and more than 100 judges and prosecutors (Roberts and Peceny 1993: 15), some of whom were said to be linked to APRA. Fujimori established secret military tribunals with unidentified, or "faceless" judges. As Roberts and Peceny conclude, constitutional democracy in Peru was undermined, in part, by its inability to resolve the inherent tension between democracy and counterinsurgency (1993: 24).

Presidential Political Calculations

Fujimori was an extremely ambitious politician. The Peruvian Constitution of 1979 prohibited the incumbent president from seeking reelection. Jaime de Althaus suggested that a disguised objective of the autogolpe was the president's personal ambition to achieve presidential reelection.[13] Under the old constitution, ex-presidents could seek reelection after one term out of office. Thus, Alan García could seek reelection in 1995, but Fujimori could not. The prospect of a challenge from García threatened the neoliberal economic reforms because it suggested that Fujimori's policies could be reversed before they had time to take root.

The very prospect of the return of García undermined investor confidence, and thus inhibited the success of the economic program. The coup would thus achieve a double purpose: to eliminate García as a political rival to enable Fujimori to change the constitution and seek reelection. Both purposes were seen as essential to the success of Fujimori's reforms. Fujimori certainly advanced his political career by changing the constitution to permit reelection, however his ulterior motives in suspending the constitution did not undermine his domestic support because his reelection was broadly supported, especially in the business community, as necessary to ensure the continuity of economic reform. As Fujimori put it, his reelection was essential in order to complete the process of "restructuring of the state."[14]

THE STABILITY OF THE PERUVIAN AUTOGOLPE

Initial reaction from the ousted Congress demonstrated its impotence. In a secret meeting on April 9, 135 members of Congress unanimously declared Fujimori morally incapable of ruling Peru. Regional Assemblies also rejected the coup. However, bold calls for popular support and resistance were made in vain. There was virtually no support for the old Congress and the leaders of the political parties. A challenge from the nation's First Vice President, Maximo San Román, who took an oath of office as head of state and talked about forming his own cabinet, was ridiculed by a sceptical public.[15]

Fujimori calculated that the public would support his crackdown on Congress. Indeed, his popularity in the past had been repeatedly shored up by attacking major institutions like the bureaucracy, the courts, and even the Catholic church. In defense of the coup, Fujimori argued that Peru did not have a real democracy, and that he would create an authentic democracy: "The democracy that we had before was just a shell and now we have to give that shell content." He stated that the coup was "not a rupture of democracy but rather a rupture of the chain of corruption," and said that people who opposed his government were free to leave the country. "Under the guise of democracy in Peru, there prevailed nothing other than a banquet of power. A party and its leader rose to power and the opposition, which had lost the elections, made them fail so they could win the next elections. When the latter rose to power the former, which had lost the elections, became an opposition as damaging as the previous one."[16]

One of Fujimori's first tasks after the autogolpe, a *sine qua non* of investor confidence, and was to persuade Economy Minister Carlos Boloña to remain in the cabinet. This meant that Foreign Minister Augusto Blacker, a supporter of the coup and a rival of Boloña, would have to resign; Prime Minister Oscar de la Puente took over foreign affairs. Boloña offered his own resignation after returning from a trip to Washington, where he saw how Fujimori's seizure of power had isolated Peru from sources of multilateral credit and assistance from the United States. He had been given a cool reception in Washington and was inclined to believe that it would be difficult to keep the economic program on track in an unfavorable international environment.

Fujimori chose Jorge Camet, president of the Confederación Nacional de Instituciones Empresariales del Perú (National Confederation of Business Institutions of Peru, CONFIEP), to be minister of industry and commerce in order to consolidate business support for his government. As president of CONFIEP Camet had been so close to Fujimori that the press called him "Kenji II," after Fujimori's son. Camet appealed for Boloña to be retained as economics minister to placate a nervous business community (trading on the stock market fell, and depositors withdrew $200 million from the banking system after April 5). Boloña was convinced to remain, which tilted the balance in favor of some form of democratic reconciliation to keep the international community from punishing Peru further, and guaranteed business participation in the post–April 5 coup coalition.

Fujimori seriously miscalculated the negative reaction to his autogolpe outside Peru. Foreign governments immediately began to isolate the regime. The United States suspended millions of dollars in economic aid and the International Monetary Fund postponed a $222 million loan. Other South American governments—notably Argentina—harshly criticized the coup and suspended all cooperation with Peru. Argentine President Carlos Menem spoke at length with President Bush on the phone after the coup. The U.S. government called the authoritarian coup a "regrettable step backwards." Assistant Secretary of State for Inter-American Affairs Bernard Aronson cancelled a meeting with the Peruvian president to signal displeasure with the coup. The OAS said it "profoundly deplored" Fujimori's measures. The general secretary, João Baena Soares, and Uruguayan Foreign Minister Hector Gross Espiell, immediately went to Lima on a fact-finding mission.

Facing international pressures, Fujimori announced he would hold a plebiscite within six months. Previously, government officials had said that a plebiscite to consult voters about the government's measures and changes to the constitution would be held within 18 months to two years. On Monday, April 13, the OAS met in Washington to coordinate international reaction to the Peruvian autogolpe. Peru's defunct Congress sent First Vice President Maximo San Román to Washington to represent them, disputing the legitimacy of Fujimori's foreign minister and asking for the support of the Peruvian ambassador to the United States, Roberto McLean. The OAS condemned the coup but stopped short of calling for economic sanctions.[17]

In late April, Fujimori called for a "national dialogue for peace and development." Political parties, business groups, and social groups were invited to participate in dialogue toward a social pact. The dialogue turned into a cacophony as thousands of groups and individuals sought input into how to transform Peru's political and legal institutions. The results of this process were never taken seriously by the Fujimori government.

In May, Fujimori met with the OAS and made a commitment to restore democratic institutions through a dialogue with the political parties and the convocation of elections for a constituent assembly. However, the Fujimori government quickly discovered that the OAS felt it had to balance its commitment to democracy with its long-standing opposition to interventionism. Such a balance was not achieved in Haiti, and the OAS wanted to be more cautious in Peru. Thus, for example, it was reluctant to intervene directly in negotiations between parties and the government. It became clear that the international community was more worried about the Shining Path, fighting drug trafficking, and the program to reinsert Peru into the international financial system than it was about democracy. It was also reluctant to intervene directly in Peruvian internal affairs. The government was aided by its record in economic policy management. Contact with U.S. government officials made it clear that the U.S. would not take a strictly constitutionalist position and demand the status quo ante, as it did in the Haitian crisis. Rather, the Fujimori government would have to "get that democratic feeling back."[18]

The international community, especially the United States, insisted that meaningful dialogue with political parties would have to be part of the final formula for democratization. The Fujimori government grudgingly agreed to talk with the opposition parties, but refused to make any compromises. A series of negotiations was held to discuss the functions and responsibilities of the new Congreso Constituyente Democrático (Democratic Constituent Congress, CCD).[19] The opposition parties wanted an assembly empowered only to reform the constitution, and the autonomy to call general elections after a six-month term, both for a new Congress and a new presidency.[20] Such an assembly was incompatible with the basic objective of the autogolpe—to expand executive power—so Fujimori rejected the proposals of the opposition parties and called for elections for an assembly that would also serve as a legislature until the end of his mandate in 1995. As a result, the "dialogue" between the government and the parties collapsed before any agreement was reached.

Two major parties, APRA and AP, boycotted the election, as did Libertad and a number of parties of the Left (PUM, UNIR, and PCP). In rejecting the CCD, most of the parties pointed to the breakdown of dialogue between the government and the parties, the lack of clear electoral rules, and the perceived intention of the government to intervene in the electoral process (Bernales 1993: 69). In a National Plenary Session of the party, APRA decided not to participate in the CCD on the grounds of persecution of their leaders by the Fujimori government. More cynical observers pointed out that APRA was so low in the polls that it may have been motivated more by the desire to avoid the embarrassingly poor election results it anticipated (Pásara 1993: 45).[21]

Not all parties agreed on the desirability of abstaining from the elections. The Movimiento Democrático de Izquierda (the Democratic Movement of the Left, MDI) was formed in September 1992 to present candidates opposed to the government. The Movimiento "Renovación" was created when Rafael Rey Rey, who was linked to the Catholic group Opus Dei, broke away from Libertad and proposed a list that supported Fujimori.

A unified list with the name Nueva Mayoría/Cambio 90 was put forward under the leadership of Jaime Yoshiyama, an engineer who had entered politics when he was invited to serve in Fujimori's cabinet, first as minister of transport, and then minister of energy and mines. The official slate was bolstered by the fortuitous capture of Abimael Guzmán Reynoso and seven other top leaders of the Shining Path in September 1992, five months after the autogolpe. Subsequently, other key members of the Shining Path's Central Committee were rounded up and imprisoned. Marta Huatay, for example, was captured the next month.

Fujimori claimed that the capture of Guzmán and other members of the Shining Path was the result of the changes in counterinsurgency legislation implemented after the April 5 autogolpe,[22] but most observers attributed it to intense and meticulous counterintelligence work by the anti-terrorism police, the DIRCOTE, under the direction of General Antonio Vidal. A majority of Peruvians did not believe that the capture of Guzmán had anything to do with the April 5, 1992, autogolpe.[23] Nevertheless, achievements in the counterinsurgency effort helped consolidate popular support for Fujimori and the new regime.[24] Fujimori demonstrated that under the new legal system Guzmán would be convicted and sentenced rather than released. During the campaign for the CCD, he called for modifications to the constitution to permit the death penalty.[25]

Despite the sustained level of popularity enjoyed by the president, the campaign for Nueva Mayoría/Cambio 90 failed to generate much enthusiasm. It became clear that Yoshiyama did not have Fujimori's popularity. Indeed, polls showed considerable dissatisfaction with the candidate of Nueva Mayoría/Cambio 90. Dissatisfaction also existed within the armed forces. Just prior to the elections, on November 13, 1992, a coup attempt demonstrated that there was substantial opposition to Fujimori's efforts to reform the political system in the armed forces. Prominent members of the political opposition were involved, some of whom were later forced into exile.

Elections for the new Congress later in the month resulted in a clear victory for the official slate (Cambio 90/Nueva Mayoría), which won a plurality of the vote and a majority of the seats.[26] The results from the election for the CCD demonstrated the continuing popularity of Cambio 90. The data in the appendix (table VIII.1) make it clear that Cambio 90 was by far the strongest party in the elections. It is also striking that support for Cambio 90 was strongest in the shantytown districts, whereas the Movimiento "Renovación" and the PPC competed with Cambio 90 for support in middle- and upper-class districts. Table 8.1 illustrates the ecological correlations between different occupational groups and support for the ten most important parties in Metropolitan Lima. There were strong and significant correlations between support for Cambio 90 and the size of the working class and informal sector in districts of Lima, and a strongly negative correlation with white-collar employees and employers. The inverse relationships held for Movimiento Renovación and the PPC, which occupied the opposite pole of the class cleavage.

The vote for the other political parties was also significantly correlated with occupational indicators. The results for the Movimiento Democrático de Izquierda were consistent with the performance of the Left in the 1980s, although the correlations are slightly weaker, perhaps because the small number of leftist voters makes it more difficult to detect strong statistical relationships. The results for FRENATRACA (Frente Nacional de Trabajadores y Campesinos) and the FIM (Frente Independiente Moralizador) suggest that these small independent groups were able to make inroads into the left-wing vote at the expense of the Left. The Coordinadora Democrática, composed in part by dissident members of APRA, was only weakly significantly correlated with white-collar employees.

TABLE 8.1
Ecological Correlations between Percent of Economically Active Population in Occupational Groups and the Informal Sector and Shares of the Vote for Political Parties in the Democratic Constituent Congress (1992)

	Workers	Employers	White-Collar Employees	Informal Sector
PPC	-0.954**	0.717**	0.951**	-0.834**
FRE	0.826**	-0.623**	-0.878**	0.823**
MDI	0.635**	-0.649**	-0.478*	0.493*
FNTC	0.820**	-0.671**	-0.824**	0.750**
SOD	-0.914**	0.861**	0.840**	-0.827**
FIM	0.708**	-0.763**	-0.686**	0.750**
COD	-0.278	-0.262	0.497*	-0.045
MIA	0.714**	-0.602**	-0.712**	0.620**
REN	-0.912**	0.881**	0.832**	-0.882**
CAM	0.909**	-0.665**	-0.924**	0.781**

Pearson's r correlation coefficients:
**significant at the 0.005 level; *significant at the 0.05 level.
N = 25 districts. Sources: See appendix to chapter 8.

Legend
PPC – Partido Popular Cristiano
FRE – Frente Agrícola del Perú
MDI – Movimiento Democrático de Izquierda
FNTC – Frente Nacional de Trabajadores y Campesinos
SOD – Solidaridad y Democrácia
FIM – Frente Independiente Moralizador
COD – Coordinadora Democrática
MIA – Movimiento Independente Agrícola
REN – Movimiento Renovación
CAM – Cambio 90

The success of Cambio 90 in achieving a majority in the CCD was a major step taken toward the institutionalization of the new regime. However, a small minority of opposition members in Congress played an important role in voicing opposition to the regime. In the opening ceremony, some opposition members of the CCD insisted on swearing their loyalty to the 1979 constitution. Among the first measures taken by the new Congress were votes to (1) approve the 1979 Constitution; (2) ratify emergency degrees by Fujimori between April 5, 1992, and December 30, 1992; (3) and confirm Fujimori as the president of the republic. Even these measures caused debate. The minority in opposition voted against recognizing Fujimori as the president and insisted his government lacked legitimacy. However, the opposition minority was unable to block the activities of the majority, which promptly set up 16 commissions to rewrite the constitution.[27]

Before the constitution could be rewritten and submitted to referendum, attention turned to the municipal elections scheduled for February 1993. This time the elections were not boycotted by the major political parties. But the results confirmed that the traditional political parties had little support, and they demonstrated the degree of political fragmentation in the wake of the collapse of traditional political parties. In Lima, 829 separate slates ran for posts in 42 districts.[28] Independent candidates were victorious throughout the country. Ricardo Belmont, the independent candidate in Lima, was swept back into office, and his movement, Obras, won even in districts of Lima where it did not present candidates due to lack of time: voters simply wrote in their preference for Obras on the ballots.[29] Belmont won 44 percent of the vote in Metropolitan Lima in a field of 40 candidates.[30] By contrast, the traditional political parties were virtually decimated. The Left won only one district; it even lost its long-time stronghold in Villa El Salvador. APRA won 3 percent of the vote in Lima, while the PPC took 2 percent. However, if the traditional political parties had reason to be disappointed with the results of the municipal race, so too did Fujimori.

Fujimori had officially presented Pablo Gutiérrez Weselby, the mayor of Chorrillos, as the candidate for the coalition Nueva Mayoría/Cambio 90. In supporting Gutiérrez, Fujimori hoped to keep the political parties off balance and promote an independent candidates as an alternative to Belmont. Gutiérrez was seen as someone identified with the urban poor and knowledgeable about the problems facing the shantytowns. Yet from the beginning it was unclear whether he would be strong enough to take on Belmont and the other major challenger, Luis Cáceres Velásquez, the ex-mayor of Arequipa and a popular favorite of Lima's middle classes. The armed forces played along with Fujimori's game, giving Gutiérrez a medal ("The Peruvian Cross for Military Merit") the day after he was chosen as the official candidate.

Initial polls showed support for Gutiérrez to be slightly ahead of the other candidates. However, immediately after announcing his candidacy, Gutiérrez began to suffer a sharp slide in popularity. Although Gutiérrez was presented as a candidate against the traditional political class, neither Cáceres nor Belmont were opponents of the government or members of the political establishment. Two weeks before the election, polls indicated that Fujimori's candidate was in third place, with most voters choosing between Cáceres and Belmont. As a result, Gutiérrez resigned, complaining about a lack of funds to publicize his works in Chorrillos. Two days later, Fujimori threw his support behind Belmont, saying: "On principle, I support the independents and not people from political parties." When asked why he changed his mind, Fujimori explained that he was convinced by the polls: "I'm guided by them, and they clearly said: 'We do not know Pablo Gutiérrez.'"[31]

TABLE 8.2

Ecological Correlations between Percent of Economically Active Population in Occupational Groups and the Informal Sector and Shares of the Vote for Political Parties in the Municipal Elections in Metropolitan Lima, 1993

	Workers	Employers	White-Collar Employees	Informal Sector
APRA	0.393	-0.605**	-0.179	0.436*
PPC	-0.604**	0.835**	0.461*	-0.637**
IU	0.706**	-0.461*	-0.656**	0.501*
LIB	-0.303	0.310	0.340	-0.617**
LIM	-0.727**	0.557**	0.772**	-0.764**
AP	0.056	-0.048	-0.070	-0.167
FRE	0.770**	-0.558**	-0.843**	0.761**
PLAT	0.511*	-0.372	-0.531*	0.493*
OBR	0.125	-0.220	-0.156	0.424*

Pearson's r correlation coefficients:
**significant at the 0.005 level; *significant at the 0.05 level.
N = 24 districts. Sources: See appendix to chapter 8.

Legend
APRA – Alianza Popular Revolucionaria Americana
PPC– Partido Popular Cristiano
IU – Izquierda Unida
LIB – Movimiento Libertad
LIM – Lima 2000
AP – Acción Popular
FRE – Frente Agrícola del Perú
PLAT – Plataforma Democrática
OBR – Obras

Results from table 8.2 show the ecological correlations between the share of the economically active population in occupational groups and the informal sector and the percent of the votes for nine political parties in Lima. Only Belmont's Obras and Cáceres's Lima 2000 won a significant share of the vote (see table VIII.2 in the appendix). The results for the Left (IU, Plataforma Democrática) APRA, and AP were consistent with past results. The correlation coefficients are slightly weaker partly because the shares of the vote were so small that it is more difficult to detect significant correlations. Lima 2000 clearly occupied the place of the traditional Right. What is noteworthy is that Belmont won the election without strong correlation with any major social group. The results suggest a significant change in his constituency from the 1989 election. Unlike 1989, when Belmont drew his support disproportionately from workers and the informal sector while employees and employers supported FREDEMO, by 1993 he drew his support evenly from across Lima. He clearly managed to pick up significant support from voters in elite districts who previously voted for FREDEMO's candidate in 1989, while not alienating his working-class constituency. Belmont's strength was his ability to avoid polarization and confrontation. However, the election results make it particularly surprising that Fujimori was unable to find a candidate capable of challenging Belmont by stealing his working-class support. Belmont showed that, for the first time since the early 1980s, it was possible to create a winning coalition that did not have a strong class base.

In April and May 1993, a year after the autogolpe, the fragility of Peru's new political arrangements was revealed by a dangerous standoff between the new legislature and the armed forces. The standoff began on April 2 when opposition Deputy Henry Pease, a member of MDI, revealed a leaked document that tied 17 officials in the armed forces to the disappearance and execution of nine university students and a professor at Enrique Guzmán y Valle University ("La Cantuta") in Chosica, near Lima. A panel was established to investigate the crime. Pease asked the minister of defense, General Victor Malca, to testify before the CCD to explain the armed forces actions. The armed forces responded by sending more than one hundred tanks into downtown Lima near the government palace. The generals issued a communique accusing the congressional opposition of orchestrating a campaign against the armed forces and serving as allies of terrorism. Then, in a surprise move, General Rodolfo Robles (who had earlier signed the military communique attacking opposition legislators) confirmed that an intelligence unit was responsible for the abductions, and that it was coordinated by Fujimori's chief advisor and top intelligence official, Vladimiro Montesinos.[32] Robles also implicated General Hermoza, the chief of the army, before fleeing to Argentina.

President Fujimori was caught between the CCD he created and his principal backers, the armed forces. The standoff quickly escalated into a constitutional crisis when opposition congressmen proposed a motion to force military officers implicated in the abuses to testify before a CCD panel. When members of the ruling coalition rejected the motion, the opposition walked out of Congress. "The majority has abdicated out of fear [of the military]. We are definitely living in a civilian-military regime," said Pease.[33] Thus, even after congressional and municipal elections, the new political equilibrium remained unstable because of the ambiguous position of the armed forces as Fujimori's *de facto* coalition base.

Faced with dissent in the military, the new regime anxiously awaited the results of the referendum on constitutional reform, which had acquired a special significance. On October 31, 1993, the measure narrowly passed when

53 percent of the voting public ratified the new constitution. Support was strongest in cities like Lima, where the referendum passed in all districts. A high level of absenteeism—around 30 percent of the electorate—was registered, and many opposition groups believed that the results were fraudulent.

The strength of the "no" vote was a major surprise to the government. Opposition to the referendum was strongest in the countryside; however, there was also an element of class-based protest in the results. The protest reflected dissatisfaction with unemployment, low salaries, and rising poverty. Although 1993 was a year of economic recovery, particularly in mining, fishing, and tourism, the benefits were not trickling down to the poor. Moreover, the continued violence, although occurring at a lower level of intensity, demonstrated that the destruction of the Shining Path would be more difficult that expected at the time of the capture of Guzmán.

Since a victory for the "yes" vote was widely expected, many voters felt free to cast a vote of protest without fearing that the outcome would create political instability. The "no" campaign capitalized on this sentiment, insisting that a "no" vote would only result in a renewed efforts to create a better constitution. In an effort to stem the loss of his support, Fujimori highlighted the seriousness of the referendum by threatening to resign if it lost. "If the 'no' wins I would reflect on this. The constitution of '79 would come into effect, strictly speaking. And in this situation I would, perhaps, have to convoke the old parliamentarians. And of course, I would have to resign or be removed. It could come to such extremes."[34]

Fujimori recognized that changes in job security and the death penalty cost votes, but he said that he was pleased with the result. He claimed that the narrow 'yes' vote gave him a stronger will to visit the shantytowns and build more schools and try to convince those who did not support him.[35] This comment reflected Fujimori's clear awareness that his support was weakest in the informal sector and the working class. Table 8.3 supports this conclusion with data on voting patterns in Lima.

Table 8.3 demonstrates that, for the first time in Fujimori's political career, working-class and informal-sector voters supported him less than employers and the middle class. However, it should also be noted that support for the referendum was roughly equivalent to support for Cambio 90 in the CCD elections (compare tables VIII.1 and VIII.3 in the appendix). The strong correlation with employers and white-collar employees reflects strong elite support for the constitutional changes, rather than a major loss of working-class support for the regime. The support of employers was guaranteed by the perception that a defeat for the referendum could result in instability that would undermine the climate for foreign and domestic investment.

TABLE 8.3
Ecological Correlations between Percent of Economically Active Population
in Occupational Groups and the Informal Sector and Shares of the Vote
for the "Yes" and "No" Campaigns in the 1993 Referendum

	Yes	No
Workers	-0.527*	0.527*
Informal Sector	-0.500*	0.500*
White-Collar Employees	0.330	-0.330
Employers	0.751**	-0.751**

Pearson's r correlation coefficients:
**significant at the 0.005 level; *significant at the 0.05 level. N=25 discricts.
Sources: See appendix to chapter 8.

EXPLAINING AUTOGOLPES: COMPARATIVE PERSPECTIVES

The Peruvian case suggests that the requirements of market reforms, institutional gridlock, and the political calculations of ambitious presidents jointly cause autogolpes. From a comparative perspective, we may hypothesize that where these three factors are all present, the chances of a successful autogolpe are high. Where one or more are absent, autogolpes are less likely, or are doomed to fail. The three establish necessary and sufficient conditions for an autogolpe. The president must believe it is in his interest to undertake an autogolpe, and must be able to make that argument convincingly to the public in order to win public support; the economic necessity for the autogolpe to ensure the continuation of market reforms must be clear in order to deflect international criticism.

Paired comparisons of the cases of Peru, Russia, Brazil, and Guatemala, using J.S. Mill's methods of agreement and difference, provide sufficient variance for a preliminary test of the hypotheses (see Przeworski and Teune 1970; Skocpol and Sommers 1980). The cases include two successful autogolpes (Peru, Russia); one failed autogolpe (Guatemala); and one country where an autogolpe was actively considered but rejected by the president (Brazil). The above hypotheses account for the variance among the cases. All three conditions coincided in the cases of Peru and Russia, but did not in the cases of Guatemala and Brazil. As a result, successful autogolpes were carried out in the first two cases, while in Guatemala the autogolpe failed, and in Brazil it was aborted prematurely.

Autogolpes are strategies for managing political opposition to economic reforms in a democratic context. International support is secured only to the extent that the temporary departure from democracy is seen as necessary to strengthen the power of the executive in handling the reform process. Since the departure from democracy is temporary, the new rules require ratification by the electorate through referenda or new congressional elections. Domestic support is unlikely if the public does not believe that the president is acting in the "public interest." The public will see the actions of the president as a "power grab" unless he is able to demonstrate that the institutional gridlock in Congress prevents him from undertaking reforms that are widely recognized as part of his mandate. Peru and Russia are the only two cases that closely fit the description of the anatomy of an autogolpe.

Russia

On September 21, 1993, Russian president Boris Yeltsin appeared on television and said, "It is my duty as president to acknowledge that the present legislature has forfeited the right to be at the major levers of power."[36] His decision to close Congress had been prepared well in advance. Indeed, a few months earlier one of Yeltsin's advisors had approached the Fujimori government for full details on how Fujimori had implemented his autogolpe.[37] Not surprisingly, Yeltsin's crackdown on Parliament was reminiscent in many of its features to the Peruvian autogolpe. He disbanded Parliament and "advised" the Constitutional Court not to convene until after the elections in December. At the same time, Yeltsin called for new parliamentary elections and a referendum on a reformed constitution.

Unlike the Peruvian autogolpe, events in Moscow quickly turned violent.[38] Ruslan Khasbulatov, chairman of the Supreme Soviet, voted to strip Yeltsin of his powers and swore in Alexander Rutskoi, the Vice President, as the rival president. On September 28, troops surrounded the parliament buildings (or White House) and the next day Yeltsin issued an ultimatum to all legislators demanding they leave the building by October 4. On October 3, demonstrators broke through the police cordon surrounding Parliament and entered the White House. In the evening, well-armed supporters of the parliament were encouraged by Rutskoi and Khasbulatov "to seize tanks and take the Kremlin by storm . . . and storm the mayor's office and Ostankino," the main television center.[39] The demonstrators obeyed, seizing the offices of Moscow's mayor and then fighting for control of Ostankino.

Yeltsin's first deputy prime minister, Yegor Gaidar, appeared on television to appeal for support to defend the Kremlin, but it was early in the morning before tanks arrived from the army to defend the government. The delay revealed divisions within the armed forces. However, once they sided with

Yeltsin, the outcome was inevitable. Tanks pounded the White House throughout October 4. In the end, Rutskoi and Khasbulatov were arrested, and at least 118 people lay dead and many more were wounded.

In his television address explaining why he had closed the Parliament, Yeltsin described the need for tough, unconstitutional measures by pointing to how Parliament was undermining economic reform: "In the past few months dozens of new anti-people decisions have been drafted and adopted. Many of them are deliberately designed to aggravate the situation. The most flagrant is the so-called economic policy of the Supreme Soviet. Its decisions on the budget, privatisation and many other areas compound the crisis and inflict huge damage on the country. . . . The intentional erosion of the existing and still weak legal foundations of the young Russian state is under way."[40]

Parliament had planned to reintroduce a budget that had been twice previously vetoed by Yeltsin, and that could have led to hyperinflation. At the same time, legislation would have been introduced to significantly weaken the president's veto powers.[41] One of the major criticisms of the shock therapy in Russia was that stabilization was undermined by excessive government spending (Brada 1993). World Bank and IMF officials were alarmed by the lack of fiscal discipline in Russia. As part of his attempt to win international support, Yeltsin brought the neoliberal reformer Yegor Gaidar back into the cabinet just prior to the autogolpe.[42] A flurry of post-coup decrees from the Kremlin—ending price controls, breaking up state monopolies, reducing state regulations—gave optimism to the international community; "Everyone has been waiting for a breakthrough," said a banker from Chase Manhattan, "We're hoping that this is it."[43] Although the United States was caught off-guard, support for Yeltsin from President Clinton was immediate (Zelikow 1994: 45).

Support for Yeltsin was reinforced by the perception that institutional gridlock had made economic reform and political stability impossible. The 1978 constitution was a Soviet-era document that did not provide a framework for market reform or democratization. Russia had neither contract law nor an election law. According to Joan Debardeleben, Russian political parties were "loose alignments and coalitions . . . elite formations with few linkages with society."[44] Yeltsin himself did not belong to a political party.

The conflict between legislature and executive began in the second half of 1992 when the alliance between Yeltsin and Khasbulatov disintegrated.[45] Parliament, which had stood with Yeltsin against the coup attempt in August 1991, began to turn against Yeltsin; its belligerent attitude was due to the disintegration of the Soviet Union and disagreements over the pace of the reform. A sharp economic crisis followed "shock therapy" (Tolz 1993: 2; see also Brada 1993; Murrell 1993), but the "reformers" in Yeltsin's cabinet were not inclined to compromise. After the autogolpe, one reformer commented, "I am sick and tired of our half-way policy, of endless compromises, of the necessity to sit at the same table with people who are my ideological enemies."[46] Yeltsin also alienated the center. "The president's unwillingness or inability to build bridges to the centrist factions in the parliament, aggravated by attacks on these factions in the pro-Yeltsin media, seemed to have contributed to the decision of many centrist deputies to move away from Yeltsin in early 1993; and they began to vote against the president's initiatives together with Communists and nationalists" (Tolz 1993: 2).[47]

A key conflict revolved around the appropriate relationship between the executive and legislature. The Law on the Russian President, adopted by the Congress of People's Deputies in May 1991, created conflicting interpretations over whether the president or the legislature were the seat of ultimate authority (Tolz 1993: 3–4). Yeltsin repeatedly challenged this law, and in doing so he created institutional enemies. Conflicts between legislature and executive were caused more by "faulty institutional structures than by clashing personalities" (Tolz 1993: 3), or even ideologies. Parliament was defending its own integrity when it "came close to passing laws depriving Yeltsin of the right to dismiss ministers and allowing criminal proceedings to be brought against officials of the executive branch who failed to implement 'normative acts' (decrees) enacted by the parliament" (Rahr 1993: 4). Ultimately, it was Yeltsin who broke the Law on the Russian President, which he had had a major hand in writing. The law had given Parliament the right to impeach the president, and it did not give the president the right to dissolve Parliament; Yeltsin, like Fujimori, was forced to admit that his actions were unconstitutional.

Another constitutional issue concerned the relationship between the various levels of government within the Russian federation. The autogolpe created a political crisis that was reflected in paralysis in the regions. In general, the executive powers in the regions were for the coup, and the regional parliaments were opposed.[48] In the past, Yeltsin and Khasbulatov had "both appealed for support to provincial leaders. While Yeltsin tended to make his pitch to the ethnically based republics, Khasbulatov capped every promise Yeltsin made and tried to win the favor of the territorially based regions (the krais and oblasts)" (Teague 1993a: 3). An August 1993 summit meeting with the leaders of the republics and regions failed to produce an agreement.

Khasbulatov and Rutskoi were largely "supported by leaders of local soviets, while Yeltsin was supported by the heads of local executives" (Teague 1993a: 4). But even the heads of the administrative regions, mostly political appointees, were not unanimous in their support of Yeltsin (Tolz 1993: 6). "Having benefited from the gridlock of the previous eighteen months, the leaders of Russia's republics and regions had no real interest in seeing an early resolution of the power struggle" (Teague 1993a: 4). One result of the auto-golpe was to strengthen the power of the federal government.

Yeltsin emerged from the confrontation with Parliament with new powers. Some observers believed that "Yeltsin was fighting not for reform but for his own personal power."[49] They pointed to a constitutional amendment to lift the age restriction barring anyone over 65 from becoming president. This would enable Yeltsin, who was 62 in 1993, to be reelected in the future.[50] Yeltsin's retreat from his promise for presidential elections on June 12, 1994, was also seen as evidence of his authoritarian tendencies.

Yet the president remained popular throughout the crisis. A majority of the population opposed the use of military force (Cline, Corning, and Rhodes 1993: 12). However, Russians also perceived an acute sense of deadlock; most could not decide who held power during the crisis, and many felt that nobody held real power. Yet support for Yeltsin was much stronger than support for Parliament. Of those polled, 72 percent supported Yeltsin and 9 percent supported Parliament before the storming; 68 percent supported Yeltsin, and 6 percent supported Parliament afterwards. Whereas 40 percent held Rutskoi and Khasbulatov directly responsible for the violence, only 8 percent blamed Yeltsin; another 40 percent blamed the entire political class, including Yeltsin (Cline, Corning, and Rhodes 1993: 14).

One reason Yeltsin may not have wanted to run for reelection at the same time elections were being held for the new assembly and the constitutional referendum was that it would look like the entire confrontation had been staged for political gain. Moreover, in a hypothetical situation in which his leadership and the constitution were simultaneously rejected in the elections, a serious constitutional crisis would have developed.[51]

After the coup, Yeltsin quickly moved to impose press censorship and ban ten political parties and movements (Teague 1993a: 2; Tolz 1993: 4). He also "invited" regional councils—most of which had demanded Yeltsin raise the siege—to dissolve themselves. A few days later, he took a harder position, and issued a decree that disbanded local soviets throughout Russia (these function at the level of cities and villages) (Tolz 1993: 6–7; Teague 1993b: 1). Yeltsin used his near-dictatorial power in the campaign for the new Parliament. He threatened to deprive political parties of media time if they criticized him or the constitution, and the media was also discouraged from criticizing the constitution.[52]

Unlike Fujimori, Yeltsin did not call elections for a constituent assembly to rewrite the constitution. The constitution was rewritten by committees appointed by the president, who did everything possible to strengthen executive power.[53] For example, they changed restrictions on the president imposed by the 1991 Law on the Russian President. Henceforth, the prime minister, chairman of the central bank, commanders-in-chief of the armed forces, and top judges would be appointed by the president, not Parliament. The president could dissolve Congress in case of a vote of no confidence; he could sack the prime minister and veto laws passed by Parliament unless a two-thirds majority in both houses overturned the veto, and finally, the president could issue decrees and referenda without legislative checks.

Russia's new constitution was approved by 52 percent of the vote, only 28 percent of the eligible voters. Elections for a new Federal Assembly resulted in a Parliament that was heavily dominated by nationalists. Ironically, the new Parliament was considered unlikely to speed up the process of economic reform. It is possible that Yeltsin's commitment to reform was never as strong as the international community believed; his commitment to democracy was even less convincing. Moreover, some observers worried that a more politicized armed forces (Foye 1993: 10), "could degenerate into the sorts of cliques and cabals that historically have been common to developing countries in Latin America, the Middle East, and Africa" (Foye 1993: 15).

What lessons can be drawn from a comparison of Peru and Russia? Yeltsin and Fujimori used autogolpes to further their political careers. Neither leader was adept in the art of political compromise, and both excelled at confrontation. Fujimori sought to establish himself as a strong leader, eliminate his rival García, and change the provision in the constitution that prohibited reelection. Yeltsin also sought to establish himself as a strong leader, eliminate his rival Khasbulatov, and pave the way for his own reelection. In both Russia and Peru, the presidents emerged with few checks against their authority. Boris Yeltsin said, "My only counterbalance is now my conscience" (Simes 1994: 71). One opinion poll in Peru indicated that only 14 percent of Peruvians believe that the separation of powers is a fundamental characteristic of democracy (Balbi 1993a: 48).

Support for Yeltsin and Fujimori came from the widespread perception that change was necessary, yet was impossible within the constraints of existing institutional rules. According to a specialist in Russian affairs, "By the time of the October events, it was clear that something had to change. Toward the end of its existence, the Congress of People's Deputies lost all credibility and sense of responsibility. Increasingly dominated by extremists, it saw its sole mission—except for enjoying the privileges of office—as going after President Boris Yeltsin and his government. It became an obstacle not only to reform, but to effective governance altogether" (Simes 1994: 67–68). Exactly the same was said about Peru before April 5, 1992.

One major difference between the Peruvian and Russian autogolpes was the international reaction. Whereas Fujimori was harshly criticized by the international community, Yeltsin received immediate support. The reasons for these different reactions were based on geopolitics, ideology, and history. The international reaction was the Achilles' heel of the "Fujicoup." However, the international community turned from hostility, to neutrality, and then to support as it became clear that Fujimori was willing to hold new elections and continue to pursue orthodox economic reforms. Peru discovered that paying its debt and implementing orthodox economic policies goes a long way toward insulating a government from international criticism for undemocratic domestic practices. Yeltsin was in an even stronger position because he came to personify the reform process in Russia for many in the West. Indeed, the United States and Western Europe dangerously identified their economic and security interests with one Russian politician (Zelikow 1994: 45).

The next two cases did not meet the conditions for successful autogolpes. In Guatemala President Serrano attempted an autogolpe anyway, with disastrous results for his own political career. In Brazil, an autogolpe was wisely avoided by President Franco. Both cases provide new insight into the causes of autogolpes.

Guatemala

On May 25, 1993, President Jorge Serrano dissolved Congress, dismissed the Supreme Court, placed the country under emergency rule, and called for elections for a constituent assembly to reform the constitution. Leading officials were placed under house arrest, and a blackout on news was imposed. In defiance of the president, Congress and the Supreme Court met and forcefully rejected the coup. The Supreme Electoral Tribunal (which was not disbanded) refused to call elections.

International reaction was harsh and swift. The members of the international community failed to see how Serrano's power grab furthered their interests in any way. The United States, which had repeatedly warned Serrano not to attempt a coup, immediately suspended all aid to Guatemala. The OAS quickly set in motion the procedures for sanctions.

Some observers believed that the armed forces were behind Serrano's move, yet the armed forces defected from his camp as soon as strong civic and business reaction emerged against the coup. The armed forces, which were initially obedient to Serrano, maintained a careful neutrality as events unfolded, stating blandly, "It is up to the political strata to restore constitutional normality."[54] However, by the end of the first week of the autogolpe Serrano had been deposed, and the armed forces had played no small role in his downfall.

On June 1, Defense Minister General José García Samayoa told Serrano that the latter no longer had the support of the military. The general then met with opposition parties and a business umbrella organization to say Serrano and his vice president had resigned. However, the next day Vice President Gustavo Espina denied he had resigned and claimed the right to the presidency, with the support of the Supreme Court.

Espina was not, however, ratified by Congress due to lack of a quorum (only 44 members of the ruling Movimiento de Acción Solidaria [MAS] and independent legislators showed up for session in a Congress of 115 seats). More radical opposition groups took to the streets in protest, with the blessing of the employers' association. Business joined unions and other popular organizations in the Unidad de Acción Sindical y Popular (UASP), as well as the opposition parties, to form the Instancia Nacional de Consenso. With Espina out of the way, Congress then elected Ramiro de León Carpio on June 5, with 106 votes out of 115. Serrano settled into asylum in Panama.[55]

In Guatemala the attempted autogolpe was seen as a power grab by a corrupt and desperate politician (Jonas 1994: 4). Serrano had tried to profit from the privatization of the electrical industry (Jonas 1994: 4). Facing a petition that was to have been presented to Congress with 5000 names calling for the president's impeachment on several charges of corruption, Serrano had vowed to Venezuelan President Carlos Andrés Pérez, who had been impeached for corruption: "They will not do to me what they did to you."[56]

Thus, little credibility could be given to his charges of corruption in Congress. Institutional gridlock existed, but it was insufficient to convince the public to support Serrano's autogolpe. The ruling party's alliance with the Christian Democrats had fallen apart, but few believed that was a convincing reason to close Congress. Corruption was more widespread in the security forces, yet they were exempted from criticism (as indeed they were in Peru).

The perception of a security threat in Guatemala was not a factor in the autogolpe. The Unidad Revolucionaria Nacional Guatemalteca (URNG) rebels were weak. Serrano had proposed agreement or cease-fire within 90 days in January 1993.[57] The proposal had failed, but progress in peace talks was reported after the government agreed to set up a Truth Commission modeled on the one in El Salvador.[58] To the extent that there was a perception of threat, it was created by the Right, which unleashed a bombing attack to pressure Serrano against reaching an agreement. More importantly, protests and clashes between police and demonstrators took the government of Jorge Serrano to the brink of a declaration of emergency in March after an increase in bus fares for students and a hike in electricity rates provoked acts of violence and unrest by students and teachers.[59] However, unrest was greater after the autogolpe than before.

Brazil

In Brazil an autogolpe was never attempted, although there are reports that one was actively considered in late 1993. In October and November of that year, President Itamar Franco was encouraged by a group of military officers and civilian politicians to stage an autogolpe modeled on the one carried out by Fujimori. One member of Franco's cabinet said that "firm actions" by Franco would have received widespread support.[60] Why did Franco refuse to stage an autogolpe? Explaining why an autogolpe did not occur in Brazil provides support for the hypotheses generated from the Peruvian case, even though it takes the analysis into the realm of speculation and counterfactuals. Brazil was brought to the brink of an autogolpe by institutional gridlock that was comparable or worse than that in the Peruvian and Russian cases. However, the likely domestic and international reaction, as well as Franco's lack of dictatorial ambition, prevented an autogolpe.

An autogolpe in Brazil would have been widely condemned by the international community. President Fernando Collor de Mello, who was praised in the international community for his commitment to economic reform, was impeached in December 1992 and charged with corruption. Whereas Collor had aggressively pursued radical neoliberal economic reforms, President Franco slowed the pace of reform. Shortly after taking office, Franco announced what his advisors called a more social-democratic rather than a neoliberal economic plan. The fight against inflation was made a lower priority, shock measures were rejected, and greater emphasis was placed on the "fight against hunger and misery." "Sectoral incentives for the economy" were proposed, including projects to start housing construction, subsidies to agriculture, and public works to develop infrastructure.[61] Brazil's apparent unwillingness to pursue rapid neoliberal reforms eliminated one of the arguments that could have been used to win international support for authoritarian rule: that a temporary departure from democratic norms was necessary in order to give drastic economic reforms time to take hold.

Despite the Franco government's gradualist approach, Finance Minister Fernando Enrique Cardoso met with intense opposition from a powerful coalition of forces both inside and outside the Congress when he presented the government's economic plan to the public in mid-1993. "This is the last attempt to conduct economic policy in democracy," Cardoso emphasized.[62] "Either we find a responsible way of governing, or democracy cannot be sustained."[63]

Cardoso's concerns were underscored by rumors of a coup during the summer of 1993. The military high command was alarmed by the existence of a current within the armed forces that wanted to impose a Brazilian version of Fujimori's autogolpe. However, the Brazilian version would have had one important variation: talk of a coup did not include President Franco.[64]

One proponent of an autogolpe, Jair Bolsonaro, was a member of Brazil's Congress. A retired army captain with military connections, Bolsonaro was a deputy of the Partido Progressista Reformador (PPR). He argued that corruption and congressional deadlock made it impossible for Brazil to control inflation and implement needed economic reforms.[65] Although members of his own party demanded a retraction, Bolsonaro's calls for a coup were echoed in other parties, even in the ruling Partido do Movimento Democrático Brasileiro (PMDB).[66]

The view that the Brazilian Congress presented major obstacles to effective economic policymaking had some merit (see, for example, Kingstone 1994). Strong entrenched interests, and a system of patronage and clientelistic politics, made it difficult to implement any coherent policy. Moreover, to implement economic reform, it was necessary to modify the constitution. Eighty percent of the federal budget was spent in ways mandated by the constitution,[67] even though the government did not have the tax revenue to cover these expenses. To balance the budget, it was necessary to raise taxes and make sharp spending cuts. However, politicians who controlled the budgetary process, and the entire Parliamentary Left, opposed any effort to modify the constitution to implement tax hikes or spending cuts.[68]

Cardoso was plagued by divisions within the ruling coalition that reflected the extent of the weakness and fragmentation of political parties in Brazil (Kingstone 1994: 386–88; Weyland 1993: 28). A constant, fluid process of alliance-making among many parties in Congress was necessary to maintain any governing coalition. While Cardoso pushed economic legislation forward he had to deal with the exit of a small center-left party and the entry of the PPR into the governing coalition.[69] After the new coalition was formed, divisions emerged within the PMDB. Cardoso's economic team was paralyzed by opposition from the governor of São Paulo, Luiz Antônio Fleury, and resignations by three government ministers from the PMDB.[70] Ultimately, Fleury moderated his position and two ministers remained in the cabinet.[71]

In October 1993 Cardoso, backed by the four parties in the ruling coalition (PMDB, PSDB, PFL, PPR) was able to place constitutional reform on the legislative agenda, over the bitter opposition of the Parliamentary Left and a broad coalition of groups in civil society.[72] Cardoso proposed a package of measures that would create a new relationship between the federal, state, and local governments; restructure state corporations; encourage foreign investment; abolish state monopolies and pork-barrel ministries like social welfare and regional integration; raise taxes; and reduce spending.[73]

Just as Cardoso was about to push forward legislation to make modifications to the constitution, a huge corruption scandal placed all economic measures on hold. Two cabinet ministers were suspended and 23 congressmen, 3 state governors, and 4 former ministers were charged with corruption. The scandal revealed the depth of wrongdoing among high officials, including members of the ruling coalition from the PMDB, PFL, and PPR. Later, the corruption scandal would be used by Cardoso to exploit the temporary weakness of the forces controlling the budgetary process; however, in October the crisis seemed to point toward the possibility of a breakdown of democracy. Franco's response was to offer to resign, which only exacerbated the perceived vacuum of authority.[74]

It was during the crisis of October and November that the idea of an autogolpe was apparently considered. Cynicism about the political system, already widespread, lead to an outcry against Congress. According to polls, 62 percent of Brazilians thought the most corrupt members of Congress would not be punished.[75] Franco claimed to have received 20 letters each day demanding the closure of Congress in this period.[76] However, he refused to "Fujimorize" Brazil, saying the country would have to find another solution to the "moral crisis." Cardoso also rejected a Peruvian-style authoritarian solution.

Potential opposition to any autogolpe would have come from Luiz Inácio "Lula" da Silva's Partido dos Trabalhadores (PT) and other groups in civil society (lawyers, journalists, some sectors of business, and the middle classes that remained hostile to the idea of a return to military rule). The PT stood a good chance of winning the presidential election in 1994, and thus would have been likely to oppose any coup attempt, and could have lead the opposition into a bruising confrontation with the president. Moreover, ties between the PT and the military were reportedly strong.[77] Both shared statist and nationalist economic objectives.

Some groups in civil society had seen the impeachment of Collor as evidence of the vitality of Brazilian democratic institutions (Lins da Silva 1993: 127; Weyland 1993: 25), and would have been reluctant to support a coup in the first year of the new administration. Support for an autogolpe was never as broad as in Peru or Russia. Above all, it would appear that Franco may not have believed that he would emerge strengthened through such a confrontation with Congress. One key difference between Brazil and Peru or Russia was that the Brazilian president was committed to democracy, highly unpopular, and far less confrontational than Yeltsin or Fujimori. According to the minister of justice, Maurício Correa, "Only Itamar's democratic spirit enabled him to resist the temptation" of staging an autogolpe.[78] Franco, unlike Collor, had been "a consistent foe of the military dictatorship" (Dos Santos 1993: 20), and he was not particularly liked by the military.

Franco was not a popular politician, nor had he received a clear mandate to implement new policies. The presidency had fallen to him only because of Collor's impeachment. His popularity had declined from 36.1 to 14.5 percent between the beginning of his mandate and the crisis in the autumn of 1993.[79] One reason for Franco's lack of popularity was precisely his lack of success in the fight against inflation, which in 1993 reached 2,450 percent.[80] Another key difference between Brazil and Peru was that there was no major national security threat in Brazil that could be used to justify authoritarian rule. In short, the conditions for an autogolpe were only partially met in Brazil.

CONCLUSION

Where economic determinants, institutional gridlock, and presidential political ambitions were all present, successful autogolpes have occurred. Where one or more of these conditions was not met, autogolpes either have failed or have not materialized.

Peru and Russia met all the conditions for an autogolpe. In both cases, a temporary departure from democracy was justified to the international community on the basis of the need to implement harsh economic austerity measures and address national security needs. Domestic support, which was required for the ratification of a new constitution, was achieved by pointing to institutional gridlock that made it difficult for the president to fulfill his mandate. Moreover, both Yeltsin and Fujimori were extremely ambitious presidents who used the confrontation with their legislatures to advance their careers. There were critical differences between the Peruvian and Russian autogolpes. Yeltsin's autogolpe was more violent, yet it won broad and immediate international support. Fujimori was more popular domestically, but he faced initially strong international criticism.

Guatemala and Brazil did not fulfill the conditions for successful autogolpes. President Serrano was widely seen as a corrupt and opportunistic president who was willing to use an autogolpe in order to preserve his own political career. President Franco was committed to democracy and a social democratic approach to economic reform. An autogolpe in Brazil would have done little to advance his policy agenda and would have provoked serious opposition, both at home and abroad. The autogolpe in Guatemala failed to win public, business, or even solid military support and it prompted a harshly critical international reaction.

Governing after an autogolpe is often more difficult than expected. Yeltsin was unable to prevent the new Parliament from pardoning legislators involved in the October 1993 crisis. President Fujimori achieved a relatively successful autogolpe. He reformed the constitution to expand executive powers; elections for the CCD in October 1992 were won by a convincing margin despite a boycott by important political parties; and the referendum in October 1993 ratified the new regime, although by a narrower margin than anticipated. Fujimori remained popular, and his support tended to come disproportionately from the informal sector and the working class. However, he also received the backing of business and Peru's middle classes.

The weakness of the new regime came from tensions within the armed forces, and between the new Congress and members of the military hierarchy. On a number of occasions these tensions threatened the stability of the new regime. Ongoing human-rights abuses by the armed forces after the coup demonstrated that it was difficult to exercise civilian oversight after the autogolpe. The consolidation of power of a small group of military commanders and advisors who were willing to meddle with the command structure of the armed forces in order to consolidate their support was one source of internal tensions. Another was the ambiguous legal and political position of the armed forces in the new regime as Fujimori's *de facto* base of power. The first problem led to a counterreaction that manifested itself in a coup attempt in November 1992. The same problem was manifested in a subsequent crisis, from April to May 1993, when a scandal over human-rights violations was precipitated by the same opposition forces in the armed forces. However, in the second crisis the problem was aggravated by the fact that it exposed the second vulnerability of the regime—the absence of civilian supremacy.

The post–April 5 political system was far less democratic than the one that preceded it. The criminal justice system was tarnished by a lack of due process; intimidation of the media intensified; opposition to Fujimori by retired members of the armed forces was silenced with criminal proceedings. Fujimori failed to resolve some of the underlying tensions that subverted the previous system, particularly the role of the armed forces in fighting subversion in the context of a democracy (Roberts and Peceny 1993). Fujimori constructed a political system which retained the appurtenances of democratic institutionality, but in which the president's *de facto* power base was clearly the armed forces.

Whether Fujimori will eventually be vindicated for his strong-arm tactics is not yet clear. What is interesting, and alarming for Latin American democrats, is the fact that while Fujimori's measures were undemocratic they were widely supported. Autogolpes involve temporary departures from democratic rule that nevertheless claim legitimacy on the basis of popular support. That no politically relevant group in Peru supported the democratic *status quo ante* indicates that the democratic institutions that were violated did not represent a political equilibrium. The high level of popularity of Fujimori, despite his autocratic style, suggests that many Peruvians believed Machiavelli's dictum that "you cannot have good laws without good arms, and where there are good arms, good laws inevitably follow" (Machiavelli 1975: 77).

APPENDIX TO CHAPTER 8

Table VIII.1

Results of the Election for the 1992 Democratic Constituent Congress

	PPC	FRE	MDI	FNT	SOD	FIM	COD	MIA	REN	CAM
Independencia	6.2	2.7	9.0	1.8	1.3	8.7	3.2	1.2	4.8	56.6
Villa El Salvador	4.7	3.4	4.8	2.7	1.0	8.8	3.1	0.8	6.0	60.6
Comas	5.9	3.1	6.5	1.7	1.3	8.4	3.8	0.8	5.0	58.7
Lurigancho	8.4	1.7	7.7	2.7	1.5	8.1	3.1	1.5	8.8	53.4
San Juan de Lurigancho	6.2	3.3	5.2	2.2	1.3	9.0	3.3	0.8	5.9	58.2
Ate	6.6	3.4	5.2	2.1	1.4	8.7	3.4	1.1	7.4	57.1
El Agustino	5.0	4.0	5.0	2.6	1.1	11.6	3.1	1.4	4.6	57.6
San Juan de Miraflores	6.5	3.4	4.7	2.1	1.3	8.5	3.6	0.8	8.5	56.9
Chorrillos	7.0	3.3	4.0	1.3	1.5	9.6	3.0	0.8	9.7	56.7
San Martín de Porres	7.4	1.6	6.2	1.7	1.6	8.2	4.2	0.8	7.5	55.5
Rímac	10.2	1.8	5.2	1.6	2.0	8.8	4.3	0.7	9.4	50.1
Lima	10.1	1.8	5.9	1.8	2.1	8.6	4.8	0.9	9.4	50.1
La Victoria	9.3	2.9	4.4	1.9	1.7	8.5	4.3	0.9	9.1	53.2
San Luis	9.1	2.5	4.9	1.9	1.8	8.5	3.6	0.8	8.8	54.7
Breña	12.0	1.2	5.6	1.4	2.2	7.9	5.8	0.8	11.1	47.5
Surquillo	10.9	1.5	4.5	1.5	1.6	7.3	4.4	0.7	10.8	53.8
Barranco	11.5	1.0	4.2	1.6	2.3	8.4	3.8	0.7	13.5	50.1
San Miguel	12.6	0.9	4.4	1.2	2.5	7.5	4.8	0.5	14.8	47.4
Surco	11.8	1.4	3.6	1.1	2.7	6.8	3.2	0.5	17.5	48.9
Lince	13.1	1.1	4.8	1.2	2.9	7.7	4.5	0.7	14.5	46.2
Magdalena	12.9	1.0	4.2	1.0	2.5	7.9	4.3	0.8	14.7	47.2
Pueblo Libre	13.5	0.7	4.9	1.1	2.7	7.0	4.4	0.5	16.0	45.9
Jesus María	14.4	1.0	5.5	1.3	3.0	7.5	4.6	0.5	14.7	44.1
Miraflores	13.9	0.7	3.0	0.9	3.5	6.3	2.8	0.5	19.9	46.2
San Isidro	14.5	0.7	2.7	0.8	3.9	6.1	2.4	0.4	21.7	44.9

Source: Tuesta (1994a).

Legend
PPC - Partido Popular Cristiano
FRE - Frente Agrícola del Perú
MDI - Movimiento Democrático de Izquierda
FNTC - Frente Nacional de Trabajadores y Campesinos
SOD - Solidaridad y Democrácia
FIM - Frente Independiente Moralizador
COD - Coordinadora Democrática
MIA - Movimiento Independente Agrícola
REN - Movimiento Renovación
CAM - Cambio 90

Table VIII.2

Results of the 1993 Municipal Election in Metropolitan Lima

Districts	APRA	PPC	IU	LIB	LIM	AP	FRE	PLAT	OBR
Independencia	3.6	1.0	5.1	1.2	21.2	6.3	0.9	6.8	47.2
Villa El Salvador	3.3	1.1	1.6	1.4	18.8	7.3	1.5	15.8	42.7
Comas	4.4	0.9	1.6	1.5	24.8	7.6	1.0	3.6	47.2
Lurigancho	3.5	2.6	1.7	3.4	36.1	17.4	0.8	2.7	25.4
San Juan de Lurigancho	3.3	0.8	1.5	1.4	26.3	6.9	1.4	5.4	46.6
Ate	2.8	1.6	3.2	1.7	28.9	8.7	1.2	2.9	42.5
El Agustino	3.0	0.7	1.4	1.3	19.3	10.0	1.5	5.3	50.9
San Juan de Miraflores	3.4	2.5	1.4	1.9	23.2	7.6	1.1	5.2	48.0
Chorrillos	2.5	1.5	0.7	2.6	26.6	10.4	1.5	4.7	43.0
San Martín de Porres	3.4	1.6	1.6	1.4	25.2	6.8	0.5	3.6	50.4
Rímac	4.6	1.4	0.9	2.1	28.0	9.0	0.4	4.6	43.7
Lima	3.5	1.1	0.9	1.5	32.7	7.3	0.6	4.2	43.5
La Victoria	3.4	1.3	0.9	1.4	29.3	6.9	1.4	3.3	47.6
San Luis	2.4	1.1	0.8	1.5	28.7	11.1	0.7	3.7	45.4
Breña	5.0	1.7	0.6	1.5	31.3	9.1	0.2	3.0	42.9
Surquillo	4.0	5.0	0.9	1.7	27.8	8.2	0.3	3.9	43.8
Barranco	3.4	2.3	0.8	2.3	30.8	8.4	0.2	3.5	44.0
San Miguel	n/a	n/a	n/a	n/a	n/a	n/a	n/a	n/a	n/a
Surco	2.2	3.2	0.5	2.5	33.6	8.0	0.4	2.7	43.3
Lince	3.2	1.6	0.4	2.0	34.1	7.8	0.2	3.0	44.0
Magdalena	3.1	2.4	0.4	2.3	31.6	9.9	0.3	3.6	42.4
Pueblo Libre	3.1	2.0	0.4	2.6	35.2	7.5	0.2	3.0	43.1
Jesus María	2.8	2.2	0.5	1.9	35.3	9.3	0.3	3.4	41.1
Miraflores	2.1	7.6	0.4	1.9	32.3	8.3	0.2	2.7	41.2
San Isidro	1.7	6.1	0.3	2.3	33.6	8.4	0.2	2.4	41.9

Source: Tuesta (1994a).

Legend
APRA - Alianza Popular Revolucionaria Americana
PPC - Partido Popular Cristiano
IU - Izquierda Unida
LIB - Movimiento Libertad
LIM - Lima 2000
AP - Acción Popular
FRE - Frente Agrícola del Perú
PLAT - Plataforma Democrática
OBR - Obras

Table VIII.3

Results of the 1993 Referendum in Metropolitan Lima

	Yes	No
Independencia	56.69	43.31
Villa El Salvador	61.53	38.47
Comas	57.60	42.40
Lurigancho	51.40	48.60
San Juan de Lurigancho	58.77	41.23
Ate	59.37	40.63
El Agustino	56.71	43.29
San Juan de Miraflores	61.93	38.07
Chorrillos	63.36	36.64
San Martín de Porres	59.24	40.76
Rímac	56.11	43.89
Lima	55.83	44.17
La Victoria	60.15	39.85
San Luis	62.46	37.54
Breña	55.93	44.07
Surquillo	62.01	37.99
Barranco	61.20	38.80
San Miguel	60.80	39.20
Surco	66.42	33.58
Lince	59.50	40.50
Magdalena	60.28	39.72
Pueblo Libre	60.31	39.69
Jesus María	58.52	41.48
Miraflores	68.30	31.70
San Isidro	69.99	30.01

Source: Tuesta (1994a).

PART V

CONCLUSION

. 9 .

POLITICAL COALITIONS AND SOCIAL CHANGE

The thesis that in the 1960s and 1970s the options for Latin America were reform or revolution form part of the lore of Latin American studies. During this period of rapid industrial modernization, the agents for change were guerrilla armies, trade unions, peasant federations, the middle sectors, radical student associations, and the armed forces. In response to a perceived threat to property relations and an armed challenge to the monopoly of coercion exercised by the armed forces, authoritarian coup coalitions were formed and justified by the need to implement painful adjustment policies (see Booth and Sorj 1983; Collier 1979; Kaufman 1979; Lowenthal 1975; O'Donnell 1973, 1988b).

More recently, students of the region have been forced to reconsider previous arguments about social and political change in Latin America. In the 1980s, fragile and restricted democratic institutions were restored to Latin America under the inauspicious conditions of debt, recession, and declining per capita income (Stallings and Kaufman 1989). There was less collectively organized protest in Latin America than in previous periods of economic stress. Instead, protest more often took the form of a multiplicity of individual actions that had the collective effect of destabilizing political institutions but did not in themselves constitute an organized alternative.

Peruvians, like Latin Americans everywhere, were not passive in the face of the social and economic deterioration of their country: they migrated to cities or foreign countries; fled into the informal economy; shifted into the harvest or trade of illicit crops; and supported populist politicians. Food riots flared up in Peru, Venezuela, the Dominican Republic, and Argentina. Evangelical Protestant sects grew and became more politicized. Political "outsiders" like Alan García, Violeta Chamorro, Fernando Collor de Mello, and Alberto Fujimori challenged the predominance of traditional political elites. These diverse responses to the crisis were symptoms of a pervasive sense of disenchantment with official institutions. Yet, change in the region emanated less from organized opposition to state policies and the interests of propertied classes than from the decisions by individuals to "opt out" of traditional institutions and seek income, power, or existential meaning under alternative arrangements (Cameron 1991c).

Few politically relevant groups saw repressive authoritarian rule as a viable or desirable response to the malaise. It was easier to wipe out student guerrillas than to stop six million peasants in the Andes from producing coca leaves. Yet the effects of the cocaine economy were vastly more subversive. Trade unions were surprisingly passive in the face of the crisis, for workers were reluctant to strike in situations where managers were looking for an excuse to fire workers to cut costs. After the land reform of the 1970s, the problem facing peasants was not how to redistribute the land of the *latifundios,* but the more difficult problem of how to stimulate investment in rural areas and reactivate the agricultural economy in a context of generalized violence and insecurity. Julio Cotler (1986) noted the phenomenon of "inorganic violence" that was the product of a desperate generation of working-class youth who could see no options within the existing political and social order.

In the 1980s and 1990s, the specter haunting Latin America was no longer (if it ever was) reform or revolution, but the disintegration of domestic political and economic institutions (Cameron 1991c: 108), and nowhere was this process more evident than in Peru. This study of the disintegration of domestic institutions has focused on the impact of the informal sector on the party system and on the factionalism in political parties in Peru. It has sought to provide an account for the instability of democracy by examining the interaction between social change and political coalitions.

REVIEW OF THE ARGUMENT

This book began by juxtaposing two views of democracy. Przeworski argued that democracy is stable when "all politically relevant forces find it best to continue to submit their interests and values to the uncertain interplay of the institution" of democratic rule (1991: 26). This important analytical insight does not tell us who the politically relevant forces are. Rueschemeyer, Stephens, and Stephens argued that capitalist development is associated with democracy because it makes the working class and other subordinate groups politically relevant forces, while weakening groups hostile to democracy such as large landowners (1992: 58). These groups have the most to gain from democracy and are its most reliable promoters and defenders (1992: 57). This equally important insight has implications, which are not explored by Rueschemeyer, Stephens, and Stephens, for the prospects of democratic consolidation when economic crisis undermines the strength and capacity for collective action of workers and other subordinate groups.

The Peruvian case provided an opportunity to explore these questions. The severe economic crisis in Peru—manifested in the growth of the informal economy—undermined the collective strength of workers, and created a volatile electorate. Coalition instability, due to the inability of political parties to adapt to these and other changes, undermined the party system, and with it the stability of democracy. An anti-system candidate captured the support of the electorate by attacking Peru's political parties and democratic institutions. To develop this argument it was necessary to explore the linkages between the collapse of the party system and electoral competition; party competition for informal sector votes; the relation between parties and their social bases and the internal factionalism within political coalitions; and the failure of political parties to deter the entry of anti-system candidates.

Peruvians witnessed the collapse of a polarized party system with clearly distinguished ideological parties that competed centrifugally for the opposed poles of the class vote. The fragmentation of the party system weakened the foundations of democratic rule. The social bases of the Peruvian Left and Right—which were sharply differentiated in the 1980s, with the Left drawing support from workers and the informal sector and the Right appealing to white-collar employees and employers—gave way to tensions within both coalitions between the leaders of the established political parties and politicians who sought to transcend the limits of class politics and build broader coalitions with groups outside the formal organized economy.

The crisis of the party system and the expansion of the informal economy were interrelated processes with dual implications. On the one hand, the relation between political parties and their social bases changed, and on the other hand, new entrants into the political system, the so-called independents, challenged the supremacy of established parties and coalitions. Independent candidates were supported by the floating electorate that was created in part by the disintegration of the formal economy.

The findings of this study have systematically linked two levels of analysis: the relation between parties and their social bases and the internal factionalism within the coalitions. The expansion of the informal sector changed the structure of opportunities in party competition. The informal sector became a majority of the electorate in the 1980s. In the eyes of most political leaders, it was no longer possible to win national elections, or municipal elections in Lima, without the support of the "marginal" or "dispossessed" masses. The center of political gravity shifted from the residential neighborhoods of the middle sectors to the shantytowns. It became necessary for both the Left and the Right to appeal beyond their traditional social bases. Yet ideological parties were tied to specific social groups and interests—workers and peasants in the case of the Left, business groups and the middle sectors in the case of the Right.

For the Left, this did not involve the wrenching conflict of an electoral trade-off. The Left could appeal to both the informal sector and organized workers, since both tended to vote the same way. However, the Left operated within two arenas: armed struggle and the Parliament. The leaders with control over the strongest party machines tied to organized social groups sought to build a mass-based alternative to existing power structures. The party bosses placed a low value on electoral competition, and saw the informal sector as a "vacillating petty bourgeoisie." The leaders of the Left with the widest electoral appeal did not have control over party machines and had fewer ties with the guilds and interest groups of the formal society. They sought to build the widest possible electoral coalition, including the informal sector and some lower-middle sector groups.

The conflict between these factions of the Left increased after 1985, and came to a climax in 1989 when the United Left coalition was registered without the membership of the two tiny reformist parties with ties to Barrantes. The division, and ultimate rupture, of the Left was a mortal blow to its electoral prospects. Plagued by infighting, the Left lost the 1985 presidential election and the 1986 municipal election in Lima, as well as the 1989 municipal and the 1990 presidential elections.

The Right was divided along similar lines. The growth of the informal sector made it necessary for the Right to formulate an appeal that would win votes in the provinces and shantytowns where many individuals had only weak ties to the formal economy. But the Right faced a major electoral tradeoff. Support for the Right was inversely related to the size of the informal sector in districts of Lima during the 1980s. In 1990, the Right united in order to increase its electoral prospects. Yet there was little consensus within the Right about strategy or policy.

The fight between the young liberals associated with Libertad and the leaders of the traditional conservative parties surfaced in 1989 with the resignation of Mario Vargas Llosa from the leadership and presidential candidacy of the Right. A formula for unity was hastily negotiated to bring Vargas Llosa back into the coalition. However, divisions remained and resurfaced in the electoral campaign in 1990. The inability of the "new" Right to present itself as distinct from the traditional conservative parties undermined its appeal with the urban informal sector.

The crisis of the traditional political parties of the Right and the Left created an "unoccupied space" in the arena of electoral competition that was quickly filled by populist politicians and movements seeking to win the support of the informal sector. Populist politicians made explicit appeals to the informal sector, yet they were unable to build enduring coalitions with the urban working class.

The failure of centrist parties to govern effectively, and the inability or unwillingness of extremist parties to occupy the center of the ideological spectrum, left an emerging electorate without effective political representation. This electorate was characterized by unstable preferences and an unwillingness to define itself in terms of traditional political options. It was linked to the growth of the informal sector, which reflected the disintegration of political and economic institutions in the face of economic crisis. The new electorate also sought to avoid polarization and political violence. This "independent" electorate turned away from traditional parties and supported political "outsiders" who shared both their profound disenchantment with political institutions and their desire for economic change.

The Centrality of Class

Rueschemeyer, Stephens and Stephens (1992: 51–63) have argued that the concept of class is central to the social sciences, and it occupies a prominent place in their own analysis of the conditions under which democracy is consolidated. They argue that the relationship between capitalist development and democracy can be explained by way industrialization strengthens the working class and other subordinate groups who have an interest in a more open political system.

The evolution of the Peruvian political system over the last decade strongly reinforces their findings, and suggests ways that their analysis may be supplemented and enhanced. The data presented in this book show powerful and persistent correlations between occupational variables and voting behavior. Moreover, the correlations remained stable throughout the period 1978–93. This indicates that despite the political instability in Peru, the cleavage between workers and employers was a powerful predictor of voting behavior. At the same time, there is evidence of a decline in support for ideological parties. A strong correlation with the size of the working class in districts tells us nothing the strength of support of workers for a given electoral coalition. The importance of the worker-employer cleavage as a determinant of voting for the Left or Right does not change the fact that most Peruvian voters did not have strong partisan attachments.

The decline in ideological and partisan attachments was linked to the creation of a massive informal sector. The transformation of the Peruvian working class in the 1980s undermined its capacity for collective action and for political influence through traditional channels. The result was that a major force for change and for political openness, the Peruvian Left, was undermined and weakened.

At the same time, the growth of the informal sector presented an opportunity for the Right to build a winning electoral coalition that would unify small and large business and formal and informal enterprises, transcending the class and ethnic divisions in Peruvian society and laying the foundations for a new liberal coalition. The success of FREDEMO would hinge on its ability to change the relatively stable patterns of voting along class lines in Peru. That task was not accomplished by the candidates of the Right, Vargas Llosa and Incháustegui. Vargas Llosa failed to project a more centrist image for the Right, and he formed an alliance with the traditional conservative parties so as to not "divide the democratic vote." However, this strategy backfired as voters turned to a more "independent" candidate, Alberto Fujimori. As a result, the Right was unable to convince its traditional backers—the economic elite—that its interests were served by adhering to democracy. Instead, they threw their support behind Fujimori, even when he refused to abide by the democratic rules of the game.

The informal sector contributed to electoral and coalition instability in Peru. The traditional party system, with organized parties and ties to interests in the formal sector, was unable to respond to the transformation of Peruvian society created by the economic crisis. Yet without strong parties and political institutions the prospects for democratic development in Peru were dismal. A candidate like Fujimori, virtually unknown until weeks prior to the first round of elections in April 1990, had few firm ties with any organized or unorganized group in Peruvian society, and no vehicle for managing the government. Fujimori, favored because he was not tainted by association with the traditional political system, was by the same token a politician without a political party.

The Role of Institutions

Democracies have been surprisingly durable in Latin America during the crisis. For example, despite drug wars, economic stagnation, and challenges to the system from guerrilla groups, the Colombian political system has undergone a major process of reform and opening. Thus, while Peruvian democracy has been undermined by adverse social conditions, it is also important to consider the serious problems of institutional design that weakened support for democracy.

Electoral rules played a decisive role in causing the collapse of the party system in Peru. In a polarized party system, in which political parties are tied to specific class-based constituencies, a system of majority rule with runoffs encourages the proliferation of candidates. Since the centrist voter was increasingly an individual whose class identity was weak, a new type of "independent" candidate emerged. This led to the collapse of the traditional party system and a process of fragmentation and proliferation of candidates. The political weight of the floating electorate was magnified by institutional rules.

To some extent, even the traditional parties of the Left and Right sought to capitalize on the growing number of floating voters without partisan attachments or ideological commitments. Vargas Llosa sought to present himself as an independent, free from traditional interests. Ultimately, however, he was doubly victimized by the French system of runoff elections. First, the requirement that the winner capture 50 percent of the vote in order to avoid a runoff set an excessively high standard for Vargas Llosa to achieve. Second, once he failed in the first round, it was impossible to walk away from the elections without denying his opponent a legitimate constitutional mandate. Thus, Vargas Llosa was forced to run for election under terms he had unequivocally rejected. Yet, the solution—a coalition government—was denied by Fujimori because he was in a strategic position to exploit class and ethnic polarization and win the second round with votes from APRA and the Left.

In the Left, the chance of being the runner-up against Vargas Llosa and then taking votes from both APRA and the Left encouraged Barrantes to split from the United Left. He felt that as an independent he had a strong chance of winning second place and depriving Vargas Llosa of a first-round victory. In so doing, however, he failed to win the backing of the independents within the United Left, and thus both factions presented nearly indistinguishable candidates. This was partly because the players in the United Left did not place the same high value on unity as the players in FREDEMO. In fact, they were operating in different arenas: armed struggle and the Parliament.

The runoff system was designed to avoid the situation where a president does not have 50 percent of the vote. But the strength of a democratic president depends more on whether he can control the Congress. The runoff system made it even more difficult to elect a president with control over the Congress. A popular president who is unable to control the Congress has an incentive to rule by decree.

Autogolpes

The recent occurrence of autogolpes in Russia and Peru, as well as the unsuccessful autogolpe in Guatemala and the unattempted one in Brazil, suggest the possibility of the emergence of new hybrid forms of democratic and authoritarian regimes in countries undergoing painful economic reforms in the context of fragile political institutions. Nevertheless, it is also important to recognize the elements of continuity between regimes created by autogolpes and past regimes, both democratic and authoritarian. Autogolpes are close to what Guillermo O'Donnell (1992) has called "delegative democracy," where presidents rule by decree rather than through representative institutions.

Autogolpes are also part of a persistent pattern of instability in Latin American regimes. For that reason, Douglas Chalmers cautions that the "politicization and changeability of regimes must always qualify interpretations of the significance of new types of regimes, even when they come in waves" (Chalmers 1977: 24). He goes on to outline what he calls the politicized state:

> When the established rules and procedures of policy-making are not buttressed by respected tradition and broadly accepted ideology, the chances are great that effective influence will by-pass such rules and procedures and that they will be altered frequently to accommodate new patterns of power. Rather than a process in which certain key steps are protected from scrutiny and evaluation by a legitimating myth, it is a politicized process in which at every crisis, and to some extent for every decision, the actors are called on to determine the way in which the system will operate. (1977: 25)

Fujimori's autogolpe provides another example of the politicized state in Latin America.

Individual Choice and Political Change

One effect of the crisis in Latin America in the 1980s was to undermine collective action and encourage the search for individual solutions and strategies for survival. Protracted crisis does not mobilize workers and encourage political confrontation. But it may have a corrosive effect on political and economic institutions as people shift out of formal institutions and engage in informal economic activities, drug trafficking, migration, speculation, or capital flight. A society that lacks organization is difficult to regulate or govern. Peru in the 1980s became a country where horrendous acts could be committed with impunity and innocent victims were often punished for crimes they never dreamed of committing (see, for example Ames 1988; Bourque and Warren 1989).

Electoral instability was another manifestation of the collapse of domestic political institutions in Peru. The electorate no longer placed much trust in organized political forces and instead demonstrated a preference for an unknown outsider over known politicians. As the response to the crisis takes the form of multiple individual actions that have the cumulative consequence of destabilizing political institutions without constituting an organized alternative, it is hard not to feel nostalgic for the days when the alternatives were captured by the romantic dichotomy of "reform or revolution."

Notes

CHAPTER 1 NOTES

1. Micro-level explanations are based on methodological individualism; macro-social approaches start with social groups. Methodological individualism can be defined as the view that "social theories must be grounded in the attitudes and behavior of individuals" (Blaug 1992: glossary). A premise of this book is that the aggregation of individual choices into social outcomes is problematic, and should be a central subject of analysis (see Elster 1989).

2. Oddly, political parties are scarcely mentioned in the "Theoretical Framework" of *Capitalist Development and Democracy* (1992: 57).

3. There has been considerable progress in recent years in defining and operationalizing the concept of the informal sector. For the purpose of the present analysis, the common structural characteristic of work in the informal economy is the absence of typical class relations. For example, Portes and Johns (1989: 116) define the informal sector as all economic activities without the following characteristics: (1) an explicit, written labor contract; (2) state regulation of wages and working conditions; and (3) a clear separation between ownership of labor and capital. For further discussion of the informal sector, see: Bernedo and Chávez O'Brien 1983; Bromley 1978, 1990; PREALC 1981; Tokman 1978, 1987; Portes 1983, 1985; Portes et al. 1986; De Soto 1989a, 1989b; Kafka 1985.

4. The words "Left" and "Right" are capitalized when referring to specific political forces; they are not capitalized when referring to points on an ideological spectrum.

5. This book does not examine the internal characteristics, organization, leadership, and emerging collective interests and identities of diverse groups within the informal sector itself (see Valentín 1991; Portocarrero and Tapia 1992; Tovar 1992 for such work). Rather, it analyzes how the political actors have sought to adjust, channel, and shape the ways in which these emerging groups are represented, excluded, coopted, or used by political "outsiders" to gain entry into the political system.

6. This case study is presented in explicitly comparative language. The variables analyzed in the Peruvian case are also present in other cases. If a convincing argument can be made that the informalization of the economy crucially influences political change in Peru, then the argument should be subsequently tested in other cases to establish its generality. My purpose here is more modest: I seek only to demonstrate that there is a relationship between the growth of the informal economy and political change in one case, and leave the task of testing the argument more broadly to further scholarship.

7. This book is concerned with legal political parties that operated within the electoral arena. The Shining Path is discussed insofar as its actions affected the beliefs and strategies of Peru's democratic political parties. There is a substantial literature on the Shining Path. See Degregori (1989, 1990, 1993), Palmer (1992), Poole and Rénique (1991, 1992), Gorriti (1990, 1993), Granados (1987), Tarazona-Sevillano (1990), Strong (1993), Guillermoprieto (1993), Starn (1991, 1992), Smith (1992a, 1992b). For a critical review of the English literature, see Koep (1993). Useful information and analysis of the Shining Path can be found in *The Sendero File,* a newsletter published by The Federation of American Scientists Fund's Project on Peru.

CHAPTER 2 NOTES

1. A more detailed discussion of the United Left is provided by Taylor (1990: 108–19); for an historical overview of political parties in Peru see Cotler (1988: 151–91).

2. The PPC and AP competed, as one PPC leader put it, for the same "political space." "Being friends, we're enemies because we dispute the same clientele. A person votes for Popular Action or the PPC and feels the same about the two parties" (cited in Daeschner 1993: 64).

3. For studies of voting in the 1960s see Powell (1976: 150–72) and Dietz (1985: 323–55).

4. The relation between income levels and voting are analyzed by Amat y León (1985: 1–14); see also Stokes (1991: 75–101).

5. In a 1987 survey, only 26–33 percent of the middle- and upper-income strata expressed complete disapproval of the prison massacres in June 1986, when the armed forces killed hundreds of political prisoners involved in a coordinated mutiny in three Lima jails, and summarily executed dozens of prisoners who were not involved in the mutiny. By contrast, 45–56 percent of the poorest strata "completely disapproved" of the massacre. Over half of the more wealthy strata were divided between 19–23 percent who completely agreed with the way the armed forces handled the mutiny, and 39–42 percent who agreed while disapproving of the "excesses" committed (APOYO, [July 1987] *Informe de Opinión* [Lima]). Similar variation in the opinions of Peruvians across class lines can be found in survey data on attitudes toward the right to job security (APOYO, [October 1985] *Informe de Opinión* [Lima]), the causes of the failure of the social pact (APOYO, [July 1985] *Informe de Opinión* [Lima]), and support for general strikes (APOYO, [May 1987] *Informe de Opinión* [Lima]).

6. These findings replicate the results of Ponce and Vallenas for 1978 (1985: 108), Roncagliolo for 1978 and 1980 (1980: 122); Tuesta for 1983 (1985) and Dietz for the same elections as well as the presidential election in 1985 and the municipal contests of 1980 and 1986 (1985: 323–55; 1986–1987: 139–63). I analyze new data from the 1989 municipal election from Tuesta (1994).

7. The distinction between the formal and informal sectors is often unclear. Workers may pursue both formal and informal income and employment opportunities, or shift between formal and informal jobs.

8. Patria Roja, which would later join UNIR, abstained in 1978.

9. Guzmán stated this in his interview in *El Diario,* Lima, 24 July 1988.

10. The term in Spanish is *clasista.*

11. This comment was made by the editors of *Quehacer* in their evaluation of the 1985 election, "Las Campañas del APRA y la IU," *Quehacer,* no. 35, 1985: 40.

12. Interview with Guillermo Nolasco, August 1988, Lima.

13. The PREALC quote continues: "wages are not the usual form of remuneration to labor, even though production is directed principally at the market; rather, one finds an abundance of activities using little capital and structured around small scale productive units, with low levels of technology and little or no formal organization."

14. Interview, July 1986, Lima.

15. I am grateful to Sinesio López for this quote.

16. Some of the informal entrepreneurs were previously union leaders and strong supporters of the United Left who were dismissed under the military government for union

agitation. An aim of the industrial park was to bring small business under municipal regulation in order to permit unionization and improve the deplorable wages and working conditions of labor in the informal sector.

17. On "democratic centralism," see Bottomore ed. (1983: 360–61).

18. I am referring here to Maoist parties that later joined the IU under a coalition called UNIR (Unión de Izquierda Revolucionaria).

19. Graffiti written on walls along the Panamerican Highway through the Maoist-controlled district of Comas in 1988 denounced the "fascist tendencies of the APRA government" ("Contra la fascistización del APRA"). "Fascist" was the term used by the Shining Path to describe the government of Alan García. The graffiti was a poor description of the government, but a good indicator of the radicalization of the UNIR.

20. De Soto is a Peruvian economist and entrepreneur whose ideas are associated with the "law and economics" school of thought. See Bromley (1990, 1992); Cueva (1988); Rivero (1990). The ILD is a think tank that received substantial support from U.S. foundations, including the United States Agency for International Development, the Inter-American Foundation, and the Liberty Fund (Bromley 1990: 332).

21. See Daeschner (1993: 13–20) for a review of how Libertad emerged out of the reaction to the nationalization of the banks. From the outset, it had a strongly class-based character and substantial financial support from Peru's economic elite. While the PPC rejected the nationalization, AP initially took a more cautious stand (Daeschner 1993: 39). This is consistent with Belaúnde's mild hostility to bankers and Peru's business elite, a major source of tension between AP and Libertad.

22. Interview with researchers in the Institute of Liberty and Democracy in Lima, August 1988.

23. "García launches mortgage-for-the masses," *The Andean Report,* October 1989: 226–227.

24. See interview with Mario Vargas Llosa, conducted by Elizabeth Farnsworth, in *World Policy Journal,* Autumn 1988: 763.

25. De Soto was critical of the influence of conservatives in Fredemo. See his interview with ORBIS (De Soto 1990: 423). Other key members of the liberal Right in the Peruvian intelligentsia were Jorge Morelli, Felipe Ortiz de Zeballos and Jaime de Althaus.

26. This was observed by the editors of *Quehacer.* See "El Fredemo y el Tercio de Vargas Llosa," *Quehacer,* no. 51, March–April 1988: 7–9.

CHAPTER 3 NOTES

1. The median-voter theorem shows that in two-party elections, candidates will move toward the electorate's median preference if voter preferences are single-peaked (Ordeshook 1992: 104–5). See Barry 1978; Downs 1957; Enelow and Hinich 1990b; and Ordeshook 1986 for a discussion. For an analysis of the political capacity of the center from the perspective of social cleavages, see Scully (1992: 6–11).

2. Catherine M. Conaghan suggested that "Peru offers an example of the dramatic reversal of the electoral standing of the right. In interviews conducted in Peru in 1986, businessmen were extremely pessimistic about the electoral future of the right. . . . But the deepening of the economic crisis under President Alan García and the policy battles between business and the García administration revived political organization of the right" (1992: 228–9). The Right responded by unsuccessfully imitating García's

strategy in 1990; when that failed, business threw its support behind Fujimori's neoliberal and authoritarian policies. These coalition dynamics are discussed in the following chapters. In order to understand the propensity to "coup-mongering" by the Right (Conaghan 1992: 232), it is first necessary to examine the electoral success and failure in government of AP and APRA, and their evolving relations with business.

3. Belaúnde insisted that AP was not a party of the Right: "The right has never been an enthusiastic supporter of ours. Never. AP has always been a party of the people. Of course the Right has respected us because they recognize our capacity to hold the masses." Interview in Lima, November 9, 1987.

4. Business leaders complained that they were unable to influence the direction of economic policy under Prime Minister Ulloa, because Ulloa paid little attention to critics, even within his party. See Conaghan (1992: 222).

5. As previously noted, the number of people in the informal sector in Lima expanded from 440,000 to 730,000 between 1981 and 1986. See Alvarado et al. (1987: 41).

6. Evidence of informal-sector voting patterns requires ecological analysis of data at the district level. This is justified by the fact that poverty and informal activities in Lima are concentrated in shantytown districts; the social structure is manifested in the demographic geography of the city (Stokes 1988: 137; Matos Mar 1985; Maria 1985; Meneses and Díaz 1978).

7. Roncagliolo (1980: 117) was first to note that in elections in the early 1980s APRA's social base was clearly distinct from the Left and particularly strong in the middle class. The only political party whose support was strong and significantly correlated with the middle class as I define it was APRA between 1978 and 1980 (see table 3.2). Afterward, APRA's support lost much of its middle class character and came to more closely approximate the social base of the Left.

8. For the full text of President García's inaugural address, see Lowenthal 1988. Unless otherwise attributed, quotes of García are taken from this source.

9. "Las campañas del APRA y la IU," *Quehacer*, 1985, no. 35, pp. 32–3.

10. These are features of the APRA party that date to its origin. For studies of APRA prior to the 1980s see North 1973; Klarén 1973; Kantor 1966; Hilliker 1971; Pike 1986.

11. On the concept of *pueblo* and *lo popular*, see O'Donnell (1988b). On the notion of the oligarchy in populism, see Laclau (1977).

12. After he was elected, Belmont threw his support behind Vargas Llosa in the second round of the presidential election in 1990. This did not prevent Fujimori from supporting his 1993 reelection bid after the official candidate of Cambio 90 dropped from the race.

13. Sectors C and D refer to lower-income groups. See chapter 6 for a discussion.

CHAPTER 4 NOTES

1. *Latin American Weekly Report,* 13 July 1989.

2. The Nash equilibrium is a widely used solution concept that refers to "an array of strategies, one for each player, such that no player has an incentive (in terms of improving his own payoff) to deviate from his part of the strategy array" (Kreps 1990: 28).

3. William H. Riker (1957) argues that small events are less subject to ambiguity than are large events. It is easier to specify initial and terminal situations in small events and to identify a finite and constant number of relevant actors.

4. *Pituco* is slang for "rich."

5. *Expreso,* 29 June 1989.

6. *La República,* 25 June 1989.

7. *La República,* 25 June 1989.

8. In 1986 the PPC elected mayors in 13 of the roughly 40 district municipalities in Lima. However, this success was partly because AP did not contest those elections.

9. This chronology is taken from a review of the weekly news magazine *Caretas,* and from the daily newspapers *La República* and *Expreso.* These sources cover a wide spectrum of views, and were checked for accuracy.

10. Orrego proposed what I have called *B* in the provinces and *A* in Lima.

11. *Caretas,* 26 July 1989.

12. See the letter of June 16, by Fernando Belaúnde Terry to Mario Vargas Llosa, reprinted in *Caretas,* 26 July 1989.

13. *Expreso,* 20 June 1989.

14. *Resumen Semanal,* DESCO, XII (524): 16–22 June 1989.

15. *Expreso,* 22 June 1989.

16. See, for example, the comments by Manuel Ulloa in *Expreso,* 22 June 1989.

17. *Expreso,* 23 June 1989.

18. The exact terms of the agreement are in *Resumen Semanal,* DESCO, XII (526): 30 June–6 July 1989.

19. The letter is reproduced in *La República,* 3 July 1989.

20. See *La República,* 10 July 1989.

21. According to the *Informativo Mensual,* DATUM of July 1989, the percent of the population in Lima that supported Vargas Llosa's candidacy rose from 20 percent in February to 46 percent in June, on the day after the resignation.

22. Belaúnde used the tripod metaphor in *La República,* 10 July 1989; Libertad politicians disputed the metaphor arguing that all actors in Fredemo should be subordinated to the need for "a great change" in Peru. Interview with Miguel Vega Alvear, National Secretary for Extension, Development and Inter-Party Relations, of the Liberty Movement, Lima, 4 August 1989.

23. *La República,* 25 June 1989.

24. *The Financial Times,* 23 June 1989.

25. The complete text of the letter is reproduced in *Caretas,* 26 June 1989; as well as DESCO's *Resumen Semanal,* XII (524): 16–22 June 1989. All subsequent quotes from Vargas Llosa's letter are taken from these sources.

26. This term was first used by defenders of the oligarchic state in the 1920s and 1930s in response to pressures for change by workers and other subordinate groups. The term denotes a link between APRA and Communism. In fact, relation between APRA and the Peruvian Left have always been more problematic than suggested by this emotionally-charged term.

27. Interview with Miguel Vega Alvear, Lima, August 4, 1989.

28. Interview with Luis Bedoya Reyes, *La República,* 25 June 1989.

29. *Expreso,* 23 June 1989.

30. *Latin American Weekly Report,* 6 July 1989.

31. The firm Mercadeo y Opinión showed that 38 percent of those surveyed believed that Bedoya was responsible for Vargas Llosa's resignation; 22 percent blamed Belaúnde, and 14 percent pointed to other leaders in AP. See *La República,* 25 June 1989.

32. *Caudillo* means "strongman."

33. *La República,* cited in the *Latin American Weekly Report,* 6 July 1989.

34. As we shall see in chapter 7, divisions reemerged within Fredemo when Vargas Llosa fell short of a first-round victory in the April 1990. Although forced to compete in a runoff election Vargas Llosa did not resign.

CHAPTER 5 NOTES

1. Related by Henry Pease, in an interview in Lima, 1988.

2. The National Election Board is the government office responsible for elections, and a tribunal to resolve disputes.

3. When the parties of the Peruvian Left ran separate slates in the 1980 presidential election they won a total of 14 percent of the vote (McClintock 1989: 131).

4. The model has been used in a previous comparative analysis of Peru and the Philippines. See Cameron (1992b).

5. The revolutionary block was composed of the Partido Unificado Mariáteguista (PUM), the Unión de Izquierda Revolucionaria (UNIR), and the Frente Obrero, Campesino, Estudiantil y Popular (FOCEP); the reformist block was made up of the Partido Socialista Revolucionario (PSR) and the Partido Comunista Revolucionario (PCR); the independent block included the Partido Comunista del Perú (PCP) and legally non-registered independent groups (Movimiento de Afirmación Socialista, or MAS, and Acción Política Socialista, APS).

6. *Latin American Weekly Report,* 14 May 1987, p. 8. The quote is attributed to Barrantes speaking in 1984.

7. This point is made by Jorge del Prado in *La República,* 9 July 1989.

8. Interview in *The Peru Report,* Vol 3(5) May 1989, pp. B3–4, cited in Roberts 1992: 363, fn 89; Diez Canseco 1992: 77–87.

9. Excellent journalistic coverage of the internal politics of the IU was published by the Peruvian daily *La República.* I am aware of the political bias of this newspaper and have used it mainly as a source of interviews and public statements, as well as to establish the timing and sequence of events.

10. The following conditions were presented by the reformist block: (1) the participation of all members of IU, including 60,000 persons excluded from the scheduled electoral process; (2) the formation of electoral committees representing all the political forces in IU; (3) freedom of all members of IU to run for office; (4) simultaneous selection of presidential and municipal candidates; (5) the withdrawal of the "exclusionary" registration of IU. See *La República,* 8 June 1989.

11. *La República,* 16 June 1989.

12. *La República,* 7 July 1989.

13. *La República,* 6 July 1989.

14. The source for the legal arguments is *La República,* 7 July 1989.

15. *La República,* 8 July 1989.

16. *La República,* 8 July 1989.

17. *La República,* 10 and 11 July 1989.

18. *La República,* 18 July 1989.

19. *La República,* 6 August 1989.

20. *La República,* 4 August 1989.

21. *La República,* 4 August 1989.

22. Interview with Henry Pease, Lima 1988.

23. Interview with Alberto Adrianzén, Lima 1989.

24. The concept of subgame perfection is a refinement of the Nash equilibrium. A strategy array in an extensive-form game is subgame perfect if the strategies form a Nash equilibrium for every proper subgame of the game tree. For an excellent nontechnical discussion of these concepts, see Kreps (1990), especially chapters 3 and 5; Tsebelis (1990), chapters 1–4; and Zagare (1990).

25. However, unity "starts with respect for the accords of the congress" said Pease. See his interview with *La República,* 6 June 1989.

26. *La República,* 7 July 1989.

27. Indeed, Barrantes initially wanted to exclude the revolutionary block from the United Left's Leadership Committee. Interview with Jorge del Prado, *La República,* 13 July 1989.

28. Interview in *La República,* 9 July 1989.

29. Interview in *La República,* 9 July 1989.

30. Alfredo Filomeno, *La República,* 21 June 1989.

31. Edmundo Murrugarra, *La República,* 23 June 1989.

32. Alfredo Filomeno in *La República,* 7 July 1989.

33. *La República,* 9 July 1989.

34. *La República,* 9 July 1989.

35. Paradoxically, the electoral rule that increased the urgency of the Right to arrive at a formula for coalition unity in the hope of winning the election in the first round encouraged Barrantes to seek a rupture of the Left in the hope of placing second in the first round and winning the runoff election.

36. *Latin American Weekly Report,* 2 February 1989, p. 9.

37. *Latin American Weekly Report,* 18 May 1989, p. 7. Taylor supports this view: "the polls predicted that in a second round contest Barrantes would obtain 51 per cent of the national vote to Vargas Llosa's 31 per cent" (1990: 113).

38. *Latin American Weekly Report,* 22 June 1989, p. 8.

39. Jorge Hurtado Pozo, quoted in *La República,* 29 June 1989.

40. *La República,* 24 July 1989

41.   *La República,* 24 July 1989.

42.   *La República,* 7 August 1989.

CHAPTER 6 NOTES

1.   See Daniele Checchi (1993) for a more formal model, based on the Peruvian experience, that "explains the emergence of populist candidates as the result of the existence of a wide informal sector in a polarized society, where pro-labour and pro-capital candidates pursue the exclusive interests of their constituencies" (1993: 1).

2.   For a review of spatial models, see Enelow and Hinich (1990a); one of the early critiques is provided by Stokes (1963); Aldrich (1983) extends the model to address party activism; issues of entry and entry deterrence are discussed by Greenberg and Shepsle (1987) and Palfrey (1984).

3.   Manuel Córdova, "El proyecto neoliberal: la oportunidad perdida," *Quehacer,* no. 64, May-June 1990, pp. 18–21.

4.   I am grateful to Julio Cotler for this observation.

5.   Manuel Córdova, "El proyecto néoliberal: la oportunidad perdida," *Quehacer,* no. 64, May-June 1990, pp. 18–21.

6.   See *Industria Peruana,* no. 529, Lima, December 1983, cited in Palma 1987: 38–39. This response possibly reflects ethnic differences as well.

7.   Mario Vargas Llosa acknowledged the opposition he faced in espousing free-market views in a recent interview: "Until now, the problem in Peru has been that even people who in their daily lives acted out of a belief in private ownership—for instance those in the informal economy—resorted to leftist vocabulary and ideas when talking about politics. And, according to that vocabulary and those ideas, private ownership was not something to be encouraged. The whole country, even the right-wing and center parties, operated under these assumptions" (cited in Farnsworth 1988b).

8.   Interview in Lima, August 4, 1988.

9.   "Old hands hold key to parliamentary vote," *The Andean Report,* Vol 19, no. 2, February 1990, pp. 26–27.

10.   In contrast with his economic proposals, Vargas Llosa's social program was mentioned almost as an afterthought. It would acquire greater salience in the second round (Daeschner 1993: 156).

11.   See Sawyer/Miller's campaign manual *Peru: the Liberal Mandate,* cited in Daeschner (1993: 112–13).

12.   *Caretas,* 5 January 1988, p. 21.

13.   "Pease: la rosa y el puño combatiente," *La República,* 8 April 1990, pp. 4–5.

14.   "Barrantes en la soledad de su castillo," *La República,* 8 April 1990, pp. 7–8.

15.   "Abril de 1990: ¿La Clave, el Segundo Puesto?" *Quehacer,* no. 62, December 1989–January 1990: 4–6.

16.   *Caretas,* 2 April 1990, p. 12.

17.   "APRA Sirvió en bandeja el segundo puesto," *Expreso,* 9 April 1990, p. 9.

18.   These data are taken from opinion poll surveys by APOYO S.A. and reported in Schmidt 1991: figure 3, pp. 34–35.

19. Vargas Llosa did not improve his image by speaking French in a postelection press conference on April 8, 1990.

20. *Caretas,* 2 April 1990.

21. By pointing out his own Japanese background, Fujimori highlighted his differences with the more European Vargas Llosa. *Caretas,* 2 April 1990.

22. *El Comercio,* 17 May 1990.

23. Alma Guillermoprieto, "Down the Shining Path," *The New Yorker,* February 8, 1993, p. 11.

24. I am grateful to the participants in a seminar at the Instituto de Estudios Peruanos for pointing this out to me.

25. Interview with Eduardo Ballón, Lima, August 11, 1992.

CHAPTER 7 NOTES

1. "Vargas Llosa propone acuerdo pero Fujimori lo rechaza," *Expreso,* 9 April 1990, p. 3.

2. "Pide a García reunión con ganadores de la contienda," *Expreso,* 10 April 1990, p. 3.

3. "Inquietud presidencial," *Expreso,* 14 April 1990, p. 4.

4. From a conversation with the press on Thursday, April 12, 1990. "Polidatos: Al hilo con FBT," *Expreso,* 11 April 1990, p. 4.

5. "Triunfo de Vargas Llosa es rechazo al APRA y comunismo," *Expreso,* 9 April 1990, p. 4.

6. "Entendimiento nacional es la única salida," *Expreso,* 9 April 1990, p. 8.

7. "Censuró terrorismo político del APRA," *Expreso,* 16 April 1990, p. 2.

8. Other members included Luis Bustamante, Felipe Ortiz de Zevallos, Raúl Salazar, Jorge Gonzáles Izquierdo, Miguel Vega Alvear, Mario Roggero, Beatriz Merino, Miguel Cruchaga, Raúl Ferrero.

9. "Sigue la incertidumbre en torno a posible retiro de Vargas Llosa," *La República,* 11 April 1990, p. 2.

10. "Sigue la incertidumbre en torno a posible retiro de Vargas Llosa," *La República,* 11 April 1990, p. 3.

11. "Sigue la incertidumbre en torno a posible retiro de Vargas Llosa," *La República,* 11 April 1990, p. 3.

12. "Vargas Llosa considera posibilidad de declinar," *Expreso,* 11 April 1990. p. 3.

13. Patricia Llosa de Vargas denied rumors that her husband was considering whether to resign, saying "I believe that the second round is now assured" before demonstrating supporters of Fredemo. Vargas Llosa left for a private cottage outside Lima. The reason given to the press was that the candidate needed to recover from the exhaustion of the electoral campaign. "Mario no ha renunciado," *Expreso,* 11 April 1990, p. 4.

14. "Sigue la incertidumbre en torno a posible retiro de Vargas Llosa," *La República,* 11 April 1990, p. 3.

15. Monseñor Vargas Alzamora denied that he had visited Vargas Llosa in secret. "Iglesia pide que Fujimori y Vargas Llosa presenten planes de gobierno," *La República,* 12 April 1990, p. 8. However, the Catholic Church clearly sided with Vargas Llosa. Vargas Alzamora denied that Vargas Llosa was an atheist: "an atheist is someone who does not believe in God and accepts no divinity. Vargas Llosa is an agnostic, who

has not defined his faith. However, he believes in God and therefore is within the Church." "Polidatos: Diferencia clara," *Expreso,* 16 April 1990, p. 2.

16. "Polidatos: Temores y temblores," *Expreso,* 11 April 1990, p.4.

17. "Cambio 90: no hay posibilidad de renuncia," *Expreso,* 11 April 1990, p. 4.

18. "Fujimori dispuesto a polemizar en cualquier terreno con Vargas Llosa," *La República,* 12 April 1990, p. 2.

19. Another argument that might have influenced Vargas Llosa was that the international press would be critical—they had been very favorable to Vargas Llosa during the campaign. Vargas Llosa was acutely conscious of his international as well as his national reputation.

20. Article 203 of the constitution stated: "If none of the candidates obtains an absolute majority, a second round will be held within the next thirty days between the candidates who have obtained the two highest relative majorities." "Segunda Vuelta," editorial, *Expreso,* 14 April 1990, p. 16.

21. "Jurado debe proclamar ganador a Fujimori," *La República,* 11 April 1990, p. 3.

22. "No hay otro salida que segunda vuelta," *Expreso,* 10 April 1990, p. 10.

23. "Segunda Vuelta," editorial, *Expreso,* 14 April 1990, p. 16.

24. "Segunda vuelta sin consignas," *Expreso,* 12 April 1990, p. 6.

25. "Acabar con Miseria y Hambre Para Derrotar al Terrorismo," *Expreso,* 9 April 1990, p. 9.

26. "Segunda vuelta es de pronóstico reservado," *Expreso,* 10 April 1990, p. 10.

27. In a meeting of the coalition's Executive Committee, Sandro Mariátegui proposed Orrego as the candidate to replace Vargas Llosa if he resigned. AP and the PPC agreed that if Vargas Llosa stepped down they would run Orrego as the presidential candidate. Ernesto Alayza would be the first vice-presidential candidate. "Contacto en Moscú," *Diario La República,* 18 April 1990, p. 4; "Polidatos: AP-PPC en guardia," *Expreso,* 11 April 1990, p. 4.

28. "Vargas Llosa acaba la cura de silencio," *Expreso,* 16 April 1990, p. 3.

29. "Sigue la incertidumbre en torno a posible retiro de Vargas Llosa," *La República,* 11 April 1990, p. 3.

30. "Chirinos Soto no declaró a nombre de Vargas Llosa," *Expreso,* 14 April 1990, p. 3.

31. "Seguiré librando muchas batallas," *Expreso,* 10 April 1990, p. 12.

32. Federico Salazar Bustamante, "Ni un paso atrás," editorial *Expreso,* 16 April 1990, p. 18.

33. Federico Salazar Bustamante, "Ni un paso atrás," *Expreso,* 16 April 1990, p. 18.

34. See "García Belaúnde pide que Fredemo escuche rechazo del pueblo al shock," *La República,* 18 April 1990, p. 13.

35. "Javier Alva Orlandini admite: 'Anunciar despidos fue grave error,'" *La República,* 12 April 1990, p. 7.

36. "El silencio estratégico," *Diario La República,* 18 April 1990, pp. 4–5; "Detrás del Bacalao," *Caretas,* 23 April 1990, pp. 16–20.

37. "Disciplinado y Ferviente Respaldo a Vargas Llosa," *Expreso,* 10 April 1990, p. 2.

38. Data by DATUM on social class and electoral preferences are in "Ultimas Tendencias," *Caretas,* 30 April 1990, pp. 10–14. See also "El Sube y Baja," *Caretas,* 14 May 1990, pp. 16–17.

39. "Vargas Llosa es el único vocero del Fredemo pero no da la cara," *La República,* 18 April 1990, p. 11.

40. "Polidatos: Mejor, no hablo," *Expreso,* 11 April 1990, p. 4.

41. "Alan García feliz con los resultados," *Expreso,* 13 April 1990, p. 3.

42. *Caretas,* 2 April 1990, p. 14.

43. "Voceros del APRA y De la IU Anticipan Apoyo a Cambio 90," *Expreso,* 10 April 1990, p. 3.

44. "Fredemo habría invertido doce millones de dólares en campaña," *La República,* 11 April 1990, p. 10.

45. Federico Salazar Bustamante, "Ni un paso atrás," *Expreso,* 16 April 1990, p. 18.

46. Interview with a spokesperson for the Left—himself a businessman of no humble origin—in June 1990, Lima.

47. "Miles pugnan por inscribirse en 'Cambio 90' o para ofrecer apoyo," *La República,* 11 April 1990. p. 5.

48. "Cambio de Estrategia," *Caretas,* 7 May 1990, pp. 16-18.

49. "Los dilemas del candidato fredemista: ¿El otro o el mismo?" *Diario La República,* 18 April 1990, p. 3.

50. Fernando Rospigliosi, "¿Puede Ganar Vargas Llosa?" *Expreso,* 13 April 1990, p. 4.

51. "Fracaso del APRA catapultó a Cambio 90," *Expreso,* 16 April 1990, p. 8.

52. "Fujimori tuvo contactos esporádicos con Sendero," *Expreso,* 11 April 1990, p. 5.

CHAPTER 8 NOTES

1. See Inter-Church Committee on Human Rights in Latin America, *The April 5th Coup: A Cure Worse than the Illness?* Ottawa: Canadian Council for International Cooperation, 1992; James Brooke, "Fujimori Sees a Peaceful, and a Prosperous, Peru," *New York Times,* 6 April 1993, p. A3. Opinion polls are notoriously unreliable in Peru because they tend to rely on small samples, overrepresent the middle- and upper-income groups, and are often conducted in a climate of fear that inhibits subjects from openly expressing their political views. Many polls incorrectly showed Vargas Llosa was going to win the 1990 election.

2. Fujimori won the 1990 election promising not to impose economic "shock" measures. Once in power, however, he implemented the harshest stabilization program ever adopted in Latin America (Chossudovsky 1991: 3).

3. Fujimori said, in explaining the coup, "I could not be stopped by this knowledge [that the constitutional order was being interrupted] because it would have meant we had to continue our coexistence with a democracy in which no one believed." "Fujimori explains why he suspended constitution; seeks to build a 'new Peru,'" *The British Broadcasting Corporation; Summary of World Broadcasts,* 7 April 1993.

4. See, for example, "Are military coups still a threat in Latin America—or is it the wrong question?" *Latin American Weekly Report,* 19 August 1993, p. 373.

5. According to Torres y Torres Lara (in Acurio et al. 1992: 21), this law could not be challenged in court (through the Tribunal of Constitutional Guarantees) because the Tribunal was dominated by sympathizers of the APRA. See the response by Alberto Borea (in Acurio et al. 1992: 26–19).

6. Under the 1979 constitution, the Congress can grant extraordinary powers to the president. However, before the President can close the Chamber of Deputies it must have rejected the government's cabinet three times. The Senate cannot legally be absolved. By closing both Houses the president acted illegally and in blatant disregard for the law.

7. "Fujimori explains why he suspended constitution; seeks to build a 'new Peru,'" *The British Broadcasting Corporation; Summary of World Broadcasts,* 7 April 1993.

8. Indeed, as early as 1990, when Fujimori was first elected, he moved into the headquarters of the armed forces. Subsequently, he collaborated more closely with the military than with Congress.

9. The following quotes of Fujimori are taken from "Fujimori explains why he suspended constitution; seeks to build a 'new Peru,'" *The British Broadcasting Corporation; Summary of World Broadcasts,* 7 April 1993.

10. "Fujimori explains why he suspended constitution; seeks to build a 'new Peru,'" *The British Broadcasting Corporation; Summary of World Broadcasts,* April 7, 1993.

11. Inter-Church Committee on Human Rights in Latin America, *The April 5th Coup: A Cure Worse than the Illness?* Ottawa: Canadian Council for International Cooperation, 1992, p. 14.

12. Critics of the coup argued that authoritarian measures would only erode the distinction between the forces of order and those of insurrection. They suggested that the most effective answer to terrorist violence was a strong civil society, and collaboration between the society and the armed forces. The Shining Path attacked mayors, political candidates, grassroots organizations, the clergy, and foreign technicians working in nongovernmental organizations precisely to weaken civil society and destroy any organized group that represented an alternative between itself and the armed forces. By weakening democracy, Fujimori played into the hands of the Shining Path, moving closer to the kind of apocalyptic confrontation that they sought.

13. "Fujimori Interviewed on Democracy, Autocracy, Death Penalty, Other Issues," *The British Broadcasting Corporation, Summary of World Broadcasts,* 2 November 1992.

14. "Fujimori presses case for re-election," *Latin American Weekly Report,* 17 June 1993, p. 268.

15. According to Teresa Tovar, San Román became an object of scorn. Interview at DESCO in Lima, 13 August 1993.

16. "Fujimori explains why he suspended constitution; seeks to build a 'new Peru,'" *The British Broadcasting Corporation; Summary of World Broadcasts,* 7 April 1993.

17. Canadian Minister of External Affairs, Barbara McDougall, took a stronger position and demanded economic sanctions.

18. Statement made on condition of anonymity by a senior State Department official in Washington D.C. on May 6, 1992.

19. One contentious issue was the size of Congress. Fujimori argued that there should be 80 members because a smaller number would make congress more "efficient." There is no reason to believe that a Congress with 80 members will be more efficient than one with 120. The efficiency of the British Parliament, one of the largest in the world, is based on disciplined and cohesive parties, a party-oriented electorate, and the centralization of power in the cabinet (see Cox 1987). Yet Fujimori—a politician who rose from obscurity, without a program or party—routinely contradicted his own cabinet and could see little value in Peru's political parties (what he called the "partidocracia").

20. *Resumen Semanal,* Año XV, no. 683, 19–25 August 1992, p. 4.21. Polls cited by Pásara showed that APRA was unlikely to win more than about 5 percent of the vote in the CCD and 3 percent in municipal elections in Lima; AP was at 6 percent of the vote for the CCD and 5 percent for the municipal election (Pásara 1993: 45).

22. "Fujimori Interviewed on Democracy, Autocracy, Death Penalty, Other Issues," *The British Broadcasting Corporation, Summary of World Broadcasts,* 2 November 1992.

23. *Resumen Semanal,* Año XV, no. 688, 23–29 September, p. 2.

24. *Resumen Semanal,* Año XV no. 687, 16–22 September 1992, pp. 4–5.

25. *Resumen Semanal,* Año XV no. 700. 16–22 December 1992.26. *Resumen Semanal,* Año XV, no. 696, 18–24 November 1992, p. 2.

27. *Resumen Semanal,* Año XVI, no. 702, 2–12 January 1993, p. 1.

28. *Resumen Semanal,* Año XVI, no. 703, 13–19 January 1993.

29. *Resumen Semanal,* Año XVI, no. 705, 17 January–2 February 1993, pp. 5-6.

30. Gustavo Gorriti, "The Unshining Path," *New Republic,* February 8, 1993, pp. 19–23.

31. *Resumen Semanal,* Año XVI, no. 704, 20–6 January 1993. p. 2.

32. General Alberto Arciniega (1994: 113) observed that under military rule Montesinos had been "accused of high treason in Peruvian military courts, cashiered, and banned from entering military installations—for which his picture was displayed at all guard posts—until he became a presidential advisor!" Yet, Fujimori tolerated no criticism of Montesinos. Enrique Zileri Gibson, the editor of *Caretas,* was charged in court and placed under conditional liberty for calling Montesinos "Rasputin." On Montesinos, see Gustavo Gorriti (1993: 22). See also Lawrence J. Speer, "Fujimori's Right-Hand Man," *San Francisco Chronicle,* May 24, 1993, p. A8.

33. Mary Powers, "Human-Rights Case Unleashes Constitutional Crisis in Peru," *The Reuter Library Report,* 25 May 1993.

34. *Resumen Semanal,* Año XVI, no. 742, 27 October–2 November 1993, p. 4.

35. *Resumen Semanal,* Año XVI, no. 742, 27 October–2 November 1993, p. 2.

36. "Russia turns its back on parliament," *The Economist,* September 25, 1993, p. 57.

37. "Spasibo, Alberto," *The Economist,* December 4, 1993, p. 50. According to Joan Debardeleben, some observers felt Yeltsin had wanted to crack down on congress since the April referendum gave him a mandate for reform, and they wondered why it took him so long. Interview, Carleton University, January 24, 1994.

38. For a good chronology, see Foye (1993); see also Brown (1993).

39. "The battle for Russia," *The Economist,* October 9, 1993, p. 57.

40. "Russia turns its back on parliament," *The Economist,* September 25, 1993, p. 57.

41. The parliament had also opposed privatization and blocked the adoption of legislation creating private ownership of land (Tolz 1993: 2).

42. "The reformer who came back," *The Economist,* September 25, 1993, p. 59.

43. "What Yeltsin Must Do," *Business Week,* October 18, 1993, p. 25.

44. Interview, Carleton University, January 24, 1994.

45. According to Elizabeth Teague (1993a: 1) Yeltsin had been at loggerheads with the Russian legislature ever since the Sixth Congress of People's Deputies in April 1992.

46. "How to get Russia Respected," *The Economist,* November 6, 1993, p. 55.

47. Among the list of political groups suspended in October were centrists, like the People's Party of Free Russia (PPFR, Rutskoi's party), which was a member of the centrist Civic Union coalition.

48. Interview, Carleton University, January 24, 1994.

49. Roy Medvedev, "Power without glory," *Manchester Guardian Weekly,* 17 October 1993, p. 12.

50. Jonathan Steele, "Yeltsin reaches for extra powers," *Manchester Guardian Weekly,* 31 October 1993, p. 3.

51. Jon Pammett, interview, Carleton University, January 24, 1994.

52. "Good grief, the good guys," *The Economist,* December 4, 1993, p. 55.

53. Jonathan Steele, "Yeltsin reaches for extra powers," *Manchester Guardian Weekly,* 31 October 1993, p. 3.

54. "Serrano 'tries a Fujimori' to avoid ending up like Carlos Andrés Pérez," *Latin American Weekly Report,* 10 June 1993, p. 253.

55. "Serrano out, León Carpio in," *Latin American Weekly Report,* 17 June 1993, p. 267.

56. "Serrano 'tries a Fujimori' to avoid ending up like Carlos Andrés Pérez," *Latin American Weekly Report,* 10 June 1993, p. 253.

57. "Serrano proposes 'peace in 90 days.'" *Latin American Weekly Report,* 28 January 1993, pp. 44–5.

58. "Progress reported in peace talks," *Latin American Weekly Report,* 1 April 1993, p. 155.

59. "Protests turn to riots and violence," *Latin American Weekly Report,* 3 June 1993, p. 245.

60. "Franco 'invited to take Fujimori road,'" *Latin American Weekly Report,* 20 January 1994, p. 17.

61. "Anti-inflation drive takes third place in Itamar Franco's new plan," *Latin American Weekly Report,* 6 May 1993, p. 193.

62. "Cardoso's 'non-plan' could become stepping-stone to the presidency," *Latin American Weekly Report,* 1 July 1993, p. 289.

63. "'Crisis of the state and of authority,'" *Latin American Weekly Report,* 29 July 1993, p. 341.

64. "Coup Rumors," *Latin American Weekly Report,* 15 July 1993, p. 321.

65. Brooke, James, "A Soldier Turned Politician Wants To Give Brazil Back to Army Rule," *New York Times,* July 25, 1993.

66. "Cheque tax passes by lower chamber," *Latin American Weekly Report,* 8 July 1993, p. 304.

67. "Cardoso unveils his tax and cuts package," *Latin American Weekly Report,* 9 December 1993, p. 567.

68. Entrenched politicians would be "reluctant to co-operate with Cardoso's economic reform programme if they thought he would derive benefits from it at the polls," reported the "Old Right begins to speak out again," *Latin American Weekly Report,* 19 August 1993, p. 377.

69. The ruling coalition was made up of the PMDB, the Partido Social Democrático Brasileiro (PSDB, Cardoso's party) and a wing of the Partido da Frente Liberal (PFL). The PSB (Socialist Party) with 9 seats was replaced by the Partido Progressista with 43 seats. See "Ruling Coalition Strengthened," *Latin American Weekly Report,* 9 September 1993, p. 418.

70. "PMDB defections stymie Cardoso," *Latin American Weekly Report,* 23 September 1993, p. 435.

71. "Cardoso to unify exchange rates," *Latin American Weekly Report,* 30 September 1993, p. 447.

72. "Constitutional reform to go ahead," *Latin American Weekly Report,* 14 October 1993, p. 470. The groups in civil society included lawyers (in the Ordem dos Advogados do Brasil, OAB), progressive Bishops, and trade unions.

73. "Cardoso falls out with Fritsch," *Latin American Weekly Report,* 7 October 1993, p. 467.

74. "Franco offers to hold early elections," *Latin American Weekly Report,* 28 October 1993, p. 503.

75. "Corruption inquiry targets contractors," *Latin American Weekly Report,* 11 November 1993, p. 518.

76. "Franco rejects the Peruvian solution," *Latin American Weekly Report,* 25 November 1993, p. 549.

77. "Taking a new look at old enemies," *Latin American Weekly Report,* 29 April 1993, p. 182.

78. "Franco 'invited to take Fujimori road,'" *Latin American Weekly Report,* 20 January 1994, p. 17.

79. The poll was conducted by the Instituto Brasileiro de Pesquisa (Ibope). See "Franco's unhappy anniversary," *Latin American Weekly Report,* 7 September 1993, p. 467.

80. "Update: Inflation in the region," *Latin American Weekly Report,* 13 January 1994, p. 11.

BIBLIOGRAPHY

Abugattás, J., et al., 1990. *Estado y Sociedad: Relaciones Peligrosas.* Lima: DESCO.

Abugattás, J., et al., 1992. *Desde el Límite: Perú, reflecciones en el umbral de una nueva época.* Lima: Instituto Democracia y Socialismo.

Abugattás, L. A., 1987. "Populism and After: The Peruvian Experience," in Malloy, J. M., and M. A. Seligson, eds. *Authoritarians and Democrats: Regime Transition in Latin America.* Pittsburgh: Pittsburgh University Press.

Acurio, G. et al., 1992. *La Democracia en Cuestión.* Lima: Centro Norte Sur/Universidad de Miami, Centro Peruano de Estudios Sociales, Instituto de Estudios Peruanos.

Adams, N. and N. Valdivia, 1991. *Los Otros Empresarios: Etica de migrantes y formación de empresas en Lima.* Lima: Instituto de Estudios Peruanos.

Adrianzén, A., 1992. "Democracia y partidos en el Perú." *Pretextos* 3: 7–19.

Adrianzén, A. and E. Ballón eds, 1992. *Lo Popular en America Latina: ¿Una Visión en Crisis?* Lima: DESCO.

Aggarwal, V. K., and M. A. Cameron, 1994. "Modelling Peruvian Debt Rescheduling in the 1980s." *Studies in Comparative International Development,* Forthcoming.

Aldrich, J., 1983. "A Downsian Spatial Model with Party Activism," *American Political Science Review,* 77: 974–90.

Alvarado, J., et al., 1987. *El Mercado Laboral Urbano y sus Interrelaciones con Otros Sectores de la Economía.* Lima: CEDEP.

Alvarez Rodrich, A., ed., 1993. *El Poder en el Perú.* Lima: APOYO.

Amat y León, C., 1985. "Ideas centrales sobre la crisis," *Socialismo y Participación,* no. 31, September.

Amat y León, C., 1987. *Niveles de Vida y Grupos Sociales en el Perú.* Lima: Universidad del Pacífico y Fundación Friedrich Ebert.

Ames, R., 1980. "Gran burguesía y movimiento popular: las dos fuerzas en pugna," *Quehacer,* Vol. 5, June: 13–24.

Ames, R., et al., 1988. *Informe al Congreso Sobre los Sucesos de los Penales,* Comisión Investigadora del Congreso (Lima).

Angell, A., 1979. "Peruvian Labour and the Military Government Since 1968," *Working Paper,* London: University of London, Institute of Latin American Studies.

Angell, A., 1984. "The Difficulties of Policy Making and Implementation in Peru," *Bulletin of Latin American Research,* 3 (1), January.

Angell, A., and R. Thorp, 1980. "Inflation, Stabilization and Attempted Redemocratization in Peru, 1975–1979," *World Development,* 8 (11).

Annis, S., and J. Franks, 1989. "The Idea, Ideology, and Economics of the Informal Sector: The Case of Peru," *Grassroots Development,* 31 (1): 9–22.

Annis, S., and P. Hakim, eds., 1988. *Direct to the Poor: Grassroots Development in Latin America.* Boulder: Lynne Rienner.

APOYO S. A., 1985. *Informe de Opinión.* Lima: APOYO S. A., July.

APOYO S. A., 1985. *Informe de Opinión.* Lima: APOYO S. A., October.

APOYO S. A., 1987. *Informe de Opinión.* Lima: APOYO S. A., May.

APOYO S. A., 1987. *Informe de Opinión.* Lima: APOYO S. A., July.

APOYO S. A., 1988. *Informe de Opinión.* Lima: APOYO S. A., February.

APOYO S. A., 1991. *Informe de Opinión.* Lima: APOYO S. A., November.

Arciniega H. A., 1994. "Civil-Military Relations and a Democratic Peru," *ORBIS,* 38 (1): 109–117.

Asamblea Nacional Popular, 1990. *La ANP Frente al Proceso Electoral de 1990.* Lima, Plaza 2 de mayo, no. 42.

Astiz, C. A., 1969. *Pressure Groups and Power Elites in Peruvian Politics.* Ithaca: Cornell University Press.

Babb, F., 1989. *Between Field and Cooking Pot: The Political Economy of Marketwomen in Peru.* Austin: University of Texas Press.

Balbi, C. R. and J. Parodi, 1981. "Los limites de la izquierda: el caso sindical." *La Revista,* vol. 5.

Balbi, C. R., 1989. *Identidad Clasista en el Movimiento Obrero Peruano: Su Impacto en las Relaciones Laborales.* Lima: DESCO.

Balbi, C. R., et al., 1990. *Movimientos Sociales: Elementos para una Relectura.* Lima: Lima: DESCO.

Balbi, C. R., 1993a. "Del golpe del 5 de abril al CCD: Los problemas de la transición a la democracia." *Pretextos* 3: 41–61.

Balbi, C. R., 1993b. "El desaparecido poder del sindicalismo," in A. Alvarez Rodrich, ed. *El Poder en el Perú.* Lima: APOYO.

Ballón, E., 1986a. "Alan, la pirámide y el movimiento social." *Quehacer,* no. 41.

Ballón, E., 1986b. "Izquierda y movimiento popular," *Los caminos del laberinto* 3: 49–57.

Ballón, E. ed., 1986. *Movimientos Sociales y Crisis: El caso peruano.* Lima: DESCO.

Ballón, E., 1991. "Las modernizaciones frustradas del los partidos políticos peruanos en la década del ochenta." Unpublished manuscript. Lima: DESCO.

Banco Central de Reservas del Perú, 1984. *En la Línea del Mapa de Pobreza: Identificación de las diferencias interdistritales en Lima Metropolitiana.* Lima: Gerencia de Investigación Económica.

Barrantes, A., 1985. *Alfonso Barrantes: Sus Propias Palabras.* Lima: Mosca Azul.

Barry, B., 1978. *Sociologists, Economists and Democracy.* Chicago: University of Chicago Press.

Becker, D., 1982a. "'Bonanza Development' and the 'New Bourgeoisie': Peru Under Military Rule." *Comparative Political Studies,* 15: 243–288.

Becker, D., 1982b. "Modern Mine Labor and Politics in Peru Since 1968." *Boletín de Estudios Latinoamericanos y del Caribe,* no. 32.

Becker, D., 1983. *The New Bourgeoisie and the Limits of Dependency: Mining, Class and Power in "Revolutionary" Peru.* Princeton: Princeton University Press.

Becker, D., 1984. "Recent Political Developments in Peru: Dependency or Post-Dependency." *Latin American Research Review,* 19 (2), April.

Becker, D., 1985. "Peru after the 'Revolution': Class, Power and Ideology." *Studies in Comparative International Development,* 20 (3), Fall.

Béjar, H., 1987. "Reflexiones sobre el sector informal." *Nueva Sociedad,* no. 90 (July–August): 89–92.

Berger, S., 1981. *Organizing Interests in Western Europe.* Cambridge: Cambridge University Press.

Bergquist, C., 1986. *Labor in Latin America*. Stanford: Stanford University Press.

Bernales, E., 1980. *Crisis Política: ¿Solución Electoral?* Lima: DESCO.

Bernales, E., 1987. *Socialismo y Nación*. Lima: Mesa Redonda.

Bernales, E., 1993. "Del Parlamento Constitucional a la ficción parlamentaria," in A. Alvarez Rodrich, ed., *El Poder en el Perú*. Lima: APOYO.

Bernedo, J., and E. Chávez O'Brien , 1983. "Los rasgos esenciales de la problemática de los estratos no organizados de la economía," *Apuntes*. Lima: Ministerio de Trabajo y Promoción Social.

Bernedo, J., and I. Yépez del Castillo, 1985. *La Sindicalización en el Perú*. Lima: Fundación Friedrich Ebert and La Pontificia Universidad Católica del Perú.

Blaug, M., 1992. *The Methodology of Economics: Or, How Economists Explain*. Cambridge: Cambridge University Press.

Bollen, K. A., and R. Jackman, 1983. "World System Position, Dependency, and Democracy: The Cross-national Evidence." *American Sociological Review,* 48: 468–79.

Boloña Behr, C., 1993. *Cambio de Rumbo*. Lima: IELM-SIL.

Bonilla, H., and Drake, P. W., 1989. *El Apra de la Ideología a la Praxis*. San Diego: Center for Iberian and Latin American Studies.

Booth, D., and B. Sorj, eds., 1983. *Military Reformism and Social Classes: The Peruvian Experience*. London: Macmillan Press.

Bottomore, T., ed., 1983. *A Dictionary of Marxist Thought*. Cambridge, MA: Harvard University Press.

Bouricaud, F., 1970. *Power and Society in Contemprary Peru*. New York: Praeger.

Bourque, S. C., and K. B. Warren, 1989. "Democracy without Peace: The Cultural Politics of Terror in Peru." *Latin American Research Review,* 24 (1).

Brada, J. C., 1993. "The Transformation from Communism to Capitalism: How Far? How Fast?" *Post-Soviet Affairs,* 9 (2): 87–110.

Bresser Pereira, L. C., J. M. Maravall, and A. Przeworski, 1993. *Economic Reforms in New Democracies: A Social-Democratic Approach*. Cambridge: Cambridge University Press.

Bromley, R., 1978. "Organization, Regulation and Exploitation in the So-Called 'Urban Informal Sector': The Street Traders of Cali, Colombia." *World Development,* 6 (9–10).

Bromley, R., 1990. "A New Path to Development? The Significance and Impact of Hernando de Soto's Ideas on Underdevelopment Production and Reproduction." *Economic Geography,* 66 (1) October: 328–348.

Bromley, R., 1992. "Informality, de Soto Style: From Concept to Policy." Paper presented at the XVII International Congress of the Latin American Studies Association, Los Angeles, September 24–27.

Brown, A., 1993. "The October Crisis of 1993." *Post-Soviet Affairs,* 9 (3): 183–195.

Bustamante, A. , 1990. "Informalidad: superando las viejas tesis," in A. Bustamante et al., *De marginales a informales*. Lima: DESCO.

Bustamante, A., et al., 1990. *De Marginales a Informales*. Lima: DESCO.

Cameron, M. A., 1989. "Cycles of Class Conflict and Regime Change: The Case of Peru, 1956-1986." Unpublished Ph.D. Dissertation, Department of Political Science, University of California at Berkeley.

Cameron, M. A. , 1991a. "Political Parties and the Worker-Employer Cleavage: The Impact of the Informal Sector on Voting in Lima, Peru." *Bulletin of Latin American Research,* 10 (3): 293–313.

Cameron, M. A. , 1991b. "The Politics of the Urban Informal Sector in Peru: Populism, Class and 'Redistributive Combines.'" *Canadian Journal of Latin American and Caribbean Studies,* 16 (31): 79–104.

Cameron, M. A., 1991c. "Canada and Latin America," in F. O. Hampson and C. J. Maule, eds., *After the Cold War: Canada Among Nations 1990-91.* Ottawa: Carleton University Press.

Cameron, M. A., 1992a. "Micro and Macro Logics of Political Conflict: The Informal Sector and Institutional Change in Peru and Mexico," in A. R. M. Ritter, et al. eds., *Latin America to the Year 2000: Reactivating Growth, Improving Equity, Sustaining Democracy.* New York: Praeger.

Cameron, M. A., 1992b. "Rational Resignations: Coalition Building in Peru and the Philippines." *Comparative Political Studies* 25 (2): 229–250.

Campero, G., 1987. *Entre la Sobrevivencia y la Acción Política.* Santiago: ILET.

Canak, W. L., 1984. "The Peripheral State Debate: State Capitalism and B-A Regimes in Latin America." *Latin American Research Review,* 19 (1): 3–36.

Canak, W. L., ed., 1989. *Lost Promises: Debt, Austerity, and Development in Latin America.* Boulder: Westview Press, pp. 216–232.

Caravedo, B., 1987. *Lima: problema nacional.* Lima: GREDES.

Carbonetto, D., et al., 1988. *Lima: Sector Informal.* 2 volumes. Lima: CEDEP.

Carbonetto, D., 1986. "El sector informal urbano: estructura y evidencias," in G. Alarco, ed., *Desafíos Para la Economía Peruana, 1985–1990.* Lima: Centro de Investigación de la Universidad Pacífico.

Cardoso, E., and A. Helwege, 1992. *Latin America's Economy: Diversity, Trends and Conflicts.* Cambridge, MA: MIT Press.

Carey, J. M., and M. S. Shugart, 1994. "Presidential Decree Authority: Toward a Theoretical Understanding." Paper prepared for the XVIII International Congress of the Latin American Studies Association, Atlanta, March 10–12.

Castañeda, J. , 1991. "The Left in Latin America Today: A Sense of Loss." *Harvard International Review,* 13, no. 3 (Spring): 7–9.

Castañeda, J., 1993. "The Intellectual and the State in Latin America." *World Policy Journal* 10, no. 3 (Fall): 89–95.

Castells, M., 1983. *The City and the Grassroots.* Berkeley and Los Angeles: University of California Press.

Castells, M., and A. Portes, 1989. "World Underneath: The Origins, Dynamics, and Effects of the Informal Economy," in A. Portes et al. eds., *The Informal Economy.* Baltimore: Johns Hopkins University Press.

Castillo Ochoa, M., 1992. *La Escena Astillada (Crisis, Acumulación y Actores Sociales).* Lima: DESCO.

Castillo Ochoa, M., and J. Joseph, 1987. "Informales: ¿Hacia un liberalismo chicha?" *El Zorro de Abajo,* no. 7 (June).

CEPAL, 1991. *Balance Preliminar de la Economía de América Latina y el Caribe, 1991.* Santiago: United Nations.

CEPAL, 1988. *El Impacto de la Crisis en Estratos Populares de los Sectores Formal e Informal: Implicancias para la Mediación y el Análisis del Subempleo.* Santiago: División de Desarrollo Social, CEPAL.

Chalmers, D. A., 1977. "The Politicized State in Latin America," in James M. Malloy, ed., *Authoritarianism and Corporatism in Latin America.* Pittsburgh: University of Pittsburgh Press.

Chaplin, D., 1976. *Peruvian Nationalism: A Corporatist Revolution.* New Brunswick, NJ: Transaction Books.

Chávez O'Brien, E., 1983. *El Sector Informal Urbano en Lima Metropolitana.* Lima: Ministerio de Trabajo-DGE/OIT/FNUAP, Seminario Población y Empleo en Lima Metropolitana.

Chávez O'Brien, E., 1987a. *El Mercado Laboral en la Ciudad de Arequipa.* Lima: Fundación M. J. Bustamante de la Fuente.

Chávez O'Brien, E., 1987b. "Los informales: del mito a la realidad." *Quehacer,* no. 49, November–December.

Chávez O'Brien, E., 1990a. "¿Votarón los informales por Fujimori?: Una reveladora encuesta." *Quehacer,* no. 64, May–June: 36–42.

Chávez O'Brien, E., 1990b. "La dinámica del empleo y el rol del SIU en un periodo de inestabilidad económica: 1985–1989." *Socialismo y Participación,* no. 49, March: 47–61.

Chávez O'Brien, E., 1990c. "El empleo en los sectores populares urbanos: de marginales a informales," in A. Bustamante et al., *De Marginales a Informales.* Lima: DESCO.

Checchi, D., 1993. "The Emergence of Populist Experiences in Latin America," in *Development Studies Working Papers.* Torino and Oxford: Centro Studi Luca D'Agliano—Queen Elizabeth House, Oxford University.

Chossudovsky, M. , 1991. "Applying the IMF Macro-Economic Stabilization Package: The Case of Peru," in H. P. Diaz et al. eds., *Forging Identities and Patterns of Development.* Toronto: Canadian Scholars' Press.

Cline, M., A. Corning, and M. Rhodes, 1993. "The Showdown in Moscow: Tracking Public Opinion," *RFE/RL Research Report* 2 (43): 11–16.

Collier, D., 1976. *Squatters and Oligarchs: Authoritarian Rule and Policy Change in Peru.* Baltimore: Johns Hopkins University Press.

Collier, D., 1979. "Overview of the Bureaucratic-Authoritarian Model," in D. Collier, ed., *The New Authoritarianism in Latin America.* Princeton: Princeton University Press.

Collier, D., ed., 1979. *The New Authoritarianism in Latin America.* Princeton: Princeton University Press.

Collier, D., and D. L. Norden, 1992. "Strategic Choice Models of Political Change in Latin America." *Comparative Politics,* 24 (2): 229–244.

Collier, R., and D. Collier, 1991. *Shaping the Political Arena: Critical Junctures, the Labor Movement, and Regime Dynamics in Latin America.* Princeton: Princeton University Press.

Conaghan, C. M., 1992. "Capitalists, Technocrats, and Politicians: Economic Policy Making and Democracy in the Central Andes," in S. Mainwaring et al., eds., *Issues In Democratic Consolidation: The New South American Democracies in Comparative Perspective.* Notre Dame: University of Notre Dame Press.

Conniff, M. L., ed., 1982. *Latin American Populism in Comparative Perspective.* Albuquerque: University of New Mexico Press.

Córdova, M., 1990. "El proyecto neoliberal: la oportunidad perdida." *Quehacer,* no. 64, May–June: 18–21.

Cornelius, W. A., 1975. *Politics and the Migrant Poor in Mexico City.* Stanford: Stanford University Press.

Cornell, A., and K. Roberts, 1990. "Democracy, Counterinsurgency, and Human Rights: The Case of Peru." *Human Rights Quarterly* 12 (4): 529–553.

Cotler, J., 1978. *Clases, Estado y Nación en el Perú.* Lima: Instituto de Estudios Peruanos.

Cotler, J., 1983. "Democracy and National Integration in Peru," in C. McClintock and A. F. Lowenthal, eds., *The Peruvian Experiment Reconsidered.* Princeton: Princeton University Press.

Cotler, J., 1985. "Una saludable indefinición," *Quehacer,* no. 35: 48–49.

Cotler, J., 1986. "The Political Radicalization of Working-Class Youth in Peru." *Cepal Review,* vol. 29.

Cotler, J., 1988. "Los partidos políticos en la democracia peruana," in J. Parodi and L. Pásara, eds., *Democracia, Sociedad y Gobierno en el Perú.* Lima: CEDYS.

Cotler, J., 1993. *Descomposición Política y Autoritarismo en el Perú.* Lima: Instituto de Estudios Peruanos.

Cox, G. W., 1987. *The Efficient Secret: The Cabinet and the Development of Political Parties in Victorian England.* Cambridge: Cambridge University Press.

Crabtree, J., 1985. "Peru: From Belaúnde to Alan García." *Bulletin of Latin American Research,* 14 (2): 75–83.

Cueva, A., 1988. *Las Democracias Restringidas de América Latina.* Quito: Editorial Planeta.

Daeschner, J., 1993. *The War of the End of Democracy: Mario Vargas Llosa Versus Alberto Fujimori.* Lima: Peru Reporting.

DATUM, 1983. *Estudio Permanente Mensual de Opinión Pública.* Lima: DATUM.

De Althaus, J., 1990. "La triste historia del centralismo distributivo," in J. Abugattás et al., *Estado y Sociedad: Relaciones Peligrosas.* Lima: DESCO.

De la Puente, L., 1965. "The Peruvian Revolution: Concepts and Perspectives." *Monthly Review,* 17 (6), November.

De Soto, H., 1989a. *The Other Path: The Invisible Revolution in the Third World.* New York: Harper & Row.

De Soto, H., 1989b. "Structural Adjustment and the Informal Sector," in J. Levitsky, ed., *Microenterprises in Developing Countries.* London: Intermediate Technology Publications.

De Soto, H., 1990. "How I Sell Capitalism to the Left." *ORBIS,* 34 (3): 413–423.

De Soto, H., and S. Schmidheiny, eds., 1991. *Las Nuevas Reglas del Juego: Hacia un desarrollo sostenible en América Latina.* Lima: Editorial Oveja Negra.

Degregori, C. I., et al., 1986a. *Conquistadores de un Nuevo Mundo: De Invasores a Ciudadanos en San Martín de Porres.* Lima: Instituto de Estudios Peruanos.

Degregori, C. I. , 1986b. "'Sendero Luminoso': Los Hondos y Mortales Desencuentros," in E. Ballón, ed., *Movimientos Sociales y Crisis: El caso peruano.* Lima: DESCO.

Degregori, C. I., 1989. *Que Difícil es Ser Dios: Ideología y violencia política en Sendero Luminoso.* Lima: El Zorro de Abajo Ediciones.

Degregori, C. I., 1990. *Ayacucho 1969-1979: El Surgimiento de Sendero Luminoso.* Lima: Instituto de Estudios Peruanos.

Degregori, C. I., et al., 1990. *Tiempos de Ira y Amor*. Lima: DESCO.

Degregori, C. I., and R. Grompone, 1991. *Demonios y Redentores en el Nuevo Perú: Una Tragedia en dos Vueltas*. Lima: Instituto de Estudios Peruanos.

Degregori, C. I., and C. Rivera Paz, 1993. *Perú 1980–1993: Fuerzas Armadas, Subversión, y Democracia*. Lima: Instituto de Estudios Peruanos.

Delich, F. J., 1970. *Crisis y Protesta Social: Córdoba, mayo 1969*. Buenos Aires: Ediciones Signos.

Deutsch, K., 1966. *Nationalism and Social Communication*. Cambridge, MA: MIT Press.

Di Tella, T. S., 1965. "Populism and Reform in Latin America," in C. Veliz, ed., *Obstacles to Change in Latin America*. London: Oxford University Press.

Diamond, L., and J. J. Linz, 1989. "Introduction: Politics, Society, and Democracy in Latin America," in L. Diamond, J. J. Linz, and S. M. Lipset, eds., *Democracy in Developing Countries: Latin America*. Boulder: Lynne Rienner.

Diamond, L., J. J. Linz, and S. M. Lipset, eds., 1989. *Democracy in Developing Countries: Latin America*. Boulder: Lynne Rienner.

Diaz Alejandro, C., 1988. "Open Economy, Closed Polity?" in *Trade, Development and the World Economy*. Oxford: Basil Blackwell.

Dietz, H. A., 1982. "Movilización, austeridad y votaciones en el Perú: las masas de Lima como objetivo, víctimas y agentes de decisión." *Socialismo y Participación*, no. 18.

Dietz, H. A., 1985. "Political Participation in the Barriadas: An Extension and Reexamination." *Comparative Political Studies* 18 (3).

Dietz, H. A., 1986–87. "Aspects of Peruvian Politics: Electoral Politics in Peru, 1978–86." *Journal of Interamerican Studies and World Affairs*, 28 (4), Winter.

Dietz, H. A., 1992. "Elites in an Unconsolidated Democracy: Peru during the 1980s," in J. Higley and R. Gunther, eds., *Elites and Democratic Consolidation in Latin America and Southern Europe*. Cambridge: Cambridge University Press.

Diez Canseco, J., 1992. "La Izquierda en el Perú: el problema nacional y la democracia," *Nueva Sociedad*, no. 117 (January–February): 77–87.

Dornbusch, R., and S. Edwards, 1991. "The Macroeconomics of Populism," in R. Dornbusch and S. Edwards, eds., *The Macroeconomics of Populism in Latin America*. Chicago: University of Chicago Press.

Dos Santos, T., 1993. "Brazil's Controlled Purge: The Impeachment of Fernando Collor." *NACLA: Report on the Americas* 17 (3): 17–21.

Downs, A., 1957. *An Economic Theory of Democracy*. New York: Harper & Row.

Drake, P. W., 1982. "Conclusion: Requiem for Populism?" in M. L. Conniff, ed., *Latin American Populism in Comparative Perspective* Albuquerque: University of New Mexico Press.

Drake, P. W., 1991. "Comment," in R. Dornbusch and S. Edwards, eds., *The Macroeconomics of Populism in Latin America*. Chicago: University of Chicago Press.

Durand, F., 1988. *Alan García y los Empresarios*. Lima: DESCO.

Durand, F., 1989. "La nueva derecha peruana: orígenes y dilemas." *Estudios Sociológicos* 8 (23): 351–374.

Durand, F., 1990. "The Peruvian Right and Democracy," in D. Chalmers et al., eds., *The Right and Democracy in Latin America*. New York: Praeger.

Eckstein, H., 1975. "Case Study and Theory in Political Science," in F. Greenstein and N. W. Polsby, eds., *Handbook of Political Science, Vol 7: Strategies of Inquiry.* Reading, MA: Addison-Wesley.

Eckstein, S., ed., 1989. *Power and Popular Protest: Latin American Social Movements.* Berkeley and Los Angeles: University of California Press.

Elster, J., 1989. *The Cement of Society: A Study of Social Order.* Cambridge: Cambridge University Press.

Enelow, J. M., and M. J. Hinich, eds., 1990a. *Advances in the Spatial Theory of Voting.* Cambridge: Cambridge University Press.

Enelow, J. M., and M. J. Hinich, eds., 1990b. "Introduction," in J. M. Enelow and M. J. Hinich, eds., *Advances in the Spatial Theory of Voting.* Cambridge: Cambridge University Press.

Evans, P., 1989. "Predatory, Developmental and Other Apparatuses: A Comparative Analysis of the Third World State," in A. Portes and D. Kincaid, eds., *Sociologial Forum,* 4 (4).

Farnsworth, E., 1988a. "Peru: A Nation in Crisis." *World Policy Journal,* 5 (4): 725–758.

Farnsworth, E., 1988b. "On Peru's Future: Alan García Pérez, Mario Vargas Llosa, Rolando Ames." *World Policy Journal,* 5 (4): 747–779.

Ferrero Costa, E., 1993. "Peru's Presidential Coup." *Journal of Democracy,* 4 (1): 28–40.

Figueroa, A., et al., 1986. *Población, Empleo y Tecnología.* Lima: Pontificia Universidad Católica del Perú.

Fishlow, A., 1991. "The Latin American State." *Journal of Economic Perspectives* 4 (3): 61–74.

Foxley, A., 1986. "After Authoritarianism: Political Alternatives," in A. Foxley, M. S. McPherson, and G. O'Donnell, eds., *Development, Democracy, and the Art of Trespassing.* Notre Dame: University of Notre Dame Press.

Foye, S., 1993. "Confrontation in Moscow: The Army Backs Yeltsin, for Now." *RFE/RL Research Report,* 2 (42): 10–15.

Flores Galindo, A., 1988. *Tiempos de Plagas.* Lima: El Caballo Rojo.

Franco, C., 1989. *Informales: Nuevos Rostros en la Vieja Lima.* Lima: CEDEP.

Franco, C., 1992. "La plebe urbana, el populismo y la imagen del 'alumbramiento,'" in A. Adrianzén and E. Ballón, eds., *Lo Popular en America Latina: ¿Una Visión en Crisis?* Lima: DESCO.

Frieden, J. A., 1991. *Debt, Development, and Democracy.* Princeton: Princeton University Press.

Galín, P., et al., 1986. *Asalariados y clases populares en Lima.* Lima: Instituto de Estudios Peruanos.

Galín, P., 1986. "Asalariados, precarización y condiciones de trabajo." *Nueva Sociedad,* no. 85 (September–October).

Galín, P., 1991. "El sector informal urbano: conceptos y críticas." *Nueva Sociedad,* no. 113, May–June: 45–50.

García Pérez, A., 1986. Interview. *Third World Quarterly,* 8 (4): 125–134.

Geddes, B., 1991. "A Game Theoretic Model of Reform in Latin American Democracies." *American Political Science Review,* 85 (2): 371–92.

Geddes, B., 1993. "Uses and Limitations of Rational Choice in the Study of Politics in Developing Countries." Paper prepared for presentation at the American Political Science Association meetings, Washington, D.C., September 1993.

Ghersi, E., ed., 1989. *El Comercio Ambulatorio en Lima.* Lima: Instituto Libertad y Democracia.

Gibson, E., 1990. "Democracy and the New Electoral Right in Argentina." *Journal of Interamerican Studies and World Affairs,* 32 (3): 177–228.

Gorriti, G., 1990. *Sendero: Historia de la Guerra Milenaria en el Perú.* Lima: Editorial Apoyo.

Gorriti, G., 1993. "The Unshining Path." *New Republic,* February 8: 19–23.

Graham, C. L., 1990. "Peru's APRA Party in Power: Impossible Revolution, Relinquished Reform." *Journal of Interamerican Studies and World Affairs,* 32 (3): 75–115.

Graham, C. L., 1992. *Peru's APRA: Parties, Politics, and the Elusive Quest for Democracy.* Boulder: Lynne Rienner.

Granados, M.J., 1987. "El PCP Sendero Luminoso: aproximaciones a su ideología." *Socialismo y Participación,* no. 37 March.

Greenberg, J., and K. A. Shepsle, 1987. "The Effect of Electoral Rewards in Multiparty Competition with Entry." *American Political Science Review,* 81: 525–37.

Grompone, R., 1986. *Talleristas y Vendedores Ambulantes en Lima.* Lima: DESCO.

Grompone, R., 1987. "El Instituto Libertad y Democracia: El difícil populismo de derecha," *Quehacer,* no. 49.

Grompone, R., 1990. "Las lecturas políticas de la informalidad," in A. Bustamante et al., *De marginales a informales.* Lima: DESCO.

Grompone, R., 1991. *El velero en el viento: Política y sociedad en Lima.* Lima: Instituto de Estudios Peruanos.

Guillermoprieto, A., 1990. "Letter from Lima." *New Yorker,* October 29: 116–129.

Guillermoprieto, A., 1993. "Down the Shining Path," *New Yorker,* February 8: 64–75.

Guzman, L. H., 1992. *Políticos en Uniforme: Un balance del poder del EPS.* Managua: Instituto Nicaragüense de Estudios Socio-Políticos.

Haak, R. et al., eds., 1987. *Estrategias de Vida en el Sector Urbano Popular.* Lima: DESCO.

Hagopian, F., 1993. "After Regime Change: Authoritarian Legacies, Political Representation, and the Democratic Future of South America." *World Politics,* 45 (3): 464–500.

Handleman, H., and T. G. Sanders., 1981. *Military Government and the Movement Toward Democracy in South America.* Bloomington: Indiana University Press.

Harsanyi, J. C., and R. Selten, 1988. *A General Theory of Equilibrium Selection in Games.* Cambridge, MA: The MIT Press.

Hartlyn, J., and S. A. Morley, eds., 1986. *Latin American Political Economy: Financial Crisis and Political Change.* Boulder: Westview.

Haya de la Torre, A., 1987. *El Retorno de la Barbarie: La Matanza en los Penales de Lima en 1986.* Lima: Bahía.

Higley, J., and R. Gunther, eds., 1992. *Elites and Democratic Consolidation in Latin America and Southern Europe.* Cambridge: Cambridge University Press.

Hilliker, G., 1971. *The Politics of Reform in Peru: The Aprista and Other Parties.* Baltimore: Johns Hopkins University Press.

Hirschman, A. O., 1979. "The Turn to Authoritarianism and the Search for Its Economic Determinants," in D. Collier, ed., *The New Authoritarianism in Latin America.* Princeton: Princeton University Press.

Huber, E., D. Rueschemeyer, and J. D. Stephens, 1993. "The Impact of Economic Development on Democracy." *Journal of Economic Perspectives* 7 (3): 71–85.

Huntington, S. P., 1984. "Will More Countries become Democratic?" *Political Science Quarterly,* 99 (2): 193–218.

Inter-Campus, 1990. *El Debate.* Lima: Universidad del Pacífico.

Inter-Church Committee on Human Rights in Latin America., 1992. *The April 5th Coup: A Cure Worse than the Illness?* Ottawa: Canadian Council for International Co-operation.

Jaquette, J., and A. F. Lowenthal, 1987. "The Peruvian Experiment in Retrospect." *World Politics* 39 (2), January.

Jochamowitz, L., 1993. *Ciudadano Fujimori: La Construcción de un Político.* Lima: PEISA.

Jonas, S., 1994. "Text and Subtext of the Guatemalan Political Drama." *LASA Forum,* 24, (4): 3–9.

Kafka, F., 1985. "Rentismo, regulación estatal y sector informal." *Finanzas Públicas,* 1 (1): 105–146.

Kantor, H., 1966. *The Ideology and Program of the Peruvian Aprista Movement.* New York: Octagon Books.

Katznelson, I., 1986. "Working Class Formation: Constructing Cases and Comparisons," in I. Katznelson and A. Zolberg, *Working Class Formation: Nineteenth Century Patterns in Western Europe and the United States.* Princeton: Princeton University Press.

Kaufman, R. R., 1979. "Industrial Change and Authoritarian Rule in Latin America: A Concrete Review of the Bureaucratic-Authoritarian Model," in D. Collier, ed., *The New Authoritarianism in Latin America.* Princeton: Princeton University Press.

Kaufman, R. R., 1986. "Democratic and Authoritarian Responses to the Debt Issue: Argentina, Brazil, Mexico," in M. Kahler, ed., *The Politics of International Debt.* Ithaca: Cornell University Press.

Kay, C., 1985. "Assessing the Peruvian 'Revolution.'" *Bulletin of Latin American Research,* 4 (2).

Kingstone, P. R., 1994. "Shaping Business Interests: The Politics of Neo-liberalism in Brazil, 1985–1992." Unpublished Ph.D. Dissertation, Department of Political Science, University of California at Berkeley.

Kitschelt, H., 1992. "Political Regime Change: Structure and Process-Driven Explanations?" *American Political Science Review,* 86 (4): 1028–34.

Klarén, P. , 1973. *Modernization, Dislocation and Aprismo.* Austin: University of Texas Press.

Koep, R., 1993. "Sendero and the 'Senderologists': A Revolutionary Movement and its Storytellers." Unpublished M.A. Research Essay, Department of Political Science, Carleton University, Ottawa.

Kreps, D. M., 1990. *Game Theory and Economic Modelling.* Oxford: Clarendon Press.

Laclau, E., 1977. *Politics and Ideology in Marxist Theory: Capitalism-Fascism-Populism.* London: New Left Books.

Lehmann, D., 1990. *Democracy and Development in Latin America.* Cambridge: Polity Press.

Letts, R., 1981. *La Izquierda Peruana: Organizaciones y Tendencias.* Lima: Mosca Azul.

Levi, M., 1988. *Of Rule and Revenue.* Berkeley and Los Angeles: University of California Press.

Levine, D., 1988. "Paradigm Lost: Dependence to Democracy." *World Politics,* 40 (3): 377–94.

Lewis, A. W. , 1971. "Economic Development with Unlimited Supplies of Labour," in A. N. Agarwala and S. P. Singh, eds., *The Economics of Underdevelopment.* Oxford: Oxford University Press.

Lins da Silva, C. E., 1993. "Brazil's Struggle with Democracy." *Current History,* 92 (572): 126–129.

Lipset, S. M., 1960. *Political Man.* Garden City, NY: Anchor Books.

Lizarzaburu T. P., 1976. "La caída del régimen Belaúndista: Un análisis político o la trágico-media de los hombres de renovación." Unpublished manuscript, Department of Social Sciences, Pontificia Universidad Católica del Perú, Lima.

Lomnitz, L. A., 1977. *Networks and Marginality: Life in a Mexican Shantytown.* New York: Academic Press.

López, J. S., 1993. "Perú, 1992: De la dictablanda a la democradura," *Quehacer,* no. 82, March–April: 35–38.

Lowenthal, A. F., ed., 1975. *The Peruvian Experiment: Continuity and Change under Military Rule.* Princeton: Princeton University Press.

Lowenthal, A. F., ed., 1988. *Latin American and Caribbean Contemporary Record, Volume V: 1985–86.* New York: Holmes and Meier.

Lynch, N., 1992. *La Transición Conservadora: Movimiento Social y Democracia en el Perú, 1975–1978.* Lima: El Zorro de Abajo Ediciones.

MacEwan, A., 1988. "Transitions from Authoritarian Rule." *Latin American Perspectives* 15 (3): 115–30.

Machacuay, S., 1990. "El 'shock,' ese viejo conocido." *Quehacer,* no. 64, May–June: 44–47.

Machiavelli, N., 1975. *The Prince.* Middlesex: Penguin Books.

Mainwaring, S., G. O'Donnell, and J. S. Valenzuela, eds., 1992. *Issues in Democratic Consolidation: The New South American Democracies in Comparative Perspective.* Notre Dame: University of Notre Dame Press.

Malloch Brown, M., 1991. "The Consultant," *Granta* 36 (Summer): 88–95.

Malloy, J., and M. A. Seligson, eds., 1987. *Authoritarians and Democrats: Regime Transition in Latin America.* Pittsburgh: University of Pittsburgh Press.

María, G. J., 1985. "Pobreza, Población y Vivienda en Distritos de Lima Metropolitana," in N. Henriquez and A. Ponce, eds., *Lima: población, trabajo y política.* Lima: Pontificia Universidad Católica del Perú.

Marshall, T. H. , 1953. "The Nature of Class Conflict," in R. Bendix and S. M. Lipset, eds., *Class, Status and Power.* New York: Free Press.

Matos Mar, J., 1985. *Desborde Popular y Crisis del Estado.* Lima: Instituto de Estudios Peruanos.

Mauceri, P., 1989. *Militares: Insurgencia y Democratización en el Perú.* Lima: Instituto de Estudios Peruanos.

Mauceri, P., 1991. "State Under Siege: Popular Mobilization and the Weak State in Peru, 1973–1990." Unpublished Ph.D. Dissertation, Department of Political Science, Columbia.

Mauceri, P.. Forthcoming. "State Reform, Coalitions and the Liberal Authoritarian Coup in Peru." *Latin American Research Review.*

Mayer, E., 1991. "Peru in Deep Trouble: Mario Vargas Llosa's 'Inquest in the Andes' Reexamined." *Cultural Anthropology,* 6 (4): 466–504.

McClintock, C., and A. F. Lowenthal, eds., 1983. *The Peruvian Experiment Reconsidered.* Princeton: Princeton University Press.

McClintock, C., 1989. "The Prospects for Democratic Consolidation in a 'Least Likely' Case: Peru." *Comparative Politics,* 21 (2): 127–148.

McClintock, C., 1993. "Peru's Fujimori: A Caudillo Derails Democracy." *Current History*, 92 (572): 112–119.

McClintock, C., 1994. "The Breakdown of Constitutional Democracy in Peru." Paper presented at the XVIII International Congress of the Latin American Studies Association, Atlanta, March 10–12.

McDonald, R. H., and J. M. Ruhl, 1989. *Party Politics and Elections in Latin America*. Boulder: Westview Press.

Menéndez-Carrión, A., 1986. *La Conquista del Voto*. Quito: Editora Nacional.

Meneses, M. and Díaz, L., 1978. *Localización Espacial y Estructura Occupacional en Lima Metropolitana*. Lima: CISEPA, Serie Población.

Ministerio de Trabajo, 1988. *Encuesta Niveles de Empleo en Lima Metropolitana 1986–1987*. Lima: Ministerio de Trabajo, DGE-DEEM, Sub-Dirección de Encuestas.

Montoya, R., 1992. *Al Borde Del Naufragio (Democracia, Violencia y Problema Etnico en el Perú)*. Lima: Cuadernos de SUR.

Moore, B., Jr., 1966. *The Social Origins of Dictatorship and Democracy*. Boston: Beacon Press.

Morales, E., 1990. *Cocaine: White Gold Rush in Peru*. Tucson: University Arizona Press.

Most, B. A., 1991. *Changing Authoritarian Rule and Public Policy in Argentina, 1930–1970*. Boulder: Lynne Rienner.

Mujica Petit, J., 1988. *Para Defender la Establidad Laboral*. Lima: CEDAL.

Murrell, P., 1993. "What is Shock Therapy? What Did it Do in Poland and Russia?" *Post-Soviet Affairs*, 9 (2): 111–140.

Nelson, J. M. et al., 1989. *Fragile Coalitions: The Politics of Economic Adjustment*. Washington, D.C.: Overseas Development Center.

Nieto M., J., 1983. *Izquierda y Democracia en el Perú, 1975-1980*. Lima: DESCO.

Nieto, M. J., 1988. "I Congreso Nacional de Izquierda Unida: Y Sin Embargo . . . Se Mueve," *Quehacer*, July–August , no. 53: 34–38.

North, L., 1973. "Origins and Development of the Peruvian Aprista Party." Unpublished Ph.D. Dissertation, Department of Political Science, University of California, Berkeley.

North, D. C., 1989 . "Institutions and Economic Growth: An Historical Introduction." *World Development*, 17 (9): 1319–32.

North, D. C., 1990. "A Transaction Cost Theory of Politics." *Journal of Theoretical Politics*, 2 (4) October: 355–367.

O'Donnell, G., 1973. *Modernization and Bureaucratic-Authoritarianism: Studies in South American Politics*. Berkeley: Institute of International Studies.

O'Donnell, G., et al., 1986. *Transitions from Authoritarian Rule*. 4 Vols. Baltimore: Johns Hopkins University Press.

O'Donnell, G., 1988a. "State and Alliances in Argentina, 1956–1976" in R. Bates, ed., *Toward a Political Economy of Development: A Rational Choice Perspective*. Berkeley and Los Angeles: University of California Press, pp, 176–205.

O'Donnell, G., 1988b. *Argentina 1966–1973: Triumphs, Defeats, and Crises*. Berkeley and Los Angeles: University of California Press.

O'Donnell, G., 1992. "Delegative Democracy?" *Kellogg Institute Working Paper,* no. 172.

O'Maolain, C. ed., 1985. *Latin American Political Movements*. New York: Longman.

Ordeshook, P. C., 1986. *Game Theory and Political Theory: An introduction.* Cambridge: Cambridge University Press.

Ordeshook, P. C., 1992. *A Political Theory Primer.* New York: Routledge.

Ortiz de Zevallos, F., 1989. *The Peruvian Puzzle.* New York: Priority Press.

Osterling, J. P., 1981. "The Informal Sector in Metropolitan Lima: The Case of its Street Vendors." Discussion paper, presented at CEDLA seminar, The Informal Sector in Third World Cities.

Palfrey, T., 1984. "Spatial Equilibrium with Entry." *Review of Economic Studies,* 51: 139–56.

Palmer, D. S., 1984. "The Changing Political Economy of Peru under Military and Civilian Rule." *Inter-American Economic Affairs,* 37 (4), Spring.

Palmer, D. S., ed., 1992. *The Shining Path of Peru.* New York: St. Martin's Press.

Palma, D., 1987. *La Informalidad, lo Popular y el Cambio Social.* Lima: DESCO.

Panfichi, A., and C. Francis, 1993. "Liderazgos políticos autoritarios en el Perú." *Debates en Sociologia,* 18: 227–47.

Paredes, P., and Tello, G., 1988a. *Pobreza Urbana y Trabajo Femenino.* Lima: ADEC-ATC.

Paredes, P., 1988b. *Las Estrategias de Contratación Laboral: La Experiencia del PROEM y sus Alternativas.* Lima: Fundación Friedrich Ebert.

Pareja Pflucker, P., and A. Gatti Murriel, 1993. *Elecciones Municipales en las provincias de Lima y Callao.* Lima: Fundación Friedrich Ebert.

Parker, D., 1987. "White Collar Unionization and Middle Class Formation: An Introduction to the Issues." Unpublished manuscript, Department of Political Science, Stanford University.

Parodi, J., 1986a. *"Ser obrero es algo relativo . . ." Obreros, Clasismo y Política.* Lima: Instituto de Estudios Peruanos.

Parodi, J., 1986b. "La Demobilización del Sindicalismo Industrial Peruano en el Segundo Belaúndismo." *Movimientos Sociales y Crisis: El Caso Peruano,* Lima: DESCO.

Parodi, J. ed., 1993. *Los Pobres, la Ciudad y la Política.* Lima: CEDYS.

Pásara, L., 1989. *La Izquierda en la Escena Pública.* Lima: CEDYS and Fundación Friedrich Ebert.

Pásara, L., 1993. "El ocaso de los partidos," in A. Alvarez Rodrich, ed., *El Poder en el Perú.* Lima: APOYO.

Pásara, L., et al., 1993. *La Otra Cara de la Luna: Nuevos Actores Sociales en el Perú.* Lima: CEDYS.

Pastor, M., Jr., and C. Wise, 1992. "Peruvian Economic Policy in the 1980s: From Orthodoxy to Heterodoxy and Back." *Latin American Research Review,* 27 (1): 83–117.

Payne, J. L., 1965. *Labor and Politics in Peru: The System of Political Bargaining.* New Haven: Yale University Press.

Perlman, J., 1986. *The Myth of Marginality.* Berkeley and Los Angeles: University of California Press.

Petras, J. F., and M. Zeitlin, eds., 1968. *Latin America, Reform or Revolution?* Greenwich, CT: Fawcett Publications.

Petras, J. F. and E. S. Herman, 1986. "'Resurgent Democracy' in Latin America: Rhetoric and Reality," in J. F. Petras, *Latin America: Bankers, Generals, and the Struggle for Social Justice.* Rowman & Littlefield.

Pike, F. B., 1986. *The Politics of the Miraculous in Peru: Haya de la Torre and the Spiritualist Tradition.* Lincoln: University of Nebraska Press.

Pinilla, C. S., 1986. *Concepción, Características y Promoción del Sector Informal.* Lima: IDESI.

Pinilla, C. S., 1988a. *La Mujer y el Sector Informal.* Lima: IDESI

Pinilla C., S., 1988b. "Políticas y programas de promoción del empleo: El PAIT y IDESI." Paper presented at a conference at the University of California at San Diego.

Ponce, A., and Vallenas, S., 1985. "Un análisis de votación diferencial en la provincia de Lima, 1978–1983," in N. Henriquez and A. Ponce, eds., *Lima: Población, Trabajo y Política.* Lima: Pontificia Universidad Católica del Perú.

Poole, D., and G. Rénique, 1991. "The New Chroniclers of Peru: US Scholars and their 'Shining Path' of Peasant Rebellion." *Bulletin of Latin American Research,* 10 (2): 133–91.

Poole, D., and G. Rénique, 1992. *Peru: Time of Fear.* London: Latin American Bureau.

Portes, A., and Walton, J., 1981. *Labor, Class and the International System.* New York: Academic Press.

Portes, A., 1983. "The Informal Sector: Definition, Controversy, and Relation to National Development." *Review* 8, no, 1: 151–174.

Portes, A., and L. Benton, 1984. "Industrial Development and Labor Absorption: A Reinterpretation." *Population and Development Review,* 10 (4): 589–611.

Portes, A., 1985. "Latin American Class Structures: Their Composition and Change during the Last Decades." *Latin American Research Review,* 20 (3): 7–39.

Portes, A., et al., 1986. "The Urban Informal Sector in Uruguay: Its Internal Structure, Characteristics, and Effects." *World Development,* 14 (6): 727–41.

Portes, A., et al., eds., 1989. *The Informal Economy.* Baltimore: Johns Hopkins University Press.

Portes, A., and M. Johns, 1989. "The Polarization of Class and Space in the Contemporary Latin American City," in L. Canak, ed., *Lost Promises.* Boulder: Westview Press.

Portocarrero, G., and R. Tapia Rojas, 1992. *Trabajadores, Sindicalismo y Política en el Perú de Hoy.* Lima: ADEC/ATC.

Powell, S. , 1976. "Political Participation in the Barriadas: A Case Study," in D. Chaplin, ed., *Peruvian Nationalism: A Corporatist Revolution.* New Brunswick, NJ: Transaction Books.

PREALC, 1981. *El Sector Informal: Funcionamiento y Políticas.* Santiago: Oficina Internacional de Trabajo.

Przeworski, A., and H. Teune, 1970. *The Logic of Comparative Social Inquiry.* New York: Wily.

Przeworski, A., 1986. "Some Problems in the Study of the Transition to Democracy," in G. O'Donnell, P. C. Schmitter, and L. Whitehead eds., *Transitions to Authoritarian Rule: Comparative Perspectives.* Baltimore: Johns Hopkins University Press.

Przeworski, A., 1985. *Capitalism and Social Democracy.* Cambridge: Cambridge University Press.

Przeworski, A., 1991. *Democracy and the Market: Political and Economic Reforms in Eastern Europe and Latin America.* Cambridge: Cambridge University Press.

Przeworski, A., and J. Sprague, 1986. *Paper Stones: A History of Electoral Socialism.* Chicago: University of Chicago Press.

Przeworski, A., and F. Limongi, 1993. "Political Regimes and Economic Growth." *Journal of Economic Perspectives* 7 (3): 51–69.

Raczynski, D., 1977. *El sector informal urbano: controversias é interrogantes.* Santiago: CIEPLAN.

Rahr, A., 1993. "The October Revolt: Mass Unrest or Putsch?" *RFE/RL Research Report,* 2 (44): 1–4.

Remmer, K., and G. Merkx, 1982. "Bureaucratic-Authoritarianism Revisted." *Latin American Research Review,* 17 (2): 3–40.

Remmer, K., 1990. "Democracy and Economic Crisis: The Latin American Experience." *World Politics,* 42 (3): 315–35.

Riker, W. H. , 1957. "Events and Situations." *The Journal of Philosophy,* 54 (3): 57–70.

Riker, W. H., 1962. *The Theory of Political Coalitions.* New Haven: Yale University Press.

Rivero, J., 1990. "'El Otro Sendero' al trasluz." *Socialismo y Participación,* 4–9 March: 79–92.

Roberts, K., 1992. "In Search of a New Identity: Dictatorship, Democracy, and the Evolution of the Left in Chile and Peru." Unpublished Ph.D. Dissertation, Department of Political Science, Stanford University.

Roberts, K. and M. Peceny, 1993. "Human Rights and U.S. Policy Toward Peru," in M. A. Cameron and P. Mauceri, eds., *The Peruvian Labyrinth.* Unpublished manuscript.

Robles, V., 1989. "Los jóvenes del Fredemo," *Quehacer,* no. 60, August–September.

Rochabrun Silva, G., 1988. "Crisis, Democracy, and the Left in Peru." *Latin American Perspectives,* no. 58, 15 (3).

Rojas Samanéz, A., 1986. *Partidos Políticos en el Perú.* Lima.

Roncagliolo, R., 1990. "Elecciones en Lima: cifras testarudas." *Quehacer,* no. 62.

Roncagliolo, R., 1980. *¿Quién Ganó? Elecciones 1931–80.* Lima: DESCO.

Rospigliosi, F., 1987. *Los Jóvenes Obreros de los '80: Inseguridad, Eventualidad y Radicalismo.* Lima: Documento de Trabajo #18. Instituto de Estudios Peruanos.

Rospigliosi, Fernando, 1988. *Juventud Obrera y Partidos de Izquierda: De la Dictadura a la Democracia.* Lima: Instituto de Estudios Peruanos.

Rueschemeyer, D., E. Huber Stephens, and J. D. Stephens, 1992. *Capitalist Development and Democracy.* Chicago: University of Chicago Press.

Sabel, C. F., 1982. *Work and Politics.* Cambridge: Cambridge University Press.

Salcedo, J. M., 1989. "IU: ¿El drama recién empieza?" *Quehacer,* no. 57, January–February: 26–40.

Salcedo, J. M., 1990. *Tsunami Presidente.* Lima: Editorial Venus.

Salcedo, J. M., 1992. "Sí hay alternativas," *Quehacer,* no. 79, September–October: 11–23.

Sanborn, C., 1989. "El Apra en un contexto de cambio, 1968–1988," in H. Bonilla and P. W. Drake, eds., *El Apra de la Ideología a la Praxis.* San Diego: Center for Iberia and Latin American Studies.

Sanchez Albavera, F., 1992. "El difícil camino de Fujimori." *Cono Sur,* 11 (2): 1–16.

Schelling, T., 1960. *The Strategy of Conflict.* London: Oxford University Press.

Schmidt, G. D., 1991. "Electoral Earthquake in Peru: Understanding the Fujimori Phenomenon." Paper Prepared for Delivery at the Annual Meeting of the Illinois Conference for Latin American Studies, Loyola University of Chicago, November 1–2.

Schmidt, G. D., 1994. "Understanding the Fujimori Tsunami: Electoral Rules and Partisan Competition in the 1990 Peruvian Elections." Unpublished manuscript, Department of Political Science, Northern Illinois University.

Scully, T. R., 1992. *Rethinking the Center: Party Politics in Nineteenth and Twentieth Century Chile*. Stanford: Stanford University Press.

Seligson, M. A., 1987. "Democratization in Latin America: The Current Cycle," in J. Malloy and M. A. Seligson, eds., *Authoritarians and Democrats: Regime Transition in Latin America*. Pittsburgh: University of Pittsburgh Press.

Sheahan, J., 1987. *Patterns of Development in Latin America: Poverty, Repression, and Economic Strategy*. Princeton: Princeton University Press.

Shepsle, K. A., 1991. *Models of Multiparty Electoral Competition*. Chur, Switzerland: Harwood Academic Publishers.

Shepsle, K. A., and R. N. Cohen, 1990. "Multiparty Competition, Entry, and Entry Deterrence in Spatial Models of Elections," in J. M. Enelow and M. J. Hinich, eds., *Advances in the Spatial Theory of Voting*. Cambridge: Cambridge University Press.

Shugart, M. S., 1992. "Guerrillas and Elections: An Institutionalist Perspective on the Costs of Conflict and Competition." *International Studies Quarterly* 36: 121–52.

Shugart, M. S., and J. M. Carey, 1992. *Presidents and Assemblies: Constitutional Design and Electoral Dynamics*. Cambridge: Cambridge University Press.

Simes, D., 1994. "The Return of Russian History." *Foreign Affairs*, 73 (1): 67–82.

Skocpol, T., and M. Sommers, 1980. "The Uses of Comparative History in Macrosocial Inquiry." *Comparative Studies in Society and History*, 12 (2).

Smith, M. L., 1992a. "Taking the High Ground: Shining Path and the Andes," in D. S. Palmer, ed., *The Shining Path of Peru*. New York: St. Martin's Press.

Smith, M. L., 1992b. "Congressional Elections Raise Questions about Peru's Future." *The Sendero File*, no. 5, November: 1–4.

Smith, P. H., 1991. "Crisis and Democracy in Latin America." *World Politics*, 43 (July): 608–34.

Snidal, D., 1986. "The Game *Theory* of International Politics," in K. A. Oye ed., *Cooperation Under Anarchy*. Princeton: Princeton University Press.

Snyder, G. H., and P. Diesing, 1977. *Conflict Among Nations: Bargaining, Decision Making, and System Structure in International Crises*. Princeton: Princeton University Press.

Squire, L., 1981. *Employment Policy in Developing Countries: A Survey of Issues and Evidence*. New York: Oxford University Press.

Stallings, B., and R. Kaufman, eds., 1989. *Debt and Democracy in Latin America*. Boulder: Westview.

Starn, O., 1991. "Missing the Revolution: Anthropologists and the War in Peru." *Cultural Anthropology*, 6 (1): 63–91.

Starn, O., 1992. "New Literature on Peru's Sendero Luminoso." *Latin American Research Review*, 27 (2): 212–26.

Stein, S., and C. Monge, 1988. *La Crisis del Estado Patrimonial en el Perú*. Lima: Instituto de Estudios Peruanos and University of Miami.

Stepan, A., 1978. *State and Society: Peru in Comparative Perspective*. Princeton: Princeton University Press.

Stephens, E. H., 1983. "The Peruvian Military Government, Labor Mobilization, and the Political Strength of the Left." *Latin American Research Review*, 18 (2).

Stokes, D., 1963. "Spatial Models of Party Competition." *American Political Science Review,* 57: 368–77.

Stokes, S. C., 1988. "Confrontation and Accommodation: Political Consciousness and Behavior in Urban Lower Class Peru." Unpublished Ph.D. Dissertation, Department of Political Science, Stanford.

Stokes, S. C., 1991. "Politics and Latin America's Urban Poor: Reflections from a Lima Shantytown." *Latin American Research Review,* 26: 75–101.

Strong, S., 1993. *Shining Path: The World's Deadliest Revolutionary Force.* London: Fontana.

Sulmont, D., 1977. *Historia del movimiento obrero en el Perú, de 1890 a 1977.* Lima: Tarea.

Tarazona-Sevillano, G., 1990. *Sendero Luminoso and the Threat of Narcoterrorism.* New York: Praeger.

Taylor, L., 1986. "Peru's Alan García: Supplanting the Old Order," *Third World Quarterly.*

Taylor, L., 1990. "One Step Forward, Two Steps Back: The Peruvian *Izquierda Unida* 1980–1990." *The Journal of Communist Studies,* 6 (3): 108–119.

Teague. E., 1993a. "Yeltsin's Difficult Road toward Elections," *RFE/RL Research Report* 2 (41): 1–4.

Teague. E., 1993b. "Yeltsin Disbands the Soviets." *RFE/RL Research Report,* 2 (43): 1–5.

Tilly, C., 1984. "Demographic Origins of the European Proletariat," in D. Levine, ed., *Proletarianization and Family Life.* New York: Academic Press.

Todaro, M. P., 1985. *Economic Development in the Third World.* New York: Longman.

Tokman, V. E., 1978. "An Exploration into the Nature of Informal-Formal Sector Relationships." *World Development,* 6 (9–10).

Tokman, V. E., 1987. "El sector informal: quince años después." *El Trimestre Económico,* 54, no. 3, July–September.

Tolz, V., 1993. "The Moscow Crisis and the Future of Democracy in Russia." *RFE/RL Research Report,* 2 (42): 1–9.

Torres Guzmán, A., 1989. *Perfil del Elector.* Lima: APOYO.

Touraine, A., 1987. *Actores Sociales y Sistemas Políticos en América Latina.* Santiago: PREALC.

Tovar, T., 1991. "El discreto desencanto frente a los actores: Modernidad, revolución y anomía en los sectores populares." *Páginas,* 111: 25–39.

Tovar, T., 1992. "La política en cielo o la oreja en el suelo. Golpe, democracia y mentalidad popular." *Páginas,* 116: 7–26.

Tsebelis, G., 1988. "When do Allies Become Rivals?" *Comparative Politics,* 20: 233–40.

Tsebelis, G., 1990. *Nested Games: Rational Choices in Comparative Politics.* Berkeley and Los Angeles: University of California Press.

Tueros, M., 1984. "Los trabajadores informales de Lima: ¿Qué piensan de la política?" *Socialismo y Participación,* no. 28, December.

Tuesta, F., 1983. *Elecciones municipales: Cifras y Escenario político.* Lima: DESCO.

Tuesta, F., 1985. *El Nuevo Rostro Electoral: Las Municipales del 83.* Lima: DESCO.

Tuesta, F., 1986. *Perú 1985: el Derrotero de una Nueva Elección.* Lima: Centro de Investigación de la Universidad del Pacífico & Fundación Friedrich Ebert,

Tuesta, F., 1987. *Perú Político en Cifras. Elite Política y Elecciones.* Lima: Fundación Friedrich Ebert.

Tuesta, F., 1994a. *Perú Político en Cifras. Elite Política y Elecciones (Segunda Edición).* Lima: Fundación Friedrich Ebert.

Tuesta, F., 1994b. "Partidos políticos y elecciones en el Perú (1978–1993)," in *Perú Político en Cifras. Elite Política y Elecciones (Segunda Edición)*. Lima: Fundación Friedrich Ebert.

Ugarteche, O., 1992. "Alberto Fujimori: entre el Ying y el Yang," *Nueva Sociedad,* no, 118, March–April: 125–31.

United States Agency for International Development, 1991. *Congressional Presentation, Fiscal Year 1992.* Washington, D.C.

Valentín, I., 1993. "Tsunami Fujimori: una propuesta de interpretación." *Los Nuevos Limeños: Sueños, Fervores, y Caminos en el Mundo Popular.* Lima: SUR Casa de Estudios del Socialismo & TAFOS Talleres de Fotografía Social.

Vargas Llosa, M., 1991. "A Fish out of Water." *Granta* 36 (Summer): 15–75.

Vargas Llosa, M., 1993. *El Pez en el Agua.* Bogota: Editorial Seix Barral.

Vargas Llosa, A., 1991. *El Diablo en Campaña.* Mexico: Ediciones El País y Aguilar Ediciones.

Vega Castro, J., 1989. *El Sector Industrial Informal y Las Políticas de   Liberalización del Comercio Exterior en el Perú.* Lima: Instituto de Investigación y Docencia.

Vega-Centeno, M., 1990. *Violencia Estructural en el Perú: Economía.* Lima: Associación Peruana de Estudios e Investigación Para la Paz.

Vigier, M. E., 1986a. *El Impacto del PAIT en el Empleo y los Ingresos.* Lima: INP-ILO.

Vigier, M. E., 1986b. "Ingresos y empleos en sectores urbanos de escasos recursos, El PAIT: Una experiencia heterodoxa." *Socialismo y Participación,* no. 34.

Villarán, F., 1990. "El fenómeno Fujimori o la crisis de las ideas convencionales," *Quehacer,* no. 64, May–June: 30–35.

Wagner R. H. , 1989. "Uncertainty, Rational Learning, and Bargaining in the Cuban Missile Crisis," in Peter C. Ordeshook, ed., *Models of Strategic Choice in Politics.* Ann Arbor: University of Michigan Press.

Wendorff M., C., 1983. "El sector informal urbano en el Perú: Interpretación y perspectivas," in N. Henriquez and J. Iguiñiz, eds., *El Problema del Empleo en el Perú.* Lima: Pontificia Universidad Católica del Perú.

Weyland, K., 1993. "The Rise and Fall of President Collor and its Impact on Brazilian Democracy." *Journal of InterAmerican Studies and World Affairs,* 25 (1): 1–37.

Wines, S. W., 1985. "Stages of Micro Enterprise Growth in the Dominican Informal Sector." *Grassroots Development,* 9 (2).

Wise, C., 1989. "Democratization, Crisis, and the APRA's Modernization Project in Peru," in B. Stallings and R. Kaufman, eds., *Debt and Democracy in Latin America.* Boulder and London: Westview.

Wittman, D. , 1990. "Spatial Strategies When Candidates Have Policy Preferences," in J. M. Enelow and M. J. Hinich, eds., *Advances in the Spatial Theory of Voting.* Cambridge: Cambridge University Press.

Wynia, G. W. , 1984. *The Politics of Latin American Development.* Cambridge: Cambridge University Press.

Zagare, F. C., 1984. *Game Theory: Concepts and Applications.* Beverly Hills, CA: Sage.

Zagare, F. C. , 1990. "Rationality and Deterrence." *World Politics,* 42 (2): 238–260.

Zelikow, P., 1994. "Beyond Boris Yeltsin." *Foreign Affairs,* 73 (1): 44–55.

NEWSPAPERS AND OTHER SOURCES CONSULTED:

Actualidad Peruana: Boletín Electrónico de la Asociación Pro Derechos Humanos (APRODEH)
Business Week
Caretas
El Comercio
Expreso
Industria Peruana
La República and *Diario La República*
Latin American Weekly Report
Manchester Guardian
Oiga
Quehacer
Resumen Semanal
Sí
The Andean Report
The British Broadcasting Corporation; Summary of World Broadcasts
The Economist
The New York Times
The Reuter Library Report
The San Francisco Chronicle
The Sendero File: Published by the Federation of American Scientists Fund's Project on Peru
The Wall Street Journal

Index